A Pictorial History
of Women in America

Members of the National League for Women's Service march during World War I. The league was formed to supplement the work of the Army, Navy, and Red Cross, and to train women to deal with fire, flood, famine, or any national calamity. NYPL

RUTH WARREN

A Pictorial History of Women in America

CROWN PUBLISHERS, INC., NEW YORK

Manufactured in the United States of America
Library of Congress Catalog Card Number: 74-83212
Published simultaneously in Canada by General
Publishing Company Limited
First Edition

The text of this book is set in 12 pt. Caledonia.
The illustrations are halftone.

Library of Congress Cataloging in Publication Data

Warren, Ruth.
    A pictorial history of women in America.
    Bibliography: p.
    Includes index.
    SUMMARY: Discusses the accomplishments of women in
America from colonization to the present. Includes
Anne Bradstreet, Eleanor Roosevelt, Bessie Smith, and
many more
    1. Women—United States—History—Juvenile litera-
ture. [1. Women—United States—History] I. Title.
HQ1410.W37 1975   301.41′2′0973   74-83212
ISBN 0-517-51845-7

To American women who have made the United States of America a great country and who have achieved their liberation by their own efforts, this book is dedicated in gratitude

ACKNOWLEDGMENTS

I acknowledge with gratitude the help of librarians at The
New-York Historical Society, the Mid-Manhattan, Riverside,
and Library of Performing Arts branches of the New York
Public Library, cooperation extended by the State of Colorado
Division of Commerce and Development, the Wyoming
State Archives and Historical Department, the Business and
Professional Women's Foundation, the Lucy Stone League,
the Jamestown Foundation, the Women's Bureau of the U.S.
Department of Labor, the Public Affairs Bureau of the U.S.
Department of State. I am grateful to many friends for the
loan and gifts of out-of-print books, to my sister, Kathleen,
for her constant encouragement, to Mary Jane Hesson for her
impeccable typing of the manuscript, and to my editor, Donna
Brooks, for interest and help.

Contents

Two Queens and One Indian Princess

TWO WOMEN SPARKED the discovery and colonization of land that was at first called the New World and later came to be known as the United States of America. Queen Isabella, who reigned jointly with King Ferdinand over Castile and Aragon (1479–1504), provided Columbus with funds for his voyage that led to the discovery of the New World in 1492. Queen Elizabeth I of England, who was crowned sixty-seven years later, issued in 1578 the first patent for English colonization of the New World's mainland. Isabella and Elizabeth lived in the exciting, challenging Age of Discovery, an era in history when mariners and royalty contemplated expanding world horizons and hoped to find a short route to the treasures of the Indies, which Marco Polo had revealed to an amazed medieval world in 1298.

Italian-born Christopher Columbus was one of many sailors on the lookout for a short sea route to the gold, the jewels, and the spices of the East. Columbus apparently read and reread his copy of the Latin version of Marco Polo's *Travels*—it was profusely annotated in his own handwriting. He must have studied routes. He listened with keen interest to maritime gossip along the waterfront. He kept an appraising eye toward the West during voyages he occasionally made in the North Atlantic. Bartholomeu Dias, a Portuguese mariner, sailed round the tip of Africa in an effort to reach the Indies in 1488, but Columbus had a different route in mind. He believed that by sailing directly west into the Atlantic sunset he would reach the treasures of the Indies. He was confident but penniless. He needed money and he needed ships. To obtain them he sought the help of a woman.

The ambitious thirty-five-year-old Columbus had a long wait after his first reassuring audience with the thirty-five-year-old, auburn-haired Queen Isabella at the Spanish Court at Cordova in May 1486. Queen Isabella seemed to understand the logic of his unorthodox proposal and she seemed responsive to his request for funds to finance his expedition. He believed that he had found not only a patroness but someone who understood his objectives and who believed in his ability to carry them out for the glory of Spain. For a time he was even put on the royal payroll. He waited confidently while months passed. The royal stipend ceased. The Royal Commission to which Queen Isabella had submitted Columbus's proposal turned down his idea as impossible. When five years had slipped away, Columbus gave up hope of assistance from Queen Isabella and prepared to seek another patron elsewhere, but friends at court urged him to try again. Queen Isabella replied promptly to Columbus's letter to her, saying she had not forgotten him and summoning him to Santa Fe where the Spanish Court was sitting out the siege of Granada in a final battle with the Moors. She enclosed a generous gift of money for his journey. It was Christmas, 1491, when Columbus again appeared before Queen Isabella to ask once more for her support, and to stress the glory and fame it would bring the Spanish throne. But again he was turned down. As he journeyed northward, a messenger overtook him. He was recalled to the court, where a friend had intervened in his behalf and promised to raise the money (some $14,000) to finance the voyage. Convinced at last that this voyage would bring glory to her throne, Queen Isabella pledged her crown jewels. By April 17, 1492, contracts were signed. By August 3, 1492, the *Santa Maria*, the *Pinta*, and the *Nina* were under sail. And in thirty-two weeks Columbus brought back to Spain Indians wearing gold and feather ornaments, exotic birds in cages, and the exciting news that he had discovered a land that he called the Indies, with inhabitants whom he called Indians. Queen Isabella and King Ferdinand rose from their thrones to greet Columbus and addressed him as Admiral of the Ocean Seas. It was a triumphant moment.

Though Columbus had not discovered the Indies, his life objective, he had discovered a new world which was to play a great role in world history. And by his voyage Queen Isabella would forever be remembered as patroness of the discoverer of that new world.

Queen Elizabeth's grandfather, Henry VII, could have sent colonists to the New World in the early 1500s after he laid claim to the land discovered by John Cabot on his 1497 voyage to the Newfoundland coast, but he did not do so, nor did Elizabeth's father, Henry VIII. Elizabeth, who ascended the English throne in 1558, fifty-four years after Queen Isabella's death, was more excited by exploration than her father and grandfather had been. She admired the daring and skill of English seamen who boldly ventured into unknown seas. She personally held shares in Francis Drake's around-the-world voyage (1577–80). However, when it came to colonization, Elizabeth had England's international relations to consider, among them Spain's reaction to England's colonial claims and a controversy brewing over the freedom of the seas. Weighing these factors, Elizabeth finally issued the first English colonization patent in 1578 to Sir Humphrey Gilbert. It authorized him to "discover, hold and occupy" for a period of six years any "remote, barbarous and heathen lands not possessed by any Christian prince or people." Sir Humphrey's reconnaissance voyages seeking colonization sites were not successful and he, himself, was lost at sea in 1583 on his way back to England from the New World. Walter Raleigh, Humphrey's half brother, and then a favorite of Elizabeth, took over the patent in 1584, and obtained permission from Elizabeth, the Virgin Queen, to call the land that he planned to colonize "Virginia" in her honor. As encouragement, Elizabeth knighted Raleigh, who promptly sent out a colonizing expedition of 108 men. They settled on Roanoke Island (now in North Carolina). They were ill-prepared for the rigors of settlement and eagerly came home when Sir Francis Drake, sailing by, offered them passage in 1586.

Raleigh's second Roanoke Island colony also failed, and Raleigh himself fell into disfavor. Then the Spanish War interrupted English colonization plans. Queen Elizabeth did not live to see any permanent English colonies founded in the New World, but she had issued the first English colonization patent, and she had strengthened England's hold on the New World by stipulating that the "forms of laws and policy of England" should prevail and that no English colonist should lose his rights by moving overseas, but rather enjoy "all the privileges of free denizens and persons

native of England." These assurances sent thousands of English colonists, knowing they had protection of their motherland, across the Atlantic for the next two hundred years and ultimately triggered the birth of the United States of America.

The first English women to arrive in the New World, the first English baby born in the New World, and the first unsolved mystery of the New World were all part of Sir Walter Raleigh's second attempt to found a colony. Ninety-one male colonists, seventeen female colonists and nine children arrived at Roanoke Island, Virginia (now in North Carolina), in the summer of 1587.

For several reasons the Roanoke Island Colony should have had the most propitious start of any of the New World colonies. John White, its governor, had already spent an entire year on Roanoke Island as a member of Sir Walter Raleigh's first all-male colony. He had explored the terrain with another observant member, Thomas Hariot, a surveyor. He had contributed drawings and watercolors for Hariot's subsequent book on Virginia, published in England after the all-male colony had disbanded and returned home in 1586. The book praised the climate, the vegetation, and the peaceful neighboring Indians. White's drawings showed Indians spearing fish, an orderly looking Indian village of houses shaped like Quonset huts surrounded by a stockade, and an apparent abundance of fish swimming in the waters near the shore.

Some of the Englishwomen who embarked for Roanoke in 1587 may have been fascinated by these pictures and by glowing tales about the Virginia country-

4 PICTORIAL HISTORY OF WOMEN IN AMERICA

side. Or they may just have been adventurous. Many of them, however, were probably told by their husbands that the family was moving to the New World.

The first baby—a girl—arrived on August 18, 1587, a few weeks after the colonists stepped ashore at Roanoke. John White was the baby girl's grandfather. Elenor White Dare, daughter of John White, was her mother. Her father was Ananias Dare, a bricklayer.

As colonists explored their island they found themselves without certain necessary supplies, and all agreed that John White should return on the waiting ship to expedite the sending of additional supplies from England. White sailed on August 27, three days after his granddaughter was christened Virginia, in honor of her new homeland. He would not see his granddaughter or his daughter, or any member of the colony, again.

Back in England, John White found that English ships and English seamen were being recruited for the forthcoming war with Spain, so his pleas to Sir Walter Raleigh for supplies for the Roanoke colony received little attention. Three years passed before John White was able to find space for himself and for supplies for the Roanoke colony aboard a three-ship trading expedition bound for the West Indies. When the fleet finally reached the Carolina coast in August 1590, it encountered tempestuous weather that took the lives of one captain and seven crew members. John White tells in his own words of the mysterious sight that greeted his final landing on Roanoke Island.

. . . It was late ere we arrived, but seeing a fire through the woods, we sounded a Trumpet, but no answer could we hear. The next morning we went to it, but could see nothing but the grass and some rotten trees burning. We went up and down the Isle, and at last found three fair Roman letters carved. C.R.O. which presently we knew to signify the place where I should find them, according to a secret note between them & me: which was to write the name of the place they would be in, upon some trees, door or post: and if they had been in any distress, to signify it by making a cross over it. For at my departure they intended to go fifty miles into the main. But we found no sign of distress; then we went to a place where they were left in sundry houses, but we found them all taken down, and the place strongly inclosed with a high Palisade, very fort-like; and in one of the chief posts carved in fair capital letters CROATAN, without any sign of distress, and many bars of iron, two pigs of lead, four fowlers, iron shot, and such like heavy things thrown here and there, overgrown with grass and weeds. We went by the shore to seek for their boats, but could find none, nor any of the ordnance I left them. At last some of the sailors found divers chests had been hidden and digged up again, and much of the goods spoiled, and scattered up and down, which when I saw, I knew three of them to be my own; but books, pictures, and all things else were spoiled. Though it much grieved me, yet it did much comfort me that I did know they were at Croatan; so we returned to our ships but had like to have been cast away by a great storm that continued all that night.

"The next morning we weighed Anchor for Croatan: heaving the Anchor a-pike, the Cable broke, by means whereof we lost another; letting fall the third, the ship yet went so fast adrift, . . . But God bringing us into deeper water; considering we had but one anchor, and our provisions near spent, we resolved to go forthwith to St.

Virgina Indians of the sixteenth century, sitting to eat a meal of fish and roast corn. The original picture was drawn by John White, governor of the Roanoke Island Colony. From engraving by de Bry

John Isle, Hispaniola, or Trinadad, to refresh ourselves and seek for purchase that winter, and the next spring come again to seek our countrymen. . . .

Written by Master John White

With one captain and seven crew members drowned in the stormy seas that raged about Roanoke and Croatan, with supplies running short, only one anchor left and the crew muttering mutinously, the three English ships set sail for the West Indies for repairs and supplies, without further effort to return to Roanoke. John White reported a plan to explore Croatan at some future time, but for an unexplained reason he never went back to hunt for his daughter Elenor and his granddaughter Virginia,

perhaps because he could raise neither interest nor money for such an expedition. The fate of the Roanoke colony has remained a mystery down through the centuries. Indian tribes in the area have claimed that the blood of Roanoke settlers flows in their veins. And the best remembered colonist of Roanoke Island has been that of Virginia Dare, the first baby (and a girl) born in the New World to English colonists. After the failure of the Roanoke settlement, no more Englishwomen crossed the sea as colonists until 1608.

No women were among the 120 English colonists who landed in Virginia on May 14, 1607, to found Jamestown, the first permanent English colony in the New

World, but an Indian woman was ultimately to play a vital role in the colony's development. The colony's sponsor, the Virginia Company, chartered in 1606 by James I, was one of the first to receive grants of land in the New World from the English Crown. To the Virginia Company the Crown conferred such powers as government of settlements, transportation of emigrants, commerce, and so on, subject to the laws of England. Numerous small investors—merchants, clergymen, knights, and ordinary citizens—put money into the enterprise. The main objective of the sponsoring Virginia Company was the discovery of gold or other valuable metals, and a shorter route to the Indies which would assure the company investors quick and abundant riches.

On that first May morning in Jamestown the labor crew (who were required to work out a term of service before they could claim land) began constructing wattle-and-daub thatched houses, a church, a fortified trading center, a stockade, and storehouses. The exploring colonists, among them Captain John Smith, took off into the woods to reconnoiter the neighborhood for Indian encampments and to look for gold and for a possible route to the Indies. After the excitement of settling their new town was over, the laborers began to be discontented. They had no stake in the venture. They had no land of their own to till. The danger of an attack by Indians was an ever-present threat. And one by one the colonists began to get sick. The Jamestown leaders had made the mistake of building their town on low-lying land near swampy areas and brackish water. The diseases to which the men succumbed were described as fluxes, agues, cramps, scurvy, burning fevers, malaria, and swellings. Day after day the exploring parties returned with the discouraging report that there was no gold, no metals, and apparently no possibility of a short route to the Indies. The only natural resource discovered that had cash value was cedar trees, which could be exported for wainscoting board. The Jamestown colony was off to a miserable start.

A woman was to raise the morale of this depressing picture. The colony was about to get a patroness. On one of his exploring trips Captain John Smith was taken captive by the Indians and brought before Powhatan, the powerful "king" of a union of Algonkin nations (called the Powhatan Confederacy), which occupied some 200 villages in the backwoods of tidewater Virginia. This is what happened to Captain John Smith as related (in the third person) in his *The Generall Historie of Virginia.*

At last they brought him [Smith] to Meronocomoco, where was Powhatan their Emperor. Here more than two hundred of those grim Courtiers stood wondering at him, as [if] he had been a monster; till Powhatan and his train had put themselves in their greatest braveries. Before a fire upon a seat like a bedstead, he sat covered with a great robe, made of Rarowcun skins, and all the tayles hanging by. On either hand did sit a young wench of 16 or 18 years, and along on each side the house, two rows of men, and behind them as many women, with all their heads and shoulders painted red; many of their heads bedecked with the white down of Birds; but every one with something: and a great chain of beads about their necks. At his [Smith's] entrance before the King, all the people gave a great shout. The Queen of Appamatuck was appointed to bring him water to wash his hands, and another brought him a bunch of feathers, instead of a towel to dry them: having seated him after their best barbarous manner . . . a long consultation was held, but the conclusion was, two great stones were brought before Powhatan: then as many as could laid hands on him, dragged him to them and thereon laid his head, and being ready with their clubs, to beat out his brains, Pocahontas the King's dearest daughter, when no intreaty could prevail, got his head in her arms, and laid her own upon his to save him from death: whereat the Emperor was contented he should live to make him hatchets, and her bells, beads, and copper . . .

Pocahontas, who was twelve or thirteen at the time, became a frequent visitor to Jamestown after her dramatic rescue of Captain John Smith. She romped around the town, naked as all Indian children were. Smith described her as full of "wit and spirit" and he frequently gave her beads and trinkets. Pocahontas brought corn when the colonists were starving. She once warned Smith of an Indian attack. Her goodwill was not lost on the colony. Pocahontas was encouraged to come to Jamestown in order to foster peaceful relations between the colony and the Indians.

One amusing and charitable little girl might save Jamestown from Indian attacks but she could not prevent the illness and starvation that continued to plague the colony. When the first supply ship arrived from England in January 1608, death had claimed 51 of the 120 colonists. The ship brought two women to Jamestown—a Mistress Forrest and her maid,

Anne Burraws, who later married a John Laydon. They were the first English couple to marry in the New World.

When Captain John Smith returned to England in 1609, Pocahontas's visits ceased, perhaps because her loyalty (or her love) had been given to him. She was missed as peace emissary between her powerful father, Powhatan, and Virginia's Jamestown colony, and so when ship captain Samuel Argall, sailing along the Potomac River with a scouting party in 1613, came upon Pocahontas, he invited her aboard, and brought her back to Jamestown to assure peace with the Powhatan Confederation. Pocahontas came willingly to Jamestown after her four-year absence. She was warmly received, treated as a guest, and began to study English and the Christian religion with the Reverend Alexander Whitaker.

At about the same time one of the most enterprising colonists at Jamestown, a thirty-year-old planter named John Rolfe, began experimenting with tobacco seed which he had imported from the West Indies. Somehow Pocahontas, then about eighteen, and Rolfe, ten years her senior, met. Pocahontas may have helped Rolfe secure Powhatan's assistance in learning the best techniques of tobacco growing. At any rate, Rolfe quickly became the most successful tobacco grower in Jamestown. He introduced others to the mysteries of tobacco raising, and Jamestown tobacco was soon exported to England, where the popularity of smoking was rapidly growing. Rolfe, meanwhile, had fallen in love with Pocahontas. He asked permission of Sir Thomas Dale, deputy governor, to marry her, and got it, since bonds between

***This statue of Pocahontas stands in Jamestown honoring the Indian woman who
helped the first Jamestown settlers to survive.*** *Virginia State Library*

the colony and the Indians would thereby be doubly secured. Pocahontas willingly agreed to the marriage. She was baptized with the Christian name Rebecca, and a church wedding ceremony took place April 5, 1614. Powhatan gave the couple some land as a wedding present, and the marriage ushered in a period of peace with the Indians. John Rolfe prospered as a tobacco grower. A son, Thomas, was born to the couple, the date of his birth unknown.

In 1616, two years after their marriage, the Rolfes were invited by Sir Thomas Dale to accompany him on a trip to England. Pocahontas, daughter of an Indian king, accompanied by Uttamatomakkin, Powhatan's chief councilor, was greeted as a princess in England. Captain John Smith presented Queen Anne with a petition that revealed for the first time Pocahontas's role in saving him from death. She herself was presented to King James and Queen Anne on January 6, 1617, and accompanied the royal couple to the theatre to see a Ben Jonson masque. Her dignity and her courtesy were much admired. When Captain John Smith visited Pocahontas in person, she turned away after greeting him and was silent for a long time. She had apparently believed him dead.

The Virginia Company was delighted by all the publicity this brought to Jamestown, and immediately arranged public lotteries to support the colony. The church was delighted that a heathen princess had been converted to Christianity.

Pocahontas was having such an exciting time in London that she did not want to go home. She begged Rolfe to stay longer, but nine months had elapsed and the Jamestown tobacco plantations needed supervision. Reluctantly, on a blustery March day in 1617, Pocahontas boarded the ship for Jamestown. As they waited for favorable winds near Gravesend at the mouth of the Thames River not far from London, Pocahontas became fatally ill either of smallpox or pneumonia or consumption, and died on March 21, 1617, at the age of 22. Her burial took place in St. George's Church at Gravesend. The church has a tablet in her memory, and two stained glass windows, presented in 1914 by the Colonial Dames of America. A statue of Pocahontas stands in Jamestown, Virginia, honoring the New World's first woman celebrity, first woman overseas "ambassador," and the first Indian woman to befriend a colony in the New World.

CHAPTER TWO

The Founding Mothers

DESPITE THE FAVORABLE publicity given the colony by Pocahontas's visit to England in 1617, despite its tobacco boom, which started in 1614, and despite a decade of peace with the Indians, Jamestown continued to deteriorate as the year 1620 approached. The death rate was appalling. Though ships were constantly arriving with new colonists, the colony's population fell from 1,000 to 866 between 1619 and 1620. Tobacco, the chief export crop, was threatened by King James's disapproval of smoking. Relations with the Indians began declining after the death of Pocahontas in 1617 and the death of the powerful and friendly Powhatan shortly thereafter. Most of the colonists considered life in Jamestown "solitary uncouthness." And in London the colony grew to have the reputation of being "a misery, a death, a hell."

As they thought about ways to revitalize the colony, the Virginia Company in London concluded that bachelor planters might "sett down satisfied" and no longer wish for their native land if they had wives and children and family roots. Someone came up with the idea of brides' ships. "Pure and spotless" English girls were to be shipped to Jamestown for "respectable" colonists who were lonely enough or enterprising enough to pay 120 pounds of tobacco for a bride. The news of a brides' ship on its way caused a sensation in Jamestown. Hitherto indolent males busied themselves clearing land and planting tobacco. And when the brides' ship was sighted, some 400 lonely bachelor planters dressed in their best doublet and breeches awaited ninety homesick and seasick English girls who eyed their future husbands apprehensively.

Every girl had the right to accept or

Women from the brides' ship arrive in Jamestown. Virginia State Library

refuse a husband. Every married couple had the right to build a house. Morale was temporarily raised in the colony. When thirty-eight more brides arrived in 1621 their price had been raised to 150 pounds of tobacco.

But the Jamestown problem had been only temporarily solved. An Indian massacre in 1622, instigated by Powhatan's brother and successor, Opechancanough, who considered that he was being pushed out of his land, took a toll of 347 colonists. And of the 128 English girls sent over to become planters' brides, only 35 were alive four years later in 1624. Almost nothing is known about the Jamestown women in these early years, not even their names. As time passed, however, their sons and daughters built themselves comfortable plantations along Virginia's rivers.

Northward, the *Mayflower* had anchored at Plymouth in December 1620, and the thirty women and girls aboard the ship were weary of overcrowded quarters, unappetizing food, and of more than two months of rolling and pitching seas. The New England shoreline which the ship had been following since November 9 did not offer much reassurance about the prospective comfort of their new homeland. It looked like a "hideous & desolate wilderness full of wild beasts & willd men."

The Pilgrims (or Saints as they are sometimes called) had come to the New World to gain religious freedom. The other passengers aboard the *Mayflower*, called Strangers, had various objectives—trade, a better life, a chance to own and develop land. There were also on that trip indentured servants (about 18 altogether)—able-bodied men who would work out their seven years of indenture (with keep but without wages) by building houses, clearing fields, felling trees, hewing timber, tending crops. And there were four waifs from the London streets, only one of whom survived. It was a heterogeneous group, and there were mutinous murmurings among the Strangers as the ship sailed northward seeking the right site for the new colony. The Pilgrim fathers were worried, and so, to give the colony unity and purpose, they wrote the Mayflower Compact aboard ship. They agreed to "combine ourselves together into a civill body politick," to frame "equall lawes, ordinances, acts, constitutions, & offices," and to promise "all due submission and obedience." Thirty-nine men of the 102 passengers aboard ship and some male servants signed the document. Women were not asked to sign, not being considered free agents ("legal chattels of their liege lords," they have been called). Husbands acted in their wives' behalf. The Pilgrim fathers believed as did most other men that a woman's mission was to bear children frequently, to cook, wash, clean, spin, and to work in the fields when needed.

Work did not start on the new town until December 25, 1620. A sheltered harbor, with an elevated lookout hill nearby and fresh water available, was chosen as the best town site. The new town was called New Plimoth (later Plymouth). A Common House was the first building raised on a twenty-foot-square elevated site,

with walls made of willow or hazel twigs bound together (wattle) and mud (daub) used as plaster. The high roof was thatched. Lots were drawn by each married man for his eventual homesite, though weeks were to pass before homes were finished. The weather was freezing cold, numbing hands and feet. Many of the exploring group were already suffering from exposure and cold. Soon death and disease stalked Plymouth.

A woman was the first Pilgrim to die in the New World. Dorothy Bradford, wife of Governor Bradford, was inexplicably drowned on December 7. Five other deaths occurred shortly after. By January the newly built Common House had been turned into a hospital. Eight persons died in January, seventeen in February, and thirteen in March. Aboard the Mayflower, still anchored offshore and still a "hotel" for Mayflower passengers, half the sailors and three mates died. At one period during the winter only seven men were well enough to tend the sick, which they did "willingly & cherfully without any grudging in ye least."

Illness so delayed the building of family homes that it was March 21, 1621, before the last passengers left the Mayflower to live ashore. The fifty or so surviving settlers waved a reluctant farewell to the Mayflower on April 5, 1621, but not one person accepted the captain's offer of a free trip back to England.

The mortality among women had been particularly high. Only five of the eighteen Mayflower wives survived. Women and young girls who lived through that first grim winter set up housekeeping in one-room daub-and-wattle cottages with thatched roofs, oiled paper windows, and a stone fireplace laid in clay, its chimney on the outside. Cooking utensils were skillets and pots that the women had brought from England. The women's russet and purple and green gowns (Pilgrim women did not wear drab gray) would have to last a long time. The colony had no sheep for wool, no poultry, no cows. The colonists waited three years for one bull and three heifers to arrive in 1624, though ships began arriving with new colonists by November, 1621.

The first grim winter over, women rejoiced at the arrival of a particularly beautiful spring. As they washed clothes in the nearby brook, using clay for soap, robins sang, bluebirds flitted from tree to tree collecting material for nests, and apple, cherry, and plum trees burst into bloom. Children brought bunches of trailing arbutus, starflowers, and jack-in-the-pulpits from the nearby woods. The first spring also brought two remarkable Indian visitors, Samoset and Squanto, who could speak some English. Squanto had learned it in England where he had been taken by an English exploring party. From Squanto, women and children learned to collect mussels and clams along the shore. Spring was the time for planting, and Pilgrim men were soon learning how to plant Indian corn along with the turnips, cabbages, parsnips, and other seeds they had brought with them from England. Some men traded with the Indians for beaver pelts to send back to England to pay off London creditors who had financed the venture and to whom the colony would be indebted for many years. Squanto also brought to the colony the most powerful

Indian chieftain of the vicinity, Massasoit, with whom the Pilgrims made a compact.

In spite of hardships, illness, and death, the *Mayflower* women and others who came after them soon learned to survive in the New World. In that first dreary seventeenth century, when the New World's terrors and problems sometimes seemed to outweigh its assets, the Founding Mothers held family units together by their indefatigable courage. Without the Founding Mothers, the Founding Fathers could not have established a new nation in the midst of the New World's primitive wilderness.

The New England Founding Mother faced one of the most bleak unfriendly New World winter climates. With no resources but her own wits and strength, she was the cook, the doctor, the household drudge for an ever-increasing family of children. She learned to keep the family alive on a cornmeal diet when famine threatened. She combed the woods for herbs to make purges, poultices, syrups, emetics. She made the straw mattresses on which most of the family slept, at first on the floor. She patched and made over old clothes. She kept the one room shack in which the family first lived lighted by night with resinous pine chips, then with candles that she made herself. She incessantly tended the smoky fireplace with its overhanging cooking pots that weighed forty pounds—heavy to lift if you were always pregnant, as most Founding Mothers were. The infant death rate was high, due to lack of medical knowledge, too frequent pregnancies, cold houses, and poor diet. When wool (with the import of sheep) became available, she kept the family in clothes by spinning, weaving, dyeing, and sewing. But above all, she created in the home a sense of security, of togetherness, of peace and, particularly in New England, a sense of destiny, of faith in God. When times got better and a new house rose on the site of the first one-room shack, the Founding Mother re-created for her family the kind of home she had known back in England, adding small luxuries as she could afford them—pewter instead of wooden plates and wooden spoons, a bedstead with a down-filled mattress, glass (sometimes leaded) windows instead of oiled paper, and a chair or two to supplement wooden benches. As she sat in church on Sunday (her only day of rest) listening to the minister preach-

ing about the horrors of hell, the New England Founding Mother must have looked with pride on the neatly dressed children at her side, must have felt gratitude for their survival.

To the south some 400 miles, the Dutch Founding Mothers of New Amsterdam faced fewer problems in the New World than New England mothers. They had come to the New World in 1624, claiming land discovered by Henry Hudson, a Dutch-employed Englishman. Instead of discovering a short route to the Indies for which he had been looking, Hudson had discovered one of the most profitable fur-bearing regions in the New World. Unlike the *Mayflower* women who had arrived at the beginning of winter, the Dutch women arrived in May so there was

Two colonial women use their feet to wash clothes. NYPL Picture Collection

Making soap and cutting it into bars. NYPL Picture Collection

time to clear land, do some planting, and build thatch shelters before the onset of winter. Two years later, Manhattan Island, the land on which they built and planted, was bought by the Dutch West India Company from the Indians for twenty-four dollars. Within a few years, New Amsterdam became a miniature Dutch village. Food was plentiful. There were vegetable farms on Manhattan Island, and weekly produce markets. Ships from the Netherlands were constantly bringing in merchandise to exchange for furs, the colony's cash crop. But there was no extravagance in those snug brick houses that began to rise in New Amsterdam in the mid-to-late 16oos. The Dutch Founding Mothers were thrifty. A primary duty of their motherhood was to teach children of the family to be thrifty, and to teach girls to be homemakers. From childhood girls learned to sew, to care for dairy animals and the poultry, to spin, brew, and cook. The Dutch family was a closely knit unit, enjoying home life together. Dutch women were serene, good-humored, charitable, and modest, one contemporary writer observed, but, he added: "There is nothing that they so neglect as reading and indeed all the arts for the improvement of the mind." However, some Dutch women of patroon families (who had been granted vast tracts of land along the Hudson River) received good educations and became mothers of distinguished sons and daughters.

Dutiful and housewifely as women were in New Amsterdam, the colony numbered among its women one who was hard-headed and shrewd in business. Margaret Hardenbrook was probably the New World's first woman of commerce. Coming as an emigrant in 1659, within a year Margaret had married Peter Rudolphus de Vries and started her own mercantile business under her maiden name (which she used throughout her career). When her husband died in 1661 she added his business to her own, shipping furs to Holland and importing European merchandise to New Amsterdam. She also owned and operated at least one ship of her own, perhaps more. Margaret Hardenbrook had the reputation of being extraordinarily frugal. Two Labadist missionaries sailing with her aboard one of her ships com-

mented on Margaret's "unblushing avarice" and "excessive covetousness," reporting that she had even stopped the ship in an attempt to retrieve a deck mop that had fallen overboard. Margaret Hardenbrook died about 1690, after a thirty-year career in commerce in the New World.

Peace and quiet did not always prevail in New Amsterdam. The Dutch had numerous encounters with the Indians, notably in 1643 when the Dutch fought the Wappinger Confederacy Indians who lived in the New Jersey and New York area. They also endured a series of autocratic rulers; the last, Peter Stuyvesant, gave up the colony without a shot being fired when four British frigates sailed into New Amsterdam harbor and demanded

Colonial woman making butter using the Dutch method. NYPL Picture Collection

surrender. The entire province came under British control and was renamed New York in 1664.

The Southern Founding Mothers—women of Virginia, Maryland, and the Carolinas—were spared much of the drudgery of housework by the availability of slave labor if they were wealthy planters' wives. Negro slaves had arrived in Jamestown in the early 1600s, and were increasingly imported to work in the tobacco, and later in the indigo and cotton fields. Southern Founding Mothers were far from indolent, however. They supervised many aspects of plantation activity —the poultry yard, the smokehouse, the kitchen garden, the dairy, and sometimes went into the fields to supervise the planting and harvesting of the crops. The Southern Founding Mother knew plantation life and its problems so well that often, upon the death of her husband, she managed the plantation alone.

Because plantations were sometimes located twenty to sixty miles from each other, they had to be self-sufficient. Women kept the larder always stocked with meat, fowl, vegetables, and the makings of very sweet and elaborate desserts to feed guests who might appear unexpectedly and remain for days. The Southern Founding Mother was doctor and nurse to her family and to the slaves. She concocted her own medicines for such ailments as fevers, spleen, hysteric fits, "evil," and agues. She had to provide clothes for the slaves. Running a plantation was like running a small town, and women (mothers, daughters, spinster relatives) managed major aspects of its complicated activities. By the 1700's less affluent Southern women were working at a variety of jobs as sextons, jailors, ferry keepers, shipwrights, running tanning yards, acting as butchers, gunsmiths, and horticulturists.

On the western fringes of the forest were frontier Founding Mothers, women who were strong, self-reliant, daring, competent, industrious. These "backwoods women" handled firearms like a man, either to protect their home against Indians or to kill deer, turkeys, hogs, wild cattle for food. There were usually no nearby towns or neighbors. They made everything needed for the home—soap, candles, clothes (spinning, weaving and sewing), and planted vegetable gardens. They cared for the cows, made butter and cheese.

Through the tireless efforts of the Founding Mothers, the family unit survived its transplanting to a primitive New World. It was a primitive and new world for them only, however. They did not realize that it was peopled with one million Indian women who had already faced and mastered its challenges.

CHAPTER THREE

Indian Women—the First American Women

IF INDIAN WOMEN and colonial women had met and become friends, life might have been easier in the first colonies. Indian women had been living in the New World for thousands of years, and had learned nature's assets and nature's hazards. Pocahontas and Powhatan, Massasoit, Squanto and Samoset, had offered friendship and peace to the first settlers. But for the most part, the colonists did not understand nor did they try to understand the rituals and traditions that bound Indian tribes together. They did not know that half the New World's two million Indian inhabitants from coast to coast were women, competent women on whom the tribe depended for survival.

The first Indian women that English colonists encountered belonged to the Algonkin and the Iroquois tribes which inhabited the Atlantic coast line. They were the cooks, the farmers, and the tailors in an Indian village. Women built the wigwams out of poles bent into a dome-shaped structure covered with birch bark in summer and matting in winter. They fetched the wood for fires, cooked all the meals, planted, cultivated and harvested corn, squash, beans, and pumpkins. They raised the children, cared for the sick, and sometimes dug graves for the dead. They collected groundnuts, and pounded them into flour. They knew the healing qualities of herbs. They wove plant fibers into baskets and cooking pots.

Indian women were strong, resourceful, and competent. They had great physical endurance. Little girls in an Indian family started early in life to build the hardy bodies needed for survival. They carried babies strapped to their backs. They foraged for wood in the forest and

An Iroquois woman pounding corn in a wooden mortar. Her clothing is made from deerskin. *American Museum of Natural History*

carried it back to the village. They learned to cook, to plant, and to tend gardens. They learned to find their way through the forest.

When the plight of an Indian village became desperate for lack of food, an Indian woman might steal away in the dead of winter to retrieve the hoard of Indian corn that she had hidden during the summer for just such an emergency. She remembered where it was. She knew her way alone. And she brought it back safely to her hungry family.

Meat was the mainstay of the Indian diet and at least four deer a day were needed to feed the one hundred people in an average-size Indian village. When men, who were the hunters, brought home a deer, which they sometimes had stalked all day, women helped butcher the deer and cook the meat. Indian women knew how to tan deerskin so that it would be pliable and soft even in rainy or cold weather. They made moccasins, skirts, and jackets out of deerskins. They made bags out of the paunch and the bladder. They used the sinews for thread, the bones for thick, blunt needles called bodkins, tail hair for embroidery or for ornaments, and antlers for tools.

Clothing for Indians was minimal, especially in summer. Children went naked up to ten years of age. Men wore a breechcloth in summer, and in winter leggings and a jacket. Women wore a deerskin wraparound skirt, held in place by a belt. Sometimes they wore a headband of embroidered skin. Teenage girls sometimes used bear fat on their long black hair to make it glossy, and carried makeup pouches of red or black paint that they

used on their cheeks or to outline their eyes.

Indian women were "liberated" women in some ways. Both Algonkin and Iroquois women owned their own wigwam homes, their "furniture" and their children. Men owned only the clothes they wore, their tools and their weapons. An Iroquois woman could divorce her husband if she wished, though in marriage she had to allow her husband to take an extra wife or two if he so desired. Iroquois women had additional status because tribal ancestry was traced through the mother.

Although a few colonists were concerned with the Indians' right to their territory, most were willing to encroach upon it without recompense. The colonists regarded the Indians with apprehension, and were often quicker to shoot them than to hold out a hand of friendship. Very rarely did women colonists express a desire to become acquainted with their Indian women neighbors. "I had often before this said that if the Indians should come, I should rather choose to be killed by them, than taken alive; but when it came to the trial, my mind changed," Mary Rowlandson said in her book *Narrative of the Captivity and Removes of Mrs. Mary Rowlandson*, a best seller of the late 1600s that went into some thirty editions. By her fortitude and her religious faith, Mary Rowlandson (c. 1635–78?) managed to survive hunger, cold, "removes" from campsite to campsite for eleven weeks and five days before she was ransomed and released on May 2, 1676.

Mrs. Rowlandson was a victim of King Philip's War, instigated by a chieftain whose real name was Metacom and who, ironically, was the son of Massasoit, who had befriended the Pilgrims when they first landed in Plymouth in 1620. King Philip resented encroachment on his land. He brooded over other wrongs besetting the New England Indians, inciting them to attack the colonists from Maine to Rhode Island for two harrowing years (1675–76). The attacks were made suddenly on isolated towns fringing the forest. With chilling warwhoops, the Indians rushed in, set fire to buildings, killed or captured cattle, tortured or killed townspeople, and disappeared into the forest carrying away captives to be held for ransom.

It was sunrise on February 10, 1676, when Indians attacked the Rowlandson home at Lancaster, Massachusetts. Mary Rowlandson, whose minister-husband was away at the time, watched friends and relatives killed and scalped. She and her seriously wounded six-year-old daughter Sarah, were taken captive, and though she did not know it at the time, so were her daughter Mary and son Joseph. As they traveled into the "vast desolate wilderness," sleeping on cold, snowy ground with only a small fire to warm them, with water to drink but no food, Mary Rowlandson comforted her dying child for nine long days. Sarah died on February 18. The Indians buried the little girl so

Pomo Indian women of California are among the finest basket weavers in America. Here a Pomo woman weaves a large "mush bowl." American Museum of Natural History

that her mother would not have to perform this sad task.

From then on life was a series of "removes" from place to place. Mary Rowlandson carried a load on her back like all the squaws; sometimes she waded across icy rivers; sometimes she climbed hills "so steep that I was fain to creep up upon my knees, and to hold by the twigs and bushes to keep myself from falling back."

Hunger, constant hunger, was Mrs. Rowlandson's chief complaint. "I cannot but think what a wolfish appetite persons have in a starving condition," she wrote, "for many times when they gave me that which was hot I was so greedy that I should burn my mouth so that it would trouble me hours after and yet I should quickly do the same again. And after I was thoroughly hungry I was never again satisfied. For though sometimes it fell out

Colonial women often had to defend themselves against hostile Indians or else be taken captive.

that I got enough and did eat until I could no more, yet I was as unsatisfied as I was when I began." As she grew more and more hungry she found "sweet and savory to the taste" soup made of horses' feet, horses' liver, and bear meat. She confesses having such a "wolfish appetite" that she would shamelessly beg for food from wigwam to wigwam. Sometimes the Indians gave her a bit of food (they had very little themselves) and sometimes they turned her away. She slept in a corner of whatever wigwam was willing to accept her. Her master had three squaws, one of whom Mrs. Rowlandson served. She described her as a "severe and proud dame" who spent much time "powdering her hair and painting her face, going with necklaces, with jewels in her ears, and bracelets upon her hands." Occasionally Mrs. Rowlandson saw her son, Joseph, and her daughter, Mary, who were captives of other tribes.

As she knitted socks for her master's squaw, Mrs. Rowlandson had time to observe Indian customs, attitudes, and behavior. She noted their lying, their stealing, their sudden brutalities, but also their acts of generosity and their impulsive friendliness. On one of her "removes" she visited King Philip who asked her to make a shirt for his son and gave her a shilling. Slowly, little by little, there emerges in the narrative of Mrs. Mary Rowlandson the growing awareness that Indians, too, were people.

Mary Rowlandson was just one of many colonial women who were taken captive by the Indians. Hannah Duston, a Haverhill, Massachusetts, housewife, was captured on March 15, 1697, with her week-old baby (whom the Indians killed) and with Mrs. Mary Neff, the child's nurse. The two women were forced to make a 100-mile march to an Indian village on an island near present-day Concord, New Hampshire. Their escape took place during the night of May 30, 1697, when Hannah Duston killed nine Indians with a hatchet, and scalped her victims to have proof of her chilling deed. The captives paddled back to safety in an Indian canoe, and Mrs. Duston, so the story goes, proudly collected 25 pounds for the scalps.

Colonial children seemed to understand the Indians better than most grown-ups. Captive children learned to love their foster Indian parents, and were often reluctant to return to their true parents when ransomed. Some never did.

One of the truly tragic aspects of the settling of the New World was the Indian question, as tribe after tribe was pushed out of their homeland. It was a question to which American women would address themselves later, in the 1800s.

CHAPTER FOUR

The Diversity of Seventeenth-Century Women

WOMEN IN THE 1600s were expected to be quiet, obedient, and rarely, if ever, to call attention to themselves in public. At various times, and in various places, however, women appeared who disregarded this enforced silence, finding their own minds a more certain guide than the rules of custom. Sometimes by choice, sometimes by circumstance, their ideas or their abilities brought them into public light. Anne Bradstreet, for instance, had no intention of publishing the poetry she wrote.

Anne Bradstreet (1612–72) wrote poetry to escape from the intellectual sterility of Puritan New England. She wrote steadily all her life in moments free of the cares of bearing eight children, homemaking, churchgoing, frequent illnesses, and moving three times.

The primitiveness of the New World startled eighteen-year-old Anne Brad-

street when she first stepped ashore in Boston in 1630. The city looked bleak and uninviting compared with the vast English estate of the Earl of Lincoln, of which her father had been manager and where she had browsed in the Earl's Tattershall Castle library and studied under eight tutors. Occasionally colonial fathers took great pains with their daughters' education, and Anne Bradstreet was one of the first emigrant daughters who had been encouraged to improve her mind. But the New World could not offer the same intellectual stimulus that Anne had enjoyed at Sempringham in Lincolnshire.

To Anne's father, Thomas Dudley, and her husband, Simon Bradstreet, the move to the New World was a progressive and logical choice. They had both been involved in the transfer of the Massachusetts Bay Company to a group of Puritans who eagerly looked forward to setting up a colony "after their own hearts" in the New World. Both men were leaders in the Puritan migration to Massachusetts of the 1630s. Both men would later become governors of Massachusetts. Anne Bradstreet faced no such future.

Members of her family knew she was writing poetry, and may have encouraged her. Her brother-in-law, the Reverend John Woodbridge, read some of her poems while on a visit to Boston and was so enthusiastic that he took a handwritten copy back to England. And he went even further. He located a publisher, circulated the poems among friends, and found eight people so enthusiastic that they offered to write dedicatory prefaces.

Anne had no idea her poems were being published. When she received the printed volume she called it a "rambling brat" and "unfit for light." Its title was certainly uninspiring—*The Tenth Muse Lately Sprung Up in America, or Severall Poems, compiled with a great variety of Wit and Learning, full of delight . . . By a Gentlewoman in those parts.* The name of the then thirty-year-old "gentlewoman" was omitted.

Seeing her poems in print gave Anne confidence to keep on writing. Her first volume of verse was a bit dull and imitative, but not the second volume published in 1678, six years after her death. Anne's later poems were more imaginative, contemplative, spontaneous, especially when she caught the moods of nature—the shady forest with its "pleasures dignified," its "stones and trees insensible of time," its crickets and grasshoppers "singing in tune."

Anne Bradstreet also wrote love poems to her husband that may seem to us too ardent to belong to Puritan Boston. But Puritans, though rigid in their religious dogma, were not prudish about sex. In fact Puritans sometimes seemed almost permissive about sex, and certainly less inhibited than Victorians of the 1800s. Sexual desire, or "concupiscence" as the Puritans called it, was considered an important part of life's cycle and Puritans treated the matter forthrightly. Anne Bradstreet's warm love for her husband is unashamedly expressed in the following lines of verse:

If ever two were one, then surely we.
If ever man were loved by wife, then thee.
If ever wife was happy in a man,
Compare with me, ye women, if you can.

Though Anne Bradstreet did not engage in any feminist crusade, an occasional reference indicates that she was not untouched by the injustice of women's inferior status. The "carping tongue" that said "my hand a needle better fits" (a reference perhaps to a Boston gossip or a Puritan clergyman) did not pass unnoticed. There is a plea for recognition of "women's worth" in this stanza in one of Anne's poems.

Nay, say have women worth or have they none?
Or had they some but with the Queen it's gone?
Nay, masculines, you have thus taxed us long,
But she, though dead, will vindicate our wrong.
Let such as say our sex is void of reason
Know it's slander now, but once was treason.

In matters of religious faith especially,

women were expected to keep silent. They could acknowledge God in their lives and in their deeds, and in private prayer, but never from the pulpit. Only the Quakers (and later also the Methodists) allowed women to participate in their meetings. The Church of England in Virginia, the Dutch church in New York, and the Catholics of Maryland all expected women to remain pious, reverent, and quiet. In the Puritan Church of Boston in Massachusetts, also, women were expected to be meek, docile, and above all silent.

Three women broke the rule of silence for women in Puritan New England in the mid-1600s. Anne Hutchinson, daughter of a twice-censured, twice-imprisoned, and "silenced" English clergyman, was compulsively outspoken in behalf of the covenant of grace, even in the face of banishment and excommunication. Mary Dyer had a compelling urge to witness for her "heretical" Quaker faith and followed a straight path to the gallows. Lady Deborah Moody, gentle but determined, took an unflinching stand for freedom of worship in dogmatic New England, and left the colony to build her own model community in more tolerant surroundings.

That these three women became protesters in Puritan New England is astonishing. The church was male, the government was male, God was male—even the Devil was male. Boston, particularly, was barren ground for dissidents. Not that the Puritan fathers had not been dissidents themselves when they rejected the Church of England, condemning its clergy for their enjoyment of "life's fleshpots," for being followed about by "flunkies in scarlet livery and gold braid," and for "making merchandise of the Church of God." The Puritan fathers emigrated to Massachusetts to restore the church to "its primitive order, libertie, and bewtie." In carrying out their purification campaign they imposed a rule of conformity that turned women like Anne Hutchinson, Mary Dyer, Lady Deborah Moody, and others against Puritan intolerance. Theocracy—the complete union of church and state—made it almost impossible for any kind of protest to be effective. The government and the church were one—an impregnable bulwark against dissident thinking. Nonconforming Bostonians had two choices in the 1600s—to be silent or to move elsewhere.

Cohesion, if not conformity, was what Boston particularly needed in the 1630s. The colony was having trouble with its charter. The Indians were restless. The French were edging down from their Canadian foothold. It was the wrong moment in the colony's history for religious nonconformists, particularly women, to trouble an already troubled Boston.

Anne Hutchinson, her husband, Will, and their children disembarked in Boston in September 1634, expecting a warm welcome from the Reverend John Cotton, whom Anne and her family had followed to Boston. Cotton had been her pastor in Alford, England, and had introduced her to a new aspect of religious thought—the covenant of grace. Now Anne and the Reverend John Cotton were in the same land again and Anne was eager to listen to his inspiring sermons. She was looking forward to more discussions on the covenant of grace—the belief that God dwells within each person, and that constant communication can be maintained directly between

This statue in Boston honors Anne Hutchinson as a "courageous exponent of civil liberty and religious toleration." Photograph by George M. Cushing

God and man. It was a doctrine not shared by the Puritan Church of Boston; in fact, they called it heresy. The covenant of grace promised that mankind, without the help of the clergy, could find inspiration and guidance by direct communication with God. The covenant of grace diminished the role of the clergy as the sole interpreters of God's will, a fact that jeopardized the clergy's lofty position in the community. The Boston church laid its theological stress on interpretation of the will of God by the clergy alone, on strict conformity to church creeds, and on the covenant of works, which included, a Puritan father once said, "secret prayer, family exercises, conscience of Sabbaths, reverence of ministers, frequenting of sermons, diligence in calling, and honesty in dealing."

The covenant of grace had not been a religious issue in Boston until Anne Hutchinson arrived. The Reverend John Cotton diplomatically had kept silent. Anne Hutchinson, however, was not a quiet woman. She soon became well known all over Boston for her skill in caring for the sick; she made friends in the community; and she enthusiastically shared her covenant of grace with other women at meetings held in the spacious house that her husband, Will, had built for her. A number of well-known Bostonians, both men and women, including young Governor Vane, began attending the meetings. For a time the magistrates and the clergy tolerated these weekly gatherings, occasionally warning Anne that outspokenness might get her into trouble. Anne Hutchinson had inherited the same contentious and fearless spirit that her father had shown, but Anne was not as easily "silenced" as her clergyman father had been in England.

The size and impact of Anne Hutchinson's weekly meetings on the Boston community soon began to concern both civic and religious leaders. Governor Winthrop later wrote in his *Journal* that "the church . . . was brought under much infamy and

neere dissolution" by Anne's "two public lectures every week in her house, whereto sixty or eighty persons did usually resort" and at which she reproached "most of the ministers (viz., all except Mr. Cotton) for not preaching a covenant of free grace, and that they had not the seal of the spirit, nor were able ministers of the New Testament." A later governor of Massachusetts, Thomas Hutchinson, a descendant of Anne Hutchinson, stated that "the whole church of Boston, a few members excepted, were her converts." The permissiveness of the covenant of grace and its intellectually liberating aspects probably attracted many members of the Boston community to Anne Hutchinson's meetings.

In September 1637, three years after her arrival in Boston, Anne received a summons to appear before Massachusetts Governor Winthrop and the magistrates for "traducing the ministers and the ministry." Facing trial for her faith did not intimidate Anne Hutchinson. In fact she may have considered it an opportunity to bring new converts to the covenant of grace. She was a brilliant logician and had a prodigious memory. The trial was probably equally enjoyable for the clergy, who relished theological argumentation and were no doubt eager to overpower a woman whose mind they grudgingly admitted was extraordinarily keen.

Anne had almost cleared herself, but at the very end she "vented her revelations," saying that "she had it revealed to her that she should come into New England, and should here be persecuted, and that God would ruin us and our posterity, and the whole state, for the same." To the Puritan fathers, who had founded their community in order to uphold the true will of God, this was heresy. And so "the court proceeded and banished her; but because it was winter, they committed her to a private house, where she was well provided, and her own friends and the elders permitted to go to her, but none else."

Ill and alone, troubled and shattered by her banishment, Anne Hutchinson day after day faced visits from the "elders," who urged her to repent, to recant, or tried to entrap her in further heresy. Will Hutchinson, a truly devoted husband, was away looking for a new home. Anne's many friends, among them some outstanding families in the community, were in jeopardy, particularly those who had signed a petition in her behalf. They were being disarmed, disenfranchised, losing their civic jobs. Anne's excommunication became inevitable. She was tried before the clergy and church of Boston in March 1638. Though the Reverend John Cotton had convinced Anne that she must make a public recantation, the clergy found errors in her "repentance and recantation," and claimed she spoke "with reservations." And so Anne was excommunicated as well as banished, a double humiliation for this concerned and genuinely sincere woman.

Several families followed the Hutchinsons into exile in 1638. Anne and Will Hutchinson moved to Aquidneck, Rhode Island, an island that they purchased with friends from the Indians. One misfortune followed another. Anne had a difficult pregnancy. Will Hutchinson died in 1642. Anne then moved to the present-day Pelham Bay Park area of the Bronx in New York with six of her youngest children. A year later, in 1643, the entire family except

one child was massacred by the Indians. Some in Boston called Anne's death a "remarkable judgement of God for her heresies." Others charged the "guilt of murder upon the colony." A tract attributed to a Samuel Groome (d. 1683) reminds Boston readers of the "barbarous action committed against Mrs. Anne Hutchinson, whom you first imprisoned, then banished, and so exposed her to that desolate condition that she fell into the hands of the Indians, who murdered her and her family, except one child," and accuses professors and clerics of "having pumped and sifted her" to "get something against her," and of "taking their opportunity when her husband and friends . . . were absent."

Of all Anne Hutchinson's many friends, Mary Dyer alone rose and walked out of the church with her after her excommunication in 1638. For this act the Dyer family—Mary, her husband, William, and their four sons—were promptly excommunicated and banished. They moved to Newport, Rhode Island, where William Dyer soon held responsible positions in the colony. When he was sent on a political mission to England in 1652, Mary Dyer accompanied her husband and remained in England for five years. There she became a convert to the Quaker faith which George Fox, founder of the Society of Friends, had begun teaching in England in 1647. Its doctrine of inner light was similar to Anne Hutchinson's covenant of grace. Its adherents believed each person was guided by the indwelling spirit of God, and they were not afraid to speak out in order to let all witness the spirit within them.

The first two Quakers to come to Amer-

MARY DYER
QUAKER

WITNESS FOR RELIGIOUS FREEDOM
HANGED ON BOSTON COMMON 1660

Mary Dyer's unwavering commitment to her religious beliefs is reflected in this statue by Quaker sculptor Sylvia Shaw Judson. Photograph by Susan Castator

ica were women, and soon Quakers were popping up everywhere in New England. One entered a Puritan meetinghouse with two bottles in his hand, which he crashed to the floor, shouting "Thus will the Lord break you in pieces." A young woman walked into a Sunday morning Puritan service in Newbury stark-naked "to show people the nakedness of their rulers." Women were allowed to speak at Quaker meetings, a permissiveness that only encouraged the Puritans to denounce Quakers as "madmen, lunaticks, daemoniacks." Boston found, in the Society of Friends, another heresy to attack, and Mary Dyer was to become its first woman victim.

Mary Dyer was prepared for persecution when she set foot in Boston in 1657 and was promptly jailed as a member of the "cursed sect of heretics called Quakers." She was willing to remain in prison as a witness to her faith, but her husband came up from Newport and secured her release. The next year, 1685, Mary Dyer was expelled from New Haven for her Quaker preaching. The following year she was back in Boston to visit two English Quaker men who had been imprisoned, though all three knew about a new law that the Puritan clergy had pushed through by a single vote banishing Quakers under pain of death. The three Quakers were banished on September 12, 1659, and were told that they would surely be hanged on Boston Common if they came back. But they were back with other Quakers in October, protesting the law. This time Governor John Endecott was forced to pass the death sentence on all three. To the loud beating of drums to drown out incendiary speeches along the way, the three

Quaker militants were led through Boston streets to the gallows. They went willingly and joyfully. The two men were hanged, but Mary Dyer, on the intercession of her son and of the governors of Connecticut and Nova Scotia, was reprieved. She quietly went back to Rhode Island. By May 31, 1660, Mary Dyer had slipped away again to Boston, determined to prove the strength of her faith by giving up her life. This time not even her husband's plea could save her. She heard the death sentence, walked through the streets to the gallows, and died a Quaker witness for freedom of conscience in Puritan Boston.

Lady Deborah Moody was also nonconformist in her religious views and a staunch proponent of civil liberty and she, too, was troubled by the intolerance of Puritan Massachusetts. The first woman to head a colony, Lady Deborah was in her mid-fifties in 1639 when she became one of the growing number of women who decided to leave England alone and take up land in the New World. She may have expected to find the New World more liberal than England; she soon discovered that it was not. She first settled in a neighborhood which later was to become Lynn; then she moved to Saugus, then to Swampscott, and for a time she had a house in Salem. But in none of these communities did she find the tolerance she was seeking. By 1643 she was being admonished for such unorthodox views as her opposition to the union of church and state and her opposition to infant baptism.

Four years of religious intransigence in Massachusetts was enough for Lady Deborah, so again she moved with a group of friends, also dissatisfied with Puritan Massachusetts, to the more tolerant atmosphere of Dutch New Amsterdam. At Gravesend on the southwest corner of Long Island she received from the Dutch a patent granting her both freedom of worship and self-government. There Lady Deborah and her companions began building a town where they could implement all their liberal ideas far away from the prying eyes and ears of the Puritan magistrates of Massachusetts. Lady Deborah paid the Indians for her land. Houses were built for convenience, comfort, and snugness against wintry Atlantic winds. Town meetings were held to decide on village improvement and security plans. A church was built where every religious faith and sect—Catholic, Protestant, Quaker—were welcome to worship according to their conscience. Lady Deborah's extensive collection of books served as a public library. In 1657 Quaker missionaries visited Lady Deborah's town and were welcomed into her home; she may or may not have become a Quaker herself. Later, however, her town became a center of Quakerism on Long Island. Lady Deborah had fifteen peaceful years in her "model" town before her death about 1658. Even Governor John Winthrop, who had called her a "dangerous woman" when she lived in Massachusetts, later wrote of her as "a wise and anciently religious woman."

Maryland was one of the few Catholic colonies along the Atlantic seaboard and one of the first colonies to pass a Toleration Act (1649) declaring that no professed Christian should be "troubled, molested or discountenanced" for his' or her religion. Lord (Cecilius) Baltimore, the colony's proprietor, who was Catholic, had inherited Maryland from his father, Lord (George) Baltimore, who had received the province from Protestant King Charles I of England in 1625. As proprietor, Lord Baltimore proposed to handle equitably his dealings with all religious faiths. "Suffer no scandall or offence to be given to any of the Protestants, whereby any just complaint may hereafter be made," Lord Baltimore told his brother Leonard Calvert, when he appointed Calvert governor of Maryland. Religious insurrection, which Lord Baltimore had so scrupulously hoped to avoid in Maryland, did inadvertently occur, bringing into public prominence and into history Margaret Brent, the first American woman who had the courage to demand the vote.

Mistress Margaret Brent, spinster, arrived in Maryland in 1638 with her sister, Mary, her two brothers, Giles and Fulke, and servants and laborers to work the land. Margaret and Mary took up 70½ acres near St. Mary's City, capital of the colony. Later Margaret acquired about 1,000 acres on Kent Island from her brother, in payment of a debt owed her. Margaret Brent soon showed herself to be a shrewd businesswoman. She raised cattle on Kent Island. She operated a mill there. She loaned money. She prosecuted her debtors with persistence, her name appearing on court records more than a hundred times, and more often as a plaintiff than as a defendant. When her brothers were away she was frequently given power of attorney to act for them.

Ingle's rebellion broke out in 1643 while Governor Calvert was in England. The rebels, who were protesting Catholic power in Maryland, became so aggressive that Governor Calvert on his return to the colony in 1644 had to import soldiers from nearby Virginia, pledging his estate and, if necessary, that of his brother the Lord Proprietor, as assurance that the soldiers would be paid. After two years of conflict, peace had scarcely been restored when Governor Calvert died in May 1647. On his deathbed he named Thomas Greene to succeed him as governor and Margaret Brent to settle his estate. "Take all and pay all" was his instruction to her.

Why Margaret Brent was appointed executrix for Governor Calvert has often been a matter of speculation. Was her sister, Anne, married to Governor Calvert? Was Governor Calvert in love with her? Or was the governor simply confident that Margaret Brent had the ability and the good judgment to meet emergencies? The appointment certainly placed considerable responsibility on Margaret's shoulders. The Calvert estate was too small to pay off the Virginia soldiers, who were restlessly demanding both money and food. And as for food, there was a corn shortage and the price of corn was high. Suits were being filed by Calvert's creditors.

Margaret Brent took immediate command. She obtained power of attorney for the Lord Proprietor. She sold some of his cattle to pay the restless soldiers. She imported corn from Virginia to feed them. She instigated proceedings to collect money due the Calvert estate. This decisive action probably saved the colony from renewed insurrection and collapse.

Margaret Brent's request for the right to vote came at about this time, perhaps as an attempt to strengthen her position. On January 21, 1648, she appeared before the Maryland Assembly, demanding two votes, one for herself, as property holder, the other as attorney for the proprietor, Lord Baltimore. If she had been a man she would have qualified for the vote on the basis of owning property, and her second request might have been granted pending instruction from the Lord Proprietor. But the assembly turned her down. Capable as she was, she was after all a woman.

Even though they refused her the vote, the assembly members loyally and emphatically stood behind Margaret when Lord Baltimore, "with bitter invectives," complained about her sale of his cattle. The assembly's reply pointed out that "as for Mrs. Brent's undertaking and medling with your Lordships Estate here . . . we do Verily Believe and in Conscience report that it was better for the Collonys safety at that time in her hands than in any mans else in the whole Province after your Brothers death for the Soldiers would never have treated any other with that Civility and respect and though they were even ready at times to run into mutiny yet she still pacified them. . . ." Margaret Brent, the assembly reported, "deserved favour and thanks from your Honour for her so much concurring to the Public Safety."

Lord Baltimore apparently was unconvinced, and continued to complain about the sale of his cattle. A power shift was taking place in London about this time, and the election of a Protestant Parliament was imminent. Lord Baltimore's concern, as a Catholic, may have been fear that the Maryland charter might be withdrawn, and that the Catholic Brents were too much in the limelight. The Brents, also, may have sensed a change. By 1651 all the Brents were established in nearby Virginia, where Margaret continued her business from a plantation, which she named "Peace." She died about 1671, apparently still a spinster and still a successful businesswoman, even without a vote.

Though Lady Deborah Moody wisely managed her Gravesend community, and though Margaret Brent was proved a skilled businesswoman in Maryland, other women, somewhat later in the century, were persecuted as the cause of a community's difficulties. The mass hysteria that led to the Salem witch hunt took place in the particularly troubled year of 1692 when the Massachusetts Bay Colony was harassed by many problems. The Indians were becoming aggressive. There was a smallpox plague. The political situation of the colony regarding England was insecure. Pirates were attacking commercial ships along the New England coast. Taxes in the colonies were rising. The ownership and boundaries of land were more and more frequently disputed. People were irritated, frustrated, and edgy. Some Puritans blamed the Devil, who, they claimed, planned to set up a kingdom in Massachusetts. It was not long before women (and a few men) were found to be the instruments through which the Devil was working.

The Massachusetts witch hunting panic began in the home of a Salem clergyman, whose daughter Elizabeth, nine, her cousin Abigail Williams, eleven, and their friends had apparently been experimenting with the occult. They listened to the stories and ideas of Tituba, a household servant from Barbados, and whether from guilt or from some sort of excitement, some of the girls became hysterical. Witchcraft was suggested as an explanation of the girls' fits and visions, and the idea quickly spread through the town. Suddenly the girls were receiving attention they had never before enjoyed. They were asked to name those who were tormenting them. The bonds of silence to which women were supposed to adhere on all matters of religion were lifted in order to rid Salem of the Devil, and a witch hunt was under way. It was an ironic end to a century that had seen one woman die and another excommunicated for expressing their religious beliefs.

Thirteen women and seven men were executed for witchcraft during the Salem witchcraft hysteria. It lasted for four frightening months. Week after week, "witches" were brought to Court. The number of young girls who were subject to fits of hysteria, blindness, or who believed they were being pinched, stuck with pins, visited in their dreams, had grown. The word of the young female accusers was taken by the magistrates in examining the "witches" rather than the testimony of church members in good standing.

The arrest, conviction, and hanging of the elderly Rebecca Nurse, a respected member of the community, and on behalf of whom thirty-nine neighbors testified as to her piety, good works, and Christian conduct, shocked Salem and the clergy into taking a more sober view of what had been going on. The Reverend Increase Mather, addressing a group of Boston clergymen, criticized the type of evidence admitted by the court, saying that it was "better that ten suspected witches should escape than one honest person should be

An accusing girl points at a Salem woman she believes to be a witch.

NYPL Picture Collection

condemned," and that "I had rather judge a witch to be an honest woman, than judge an honest woman to be a witch." One by one people stood up in church and publicly admitted their guilt for false testimony or false accusations. A fast day was declared for the entire community on January 14, 1697. Judge Samuel Sewall made public acknowledgment of guilt of the Court on December 24, 1697. Standing in church, head bowed, he took the "blame and shame," with members of the congregation listening silently and remembering the death of nineteen of their neighbors.

By the end of the 1600s twelve English colonies along the east coast of the New World had thriving settlements, and so much land was still available that both women and men were being offered sizable tracts to come as settlers. A surprising number of enterprising women (true daughters of the adventurous Queen Elizabeth) did emigrate alone to the colonies, though relatively few names of these women emigrants have survived. Maryland's generous land offers to women brought, besides Margaret Brent, Mary Tranton, Frances White, Elizabeth Beach, and Winifred Seaborne. Some of these women brought servants, claimed large tracts of land and established thriving plantations. Maryland men occasionally protested because single women remained single, and suggested that a law be passed compelling women to "marry within seven years after land shall fall to her," but no such law was ever passed.

The terms of land grants varied from colony to colony. Maryland, as one example, had the head-right system, which

meant that any man or woman affluent enough to bring over servants was given 100 acres free for each able-bodied man, and 50 acres free for each woman or child. The colony's proprietor collected an annual two shillings (later four) per 100 acres.

Elizabeth Poole settled in Taunton, Massachusetts, in the late 1600s. Taunton's great seal, adopted January 1, 1865, bears a woman's figure, which may be hers, and the motto Dux Femina Facti [a woman was the leader of things accomplished]. One of Elizabeth Poole's alleged accomplishments was to form a joint stock company in 1652, capitalized at 600 pounds, for the manufacturing of iron bars. This iron bloomery, built on the Cohannet River, was one of the first, if not the first, successful iron production plant in the New World.

Elizabeth Haddon's father, who had no sons, sent his twenty-year-old daughter to oversee 400 acres of land in New Jersey that he had acquired in 1689. Within a year she had started a colony, built a comfortable home, and married John Estaugh, a Quaker missionary to whom she had the courage to propose marriage. Haddonfield, New Jersey, bears her name. Longfellow tells her story in the Theologian's Tale in *Tales of a Wayside Inn*.

Women without money, who wished to leave England for adventure or to escape an unwanted marriage, or for other reasons, sometimes came as redemptioners, binding themselves to be sold into service by the master of their ship in return for free passage. In some colonies, Carolina for example, indentured women (after their term of service was completed) were offered land grants, though smaller than those offered men. In Maryland, indentured women received, at the end of their term of service, a pair of shoes and stockings, two white linen caps, a blue apron, a waistcoat, a petticoat, and a new shift of white linen.

London's Bridewell Penitentiary offered another less welcome source of women for the New World; shipping women prisoners off to the New World was a convenient way of emptying London's already crowded prisons. Trepanning (kidnapping) became a money-making device of enterprising shysters who combed London streets on sailing days, dragging women and children to the waterfront to be forcibly shipped off to the New World, and upon arrival "decked out for sale."

One of the chief anxieties of the early colonies was getting male colonists to establish roots in the New World so they would be contented, industrious, beget children, and stop complaining. Colony publicists painted glowing pictures of life in their colonies to attract women settlers. But some young women found life across the Atlantic far from a joyous holiday. One young woman of twenty, arriving penniless in South Carolina, married, worked side by side with her husband felling trees, operating the whipsaw, going

without bread, and working "like a slave." Another woman wrote her sister not to come to the New World because of "the Small pox which has been mortal to all sorts of the inhabitants" and because of an "earthquake and burning of the town or one third of it," and because of "great loss of cattle which I know by what has been found dead of mine."

At the turn of the seventeenth century the French, who had established a colony in Louisiana, needed women homemakers desperately. Louisiana had only twenty-seven French families in 1717. Louis XIV adopted the "brides' ship" idea that the English had used at Jamestown, and sent twenty girls of "unspotted reputation and upright lives" to Louisiana. The girls, Parisian born and with gourmet tastes, turned up their noses at the coarse, unappetizing Indian cornmeal bread Louisiana had to offer them. Their revolt is known as the Petticoat Rebellion. France's second Louisiana brides' ship, which arrived in 1728, proved more successful. The girls, known as *filles à la cassette* (girls supplied with caskets of clothing for their debut in the New World), were so carefully chosen and so closely chaperoned that they formed a female aristocracy of Louisiana wives.

CHAPTER FIVE

Three Women Religious Leaders

NEW GENERATIONS OF colonists, some 360,-000 of them, began to enjoy life's comforts by the early 1700s. One hundred years had passed since the first courageous women and men had set foot timorously in the New World. Frame houses, with glass windows and cast iron stoves, had replaced log cabins and shacks. Trees had been felled, fields planted, and a lucrative trade had been set up with the West Indies and Britain. Prices for wheat, tobacco, sugar, and rice were high. Newspapers, which were being published in all the major cities by the 1730s—New York, Williamsburg, Charleston, Philadelphia, Boston, Annapolis, Newport—kept people informed about happenings in the colonies and helped develop a sense of unity and togetherness. Life was more sophisticated in the major cities. Boston women were trying to be as fashionable and witty and to entertain as aristocratically as women at the British Court of St. James. Harvard students were being accused of frivolity, and, according to one prominent colonist, of "stealing, lying, swearing, idleness, picking of locks, and too frequent use of strong drink." Horse racing was a sport for which society and townspeople turned out by the hundreds in Virginia. Colonists were also beginning to resent being called "colonials," an indication that political attitudes were changing. People's minds were stirred in many directions, toward changes in religious sentiments, toward changes in duties and obligations, and above all toward a change in the representative relationship between themselves and the British Parliament. Williamsburg had frequent visiting troupes of actors. New York and Philadelphia had theatres. Puritanism was fading away, and colonists, whose new neighbors might be Mennonites, Presbyterians, Baptists, Methodists, Catholics, or Quakers, were ready to take a new look at religion. The Great Awakening, a wave of evangelistic preaching that swept the country, starting in the 1730s, found colonists ready to explore new emotional ways to God.

Do but consider what it is to suffer extreme torment forever and ever; to suffer it day and night, from one day to another, from one year to another, from one age to another, from one thousand ages to another, and so, adding age to age, and thousands to thousands, in pain, in wailing and lamenting, groaning and shrieking and gnashing your teeth; with your soul full of dreadful grief and amazement, with your bodies and every member full of racking torture, without any possibility of getting ease; without any possibility of moving God to pity by your cries . . . but will remain to roast through eternity . . .

With words such as these Congregational theologian-clergyman Jonathan Edwards sparked the flame of the Great Religious Awakening that swept the American colonies in the early 1700s from Georgia to New England, with audiences rising to their feet and shouting in anguish, "What shall I do to be saved?" Edwards himself was a mild, scholarly man, devoted to his wife, Sarah Pierrepont Edwards, a religious mystic whose experiences had a profound effect upon him. Edwards's *A Faithful Narrative of the Surprising Work of God in the Conversion of Many Hundred Souls in Northhampton*, published in 1736, after Edwards had held his famous Northampton revival (1734–35), had far-reaching consequences. The

Reverend George Whitefield, a close friend of Methodist divine John Wesley, read *A Faithful Narrative* in Savannah, Georgia, and started preaching his way north. Whitefield's sermon in Philadelphia was so powerful that skeptic Benjamin Franklin poured every penny (even the gold) in his pocket into the collection plate. Whitefield rode north 800 miles, preaching 175 sermons, sometimes pacing the platform, shouting, gesturing. Audiences went wild with religious ecstasy. In England, John Wesley, who was to found the Methodist Church in England, read *A Faithful Narrative* as he walked from London to Oxford, and he, too, began preaching with similar ecstatic results.

Three women during this period founded religious communities that brought a new ordering of values into the lives of the people who participated in them. The acceptance of Jemima Wilkinson, Barbara Heck, and Mother Ann Lee, as women with relevant religious messages may have been facilitated by the emotionalism that women and men had shared side by side at Great Awakening revival meetings.

Jemima Wilkinson (1752–1819) was a devout young Quaker who had been dismissed from the Society of Friends for attending meetings of a New Light Baptist group in her hometown of Cumberland, Rhode Island. The New Light Baptists were a separatist group which permitted women to speak in meetings. After recovering from a serious illness in October 1776, Jemima Wilkinson claimed that during her illness she had died, and had been sent back to preach to a sinful world. From then on she called herself Publick Universal Friend, and would not answer to any other name during the forty years she traveled and preached (even during Revolutionary years) throughout Rhode Island, Massachusetts, Connecticut, and later Pennsylvania. Repent, forsake evil, and prepare for God's judgment were the basic admonitions of her preaching. There was an aura of Messianic mysticism about her that attracted a large following, among them many well-established citizens. The Publick Universal Friend sometimes made prophecies, sometimes interpreted dreams, and occasionally attempted faith healing in the early years of her mission. In the 1780s she established a settlement where her followers could seclude themselves from the "wicked world." She was opposed to violence, and she spoke out against slavery long before other women addressed the public. The movement, which lasted forty years, did not survive after Jemima Wilkinson's death in 1818, and the followers of the Publick Universal Friend gradually dispersed.

Barbara Heck (1734–1804), known as the mother of American Methodism, arrived in New York City in 1760 with a group of Methodists who had been converted to Methodism by one of John Wesley's itinerant Methodist preachers. The group practiced its religion quietly in members' homes in New York for six years. On a fall day in 1766, Mrs. Heck found some of the group playing cards. This "wickedness" shocked her. Throwing the cards into the fire, she rushed to Philip Embury, her cousin and a lay preacher, urging him to save the group from worldliness. A Methodist Society was formed in New York, and by 1768, through the ef-

forts of Mrs. Heck, a Methodist church was erected on John Street in New York, the first center of Methodism in the United States. The Hecks moved frequently in the next twenty years, with Mrs. Heck actively organizing Methodist churches at each new home site—at Camden in upper New York State in 1770, in Canada at Sorel (near Montreal) in 1774, in Augusta Township near present-day Maynard (Canada) in 1778.

Mrs. Heck's religious movement was hers alone. She was apparently not in touch with the Great Religious Awakening Movement in America. She apparently had no contact with the Reverend George Whitefield during his 1769 visit to the United States, nor with Francis Asbury whom John Wesley appointed general superintendent of Methodism in America in 1771. Barbara Heck's devotion to Methodism continued unabated throughout her life and is commemorated today by the John Street Methodist Church in New York that stands on or near the site where, through Barbara Heck's efforts, the first Methodist church in America was built in 1768.

As early as 1810 another woman, Mother Seton (1774–1821), had founded and become head of the first sisterhood established in America which became the Sisters of Charity of St. Joseph's. She is also credited with founding the first Catholic school system in the United States. In 1963 she was beatified and in 1974 was being considered for canonization.

Mother Ann Lee (1736–1784), brought the Shaker religion to America in 1774 after having a revelation that New England (and not old England) was the

Shaker women doing their religious dance. NYPL Picture Collection

place where the gospel would take root and flourish. Like the Publick Universal Friend, Mother Ann Lee found her first converts among New Light Baptists and others stirred by the Great Religious Awakening of the 1700s. Mother Ann Lee was converted to Shakerism after a hard life working in an English textile mill, and an unhappy marriage. As she was recovering from a complete physical breakdown she felt born "into the spiritual kingdom" and felt for the first time that she had a mission in life. Quakers with whom she had previously taken refuge introduced her to a new religious group. They were called "Shakers," because of the shouting, singing, speaking in new tongues, and shaking that was a part of their worship. Mother Ann Lee was soon a leader in the

Shaker movement. She came to America in 1774.

Four years passed, and Mother Ann Lee and the seven followers who came with her to America established themselves quietly in Watervliet (near Albany), New York, before an opportunity to preach presented itself. Again it was the New Light Baptists of the Great Religious Awakening Movement who came to Mother Ann Lee in 1780 and asked to hear her message. Many conversions followed. Mother Ann Lee carried her message through New England and into eastern New York State. Her magnetic personality, her high ideals, her visions and revelations, gained for her great respect as well as converts from all walks of life. Eleven communities were established before her death in 1784. The

The graceful lines of Shaker design can be seen in the bonnet and basket of this present-day Shaker sister. Photograph by W. F. Winter

movement reached its peak between 1830 and 1860 when more than 6,000 Shakers had established some 19 communes, all stressing Mother Ann Lee's goals for an ideal religious community.

Mother Ann Lee was one of the first American women to take a stand for the complete equality of men and women. Shaker men did the farm and shop work. Women did the housework, cooking, tailoring. The Shakers believed in celibacy, so they occupied separate quarters, but men and women met together for meals and worship. The Shakers were industrious and ingenious. They invented the circular saw, the clothespin, the flat-sided broom, automated seed planters, and several labor-saving tools. Their craftsmanship expressed outwardly their inner ideals and goals. The clean, graceful lines of Shaker furniture is still much sought after and often imitated today.

In the 1970s the Shakers still had two surviving communes. In 1972 there were fourteen surviving members of this longest experiment in Christian celibate communal living in America. The long duration of the Shaker movement is a monument to Mother Ann Lee's faith in a higher plane of living close to "Christ who dwells within me."

CHAPTER SIX

A Southern Family and a Northern Family

YOU HAD TO be married by twenty—well, at least by twenty-five. Otherwise you would risk becoming an old maid, and that was the worst thing that could happen to a teen-age girl on a Southern plantation in the early 1700s. To be called an "old virgin," a "pitiable encumbrance" or a "stale maid" meant that you had lost your chances for a husband practically forever, and would have to live out your life on your family's plantation, supervising the poultry yard or the kitchen garden. Southern girls concentrated on getting married, and sometimes they were married as early as thirteen or fourteen.

Balls were a good place for young people to meet, and there were many balls in the Southern colonies of Virginia, Maryland, and the Carolinas. Most teen-agers loved dancing and would dance minuets, jigs, reels, and country dances as long as

the music (violins and French horns) played. Dressed in hoop petticoats with tight-fitting bodices cut very low, hair piled high in puffs and curls, teen-age girls flirted discreetly with prospective beaus. Sometimes dances and house parties lasted for several days.

Young people were able to see one another more privately after the girl's father and the suitor's father exchanged letters stating their willingness to allow the two young people the privilege of formal courting. The father of each determined what financial contributions would be made in the event of marriage. Young women of wealth were warned against "fops," "rakes," "drunkards," and "fortune seekers." Prospective bridegrooms frankly discussed and weighed the advantages of brides with a "handsome fortune."

There were few public schools, and compulsory education was unheard of. Plantation owners' daughters were trained for one career only—marriage. Girls received lessons from private tutors or in private classes, in such subjects as French, drawing, reading, writing, accounts, playing the harpsichord, singing, dancing. And there were homemaking pursuits that every girl had to learn in order to prepare herself for marriage—sewing, spinning, cooking, taking care of the garden and the poultry, and preparing elaborate menus that were part of plantation life. There were slaves to do the hard work, but women had to know how the work was done and supervise the servants.

The first schools, which began opening in the 1700s, had a very limited curriculum for girls. To teach girls to read the Bible, write a good hand, a good letter, and to sew were the objectives of most girls' schools. Girls ended their schooling at the age of twelve, boys at fourteen. Tradesmen, merchants, and other villagers who could afford to pay for their daughters' education sent the girls to parsons' schools or subscription schools that were financed by a group of parents. The idea of free education was being discussed in the South, but an attempt to open a free school in Maryland in 1723 was unsuccessful.

Eliza Lucas Pinckney was an exceptionally well-educated southern woman. When Eliza Lucas arrived with her family in South Carolina in 1738, the eight original promoters of the Carolinas had already turned their proprietary grant back to the Crown, having discovered that neither silkworm culture, real estate, olive growing, wine production nor currant growing was the get-rich-quick venture that they had anticipated. It took teen-ager Eliza Lucas to cultivate successfully a profitable cash crop that no one else had thought of . . . a crop that was to help sustain the South Carolina economy for thirty years.

The Lucases had come to South Carolina from Antigua in the West Indies where Eliza's father, Lieutenant Colonel Lucas, was stationed. Because the West Indies climate did not agree with Eliza's mother, the family left Antigua and settled in Wappo Creek, South Carolina, seventeen miles from Charles Town. A crisis in Antigua, however, soon forced Eliza Lucas's father to return to the West Indies, leaving his seventeen-year-old daughter in charge of their plantation.

Both father and daughter were interested in agricultural experiments. "I love the vegitable world extremely," Eliza once wrote her father, and so did he. Eliza browsed in Virgil to find out how crops were cultivated in ancient Italy. And when her father sent her seeds from the West Indies—ginger, cotton, lucern, cassaba, and indigo—she planted them and nursed them along, reporting to her father from time to time that the cotton and most of the ginger had been "cut off by the frost," that the lucern was "dwindling," and that the "frost took the indigo seed before it was dry." These casualties did not discourage Eliza. She kept on experimenting, particularly with indigo, which was at that time highly prized in Europe as a dye. Preparing indigo for market was a difficult and tricky process, and when Eliza was ready to master its intricacies, her father sent an overseer from the West Indies to teach her the routine of cutting the leaves at exactly the right time, soaking them in

putting my design in Execution. I suppose according to custom you
will show this to yr Uncle and Aunt, "she is a good girl says Mrs Pinckney
she is never Idle and always means well" tell the little Visionary
says your Uncle come to town and partake of some of the amusements
suitable to her time of life", pray tell him I think there is, and what
he may now think, whims and projects may turn out well by and by
out of many surely one may hitt.

I promised to tell you when the mocking bird began to sing,
the little warbler has done wonders, the first time he opened his
soft pipe this spring, he inspired me with the spirit of Rymeing
and produced the 3 following lines while I was lacing my Stays

Sing on thou charming mimick of the feathered kind
and let the rational a lesson learn from thee
to Mimick (not verses) beside yourself but harmony

If you let any mortal see this exquisite piece of poetry you
shall never have a line more than this specimen,
and how great will be your loss you who have seen the above may
judge as well as
Yr m. obed. Servt.
Eliza. Lucas

I hope you never forget to pay
my Mamma's and my best respects
to Colo Pinckney and Lady

Part of a letter showing Eliza Lucas's signature in which she writes that she is cultivating a large plantation of oaks "which I look upon as my own property, whether my father gives me the land or not." South Carolina Historical Society

vats, fermenting them to the proper color, drawing off into another vat, beating until thick, allowing setting to take place and the sediment to form into cakes ready for shipment. Eliza let her first good crop go to seed, which she distributed among her neighbors so they could participate in this new Carolina crop project. By 1746 some 40,000 pounds of indigo were shipped to England, the next year 100,000 pounds and shipments continued uninterrupted until the Revolutionary War.

Another of Eliza's agricultural projects was to plant a forest of oak trees so that when they reached maturity they could be used for shipbuilding. She also planted a fig orchard. Meanwhile she was reading John Locke "over and over again" to see "wherein personal Identity consisted and if I was the very same Selfe"; she was studying law books to learn how to make wills; and she was teaching her young sister, Polly, along with two black girls how to read. By seven o'clock each morning she was walking through the plantation to see if all the servants "were at their respective business."

In 1744, at the age of twenty-one, Eliza married Charles Pinckney, twenty years her senior. Silk raising became her next business project; she raised silkworms, reeled the cocoons, and supervised the process of weaving it into cloth. When her first child was only a few months old, she sent to London for a new toy to teach him to "play himself into learning" and hoped to teach him his letters when he was old enough to speak. The Pinckney family, two sons and one daughter, spent five years in England from 1753–1758, because Charles Pinckney had been appointed commissioner for the colony. Upon their return to South Carolina, Mr. Pinckney died, and Eliza found herself managing seven separate landholdings belonging to her husband's estate.

Eliza Pinckney's intelligence, vigor, and industry served as a fine model to her children. Her two sons fought in the Revolutionary War, one as an aide to George Washington. Her son Charles represented South Carolina at the Constitutional Convention. Her son Thomas was governor of South Carolina in 1787.

The togetherness of the colonial family group, from the Carolinas to Maine, was one of its endearing aspects. Someone was always ready to lend a helping hand, or even supervise a plantation, as Eliza Lucas Pinckney had done. There was ungrudging willingness to be caretakers of kin, regardless of infirmity or penury. There was always room (and usually work) for a grandmother or a spinster aunt or an orphaned child on a Southern plantation, in an aristocratic brick house on Boston's Beacon Hill, in a log cabin on the edge of the forest, or in a modest clapboard house in a New Jersey village.

One of the most exemplary of colonial caretaker families was the Benjamin Franklin family. Jane Franklin Mecom (1712–1794) was Franklin's favorite sister. The two corresponded all their lives; one of Franklin's last surviving letters was written to Jane, the "crooked line," he explained, being occasioned by his lying ill in bed. Jane had a hard life. Her husband was often ailing, two sons died insane, and she watched over her father and mother in their old age, taking in boarders and selling notions to support her household. Franklin admired his sister's bravery; Jane was proud of her brother's prosperity and the variety of his accomplishments. Jane frequently sent Franklin soap that she made and his favorite preserved fish. He sent her gold pieces or slipped currency into his letters or sent merchandise that she could sell in Boston. After Franklin's death, Jane lived for four years in the old Franklin family house in Boston, which Ben Franklin had left her in his will. She never knew that Franklin had written more letters to her during his lifetime than to anyone else.

Deborah Read (c. 1707–1774) became Benjamin Franklin's common-law wife in 1730. She was not his social or intellectual equal—a fact they both accepted—and though it made their marriage somewhat unconventional, it did not interfere with the warmth of their relationship, which lasted 44 years. Deborah competently managed the stationery and book shop attached to the Franklin printing shop in

Philadelphia. She looked after the household, and during the fourteen years Franklin was in England and France on behalf of American political interests, she had the power of attorney and corresponded with him on business and family affairs. From England, Franklin sent his wife presents —"a fine piece of Pompadour satin," a Turkey carpet, a box of cheese, a "gimcrack corkscrew," a crimson satin cloak, English china, a "little instrument to core apples," "seven yards of printed cotton, blue ground, to make you a gown," and a "large fine jug for beer, to stand in the cooler. I fell in love with it at first sight; for I thought it looked like a fat jolly dame, clean and tidy, with a neat blue calico gown on, goodnatured and lovely, and put me in mind of somebody." Deborah in turn sent her husband American food, which he craved—cornmeal, buckwheat flour, apples, cranberries, dried

Mrs. Deborah Franklin. NYPL Picture Collection

Benjamin Franklin holding a political discussion in the comfortable setting of his Philadelphia home.

peaches, nuts. Deborah Franklin died on December 19, 1774, while Franklin was still overseas. As he faced his homecoming in 1775 he spoke sadly of the loss of "my old faithful companion" and of his long marriage during which each endeavored to make the other happy.

In 1737, Franklin's older brother James died. His widow, Ann S. Franklin (1696–1763), took over the printshop in Newport, Rhode Island, and with the help of two daughters, Elizabeth and Mary, ran the business. In his youth, Ben had been a runaway apprentice in his brother's printshop, and to make amends for this, he educated his brother's son, trained him as a printer, and sent him back to Newport

with new type. Ann Franklin, meanwhile, had become colony printer. At her death in 1763, she was eulogized as a "woman of great Integrity and Uprightness" and "as a compassionate benefactor to the Poor."

The Franklins had a son, who died of smallpox in childhood, and a daughter, Sarah. Sally Franklin Bache (1743–1808) studied reading, writing, grammar, arithmetic, penmanship, needlework, French, and music, and learned to play the armonica, a musical instrument invented by her father. In 1767, at the age of twenty-four, she married a Philadelphia merchant by the name of Richard Bache. Franklin, who was in England, was dubious about the marriage and the future prospects of his son-in-law and gave instructions to his wife about the amount of money to be spent on clothes and furnishings for the bride. The marriage worked out prosperously and happily, the couple living in the Franklin home where seven children were born. Although constantly urging her to be thrifty, Franklin frequently pampered his daughter by sending her clothes—a muff and tippet, gloves, a silk negligee—and lavender water.

Sally kept her father informed about the goings-on in the colonies. Twice during the Revolutionary War when the British army advanced and she had to flee Philadelphia, Sally packed up her father's treasured possessions and books and sent them out of town. She raised money in Philadelphia to provide American Revolutionary soldiers with clothing, and the Franklin home was a center for the cutting and sewing of 2,200 shirts for Washington's army. "If there are in Europe any women who need a model of attachment to domestic duties and love for their country, Mrs. Bache may be pointed out to them as such," a French acquaintance of her father's wrote Franklin after a visit with the Baches in Philadelphia. In 1785 Franklin came back to spend his last five years comfortably and peacefully in Philadelphia with his grandchildren and his daughter, who had taken her mother's place in maintaining the closeness and solidarity of the Franklin family group.

CHAPTER SEVEN

Women During Revolutionary Years

FIFTEEN YEARS BEFORE the Declaration of Independence was signed, newspapers of various sizes and shapes, various type styles, lengths and widths, were carrying news of the worsening relationship between the colonies and Great Britain. Everyone seemed to have an opinion to express. From Maine to Georgia, in newspaper columns, broadsides, pamphlets, even in almanacs, political thought took the form of argument and counterargument, letters, sermons, essays, and speeches. Printed material was passed from hand to hand and read eagerly. John Adams wrote to Jefferson about this proliferation of material:

> The Revolution was in the minds of the people, and this was effected from 1760 to 1775, in the course of fifteen years before a drop of blood was shed at Lexington. The records of thirteen legislatures, the pamphlets, newspapers in all the col-

onies, ought to be consulted during that period to ascertain the steps by which the public opinion was enlightened and informed concerning the authority of Parliament over the colonies.

Women entered the field of newspaper publishing early in the century—some thirty women altogether. They usually did not choose this profession, but, as widows, they took over their husbands' businesses in order to support large families of children. These early women newspaper publishers competently edited copy, set type, and solicited printing jobs in competition with male colleagues.

Elizabeth Timothy, the first American woman to publish a newspaper, was one of the early widow-printers, publishing the weekly *South Carolina Gazette* from her husband's printing shop in Charleston, South Carolina. Benjamin Franklin, Timothy's copartner, had nothing but praise for Elizabeth Timothy, a Dutch woman by birth, and a meticulous account-keeper. With four children to support, she handled the business so thriftily that she was able to purchase it outright from Franklin at the expiration of the Franklin-Timothy partnership and turn it over to her son Peter in 1746. She immediately opened a small stationery store where she sold "Pocket Bibles, Primmers, Hornbooks and Reflections on Courtship and Marriage," prospering to such an extent that she left three houses, some land, and eight slaves at her death in 1757.

Her son, Peter Timothy, was forced to leave Charleston with his family during the British occupation and moved to Philadelphia. In 1782 Peter Timothy and two daughters were lost at sea on their way to the West Indies. His wife, Ann Timothy, returned to Charleston, and like her mother-in-law, Elizabeth Timothy, she began republishing her husband's newspaper, under the new name of the *State Gazette of South Carolina*. She became Printer to the State (printing official notices and legal documents) from 1785 to her death in 1792.

The name of Catherine Zenger (born Anna Catherine Maulin) is rarely mentioned in connection with the famous Zenger freedom-of-the-press trial that took place in New York City in 1735. But during the more than eight months that her husband, Peter Zenger, spent in jail awaiting trial on the charge of printing seditious libels against Colonel William Cosby, British Royal Governor of New York, it was Catherine Zenger who kept the printshop running. She set type, read proof, did some of the writing, and, with the help of

a journeyman printer, got her husband's accused *New-York Weekly Journal* off press. During this time she communicated with her husband about newspaper copy through a hole in his prison door. Zenger was defended so ably by the distinguished and elderly Andrew Hamilton of Philadelphia that he was acquitted by the jury in a decision that stands as the first great victory for freedom of the press.

When Zenger died in 1746, Catherine continued to publish the *New-York Weekly Journal* for two years and to accept printing jobs, including an Almanack published in 1749, which bears the imprint of the "Widow Catherine Zenger, at the Printing Office in Stone Street."

After the death of her husband, Anna Catherine Green (c. 1720–75), at the age of forty-five and having given birth to fourteen children, became publisher of the *Maryland Gazette* in 1767. Of particular significance in her newspaper career is the fact that she courageously printed news of resistance to the Townshend Acts, news of the Boston Tea Party, and of the Boston Port Act of 1774.

The Goddard family—widow Sarah Goddard, daughter, Mary Katherine, and son, William, successively published the *Providence Gazette* (1766–1768), the *Pennsylvania Chronicle* (1768), and the *Maryland Journal* (1773), Baltimore's first newspaper. From the *Maryland Journal* in January 1777 came the first printed copy of the Declaration of Independence with the signers' names. Mary Katherine Goddard's name appeared on the newspaper's masthead.

Women were applauded and commended by press and patriots for their

Catherine Zenger, who managed her husband's New-York Weekly Journal *while he was in jail, consults with him about newspaper copy through the prison door. Zenger Memorial Room, Federal Hall, New York City*

"display of zeal" in boycotting British products in the period before the Revolutionary War. "All domestic pleasures and enjoyments are absorbed in the great and important duty you owe your country," wrote Abigail Adams,

> for our country is, as it were, a secondary god, and the first and greatest parent. It is to be preferred to parents, wives, children, friends and all things, the gods only excepted, for if our country perishes, it is as impossible to save the individual, as to preserve one of the fingers of a mortified hand.

As public anger spread about the Revenue Act of 1764, which levied taxes on sugar, wine, silk, and linen, the Stamp Act of 1765 which required stamps to be affixed to legal papers and documents, and the Townshend Acts of 1767, which levied duties on English products imported into the colonies such as paper, glass, and particularly tea, Daughters of Liberty clubs began to spring up in the thirteen colonies. They intended to prove that the colonies could be self-sufficient and to protest taxation without representation, a grievance that, ironically enough, women were to endure for many years to come.

At the first Daughters of Liberty meeting, which took place in Providence, Rhode Island, in 1766 seventeen young women spent the day spinning, triggering the popularity of spinning matches. Homespun began to be worn as a protest. The graduating class of Rhode Island College (later Brown University) was clothed in suits of American homespun manufacture in 1769, as was the graduating class at Harvard in 1768.

Tea was one of the products most difficult for women to give up. It was the basis of all entertaining, and was served ceremoniously with a "gaudy equipage" of cups, saucers, cream bucket, silver sugar tongs, tea chest, and excellent blends of "Hyson, Congo and best double-fine." But women patriotically gave up tea. In Virginia, women stated that by the consumption of tea they would be "supporting Commissioners & other Tools of Power" and swore to refrain from drinking tea "until those Creatures, together with the Boston Standing Army are removed, and the Revenue Acts repealed." Three hundred Boston women resolved on January 31, 1770, "totally to abstain from the Use of Tea," and to absolutely refuse it "if it should be offered to us upon any Occasion whatsoever" until the "late Revenue Acts are repealed."

Women were inventive in finding tea substitutes. Liberty Tea was a brew made from loosestrife, a well-known and abundantly growing herb. This plant was pulled up by its roots, stripped of its leaves, the stalks boiled, then the leaves boiled in the stalk liquid. The leaves were then dried in the oven. Labrador Tea (also called Hyperion) was another tea substitute. It was brewed from raspberry leaves. Sage tea, ribwort tea, and currant tea were other tea substitutes.

The women of North Carolina carried their patriotism even beyond their sisters in other colonies. Matrons of Edenton, North Carolina, went so far as to pass resolutions on October 25, 1774, commending the Provincial Congress for its firm stand against British taxes and declaring that they would neither drink tea nor wear clothes of English manufacture until the tax was abolished. A mezzotint titled *A*

Society of Patriotic Ladies at Edenton in North Carolina was later printed in London as a caricature of the Edenton ladies' unabashed declaration.

When war broke out in 1775, women unhesitatingly sent their husbands and sons to battle, contributed their melted-down leaded window panes, pewter heirlooms, and clockweights to be used for bullets. They ran the farms and plantations while their husbands and sons were away. Inflation plagued the women, as shortages rapidly developed and prices skyrocketed. Linen was twenty dollars a yard, molasses twenty dollars a gallon (it came from the West Indies), and sugar four dollars a pound. "I cannot get a common winter coat and hat but just under 200 pounds," Sarah Franklin Bache wrote her father, Benjamin Franklin. And Abigail Adams wrote her husband, John Adams in June, 1778, that it was "as much as I can do to manufacture clothing for my family who would else be naked."

Women also learned to endure the terrors of war alone. "The house this instant shakes with the roar of cannon," Abigail Adams wrote John Adams from her Braintree, Massachusetts, home on March 2, 1776. "I have been to the door and find it is the cannonade from our army . . . No sleep for me to-night." Women watched their homes and all their possessions go up in flames, watched their cattle butchered, their food supplies commandeered by British troops. They were constantly uncertain whether to flee or to stay, as they lay awake listening attentively to determine if the sounds of battle were approaching or receding.

When the opportunity presented itself,

An old engraving titled **Heroic Women of the Revolution** *shows women in scenes of bravery and sacrifice. NYPL Picture Collection*

women did not hesitate to make bold decisions. Catherine Schuyler burned the entire wheat harvest at her home near Albany, New York, in July 1777 rather than let it fall into the hands of General Burgoyne's advancing army. Lydia Darrah, a Philadelphia Quaker, listened at the keyhole one night while British officers were holding a conference in her commandeered home in Philadelphia. Then, before sunrise, she stole away to warn Washington's forces of British battle plans. Several times during the Revolutionary War Eliza Lucas Pinckney was obliged to face British soldiers entering her plantation home at night. On one occasion, Mrs. Pinckney and her granddaughter who were sleeping in the same room were awakened by a frightened young girl entering their bedroom crying out, "Save me, save me, the British soldiers are after me." Mrs. Pinckney told the young lady to get into her own bed and lie there quietly. Then, with dignity and outrage she went down to face the soldiers who slunk away into the darkness, cowed by her indomitable and fearless courage.

Tory women, those loyal to the British, suffered greatly during the war. Their husbands were most often the officials appointed by the Crown, the governors of the colonies, the clergy, and sometimes large landowners, businessmen, merchants and tax collectors. Some Tory families left the country, immigrating to Jamaica or Canada or Nova Scotia; some returned to England; some Loyalists simply remained silent and stayed on as citizens of the new republic. Some Tories suffered loss of their property, their businesses, their plantations, by destruction or confiscation.

Two of the most observant and intellectual women of the Revolutionary War period were Abigail Smith Adams (1744–1818) and Mercy Otis Warren (1728–1814). Neither Mrs. Adams nor Mrs. Warren hesitated to speak out when they disapproved of the deliberations of Congress nor did they hesitate to air their views on the Declaration of Independence or the Constitution. Neither woman had any formal schooling. Abigail Adams's father was a graduate of Harvard and a Weymouth, Massachusetts, clergyman. She was a voracious reader in the family's well-stocked library and taught herself French, but never studied Latin. Mercy Warren came from a lawyer-merchant-farmer family. She learned by sitting in with her brothers while they were being tutored, and by reading in the family library. Both Mrs. Adams and Mrs. Warren participated in discussions at the family fireside. Both were married while in their twenties—Abigail at twenty-one to John Adams, Mercy at twenty-six to James Warren. Each woman had five children.

Abigail became the wife of one president and the mother of another president, John Quincy Adams. In her own right she became famous as a letter writer. While her husband was in Europe or serving as a delegate to the first Continental Congress, Abigail Adams took charge of her husband's business affairs, the farming, the education of the children, and found time to write the entertaining and thoughtful letters that kept her husband (and future generations) informed of the course of the Revolutionary War events and her observations on the problems of the emerging new republic.

"I am more and more convinced," she wrote to John Adams in 1775,

> that man is a dangerous creature; and that power, whether vested in many or a few, is ever grasping. . . . If we separate from Britain, what code of laws will be established? How shall we be governed, so as to retain our liberties? Can any government be free, which is not administered by general stated laws? Who shall frame these laws? Who will give them force and energy? . . . When I consider these things, and the prejudices of people in favor of ancient customs and regulations, I feel anxious for the fate of our monarchy or democracy, or whatever is to take place.

In a now famous letter that Abigail wrote to her husband while the Second Continental Congress was deliberating, she gently reminded him that the balance of power between men and women was not equal.

> . . . And, by the way, in the new code of laws which I suppose it will be necessary for you to make, I desire you would remember the ladies and be more generous and favorable to them than your ancestors. Do not put such unlimited power into the hands of the husbands. Remember, all men would be tyrants if they could. If particular care and attention is not paid to the ladies, we are determined to foment a rebellion . . . and will not hold ourselves bound by any laws in which we have no voice or representation.

Mercy Otis Warren became famous as the first American woman historian. Her home was a meeting place for antiroyalist political leaders such as John Adams and Samuel Adams. Her husband was a member of the Massachusetts Legislature, her brother a former king's advocate. Mercy

Mercy Otis Warren. NYPL Picture Collection

Warren herself wrote (under a pseudonym) political satire in pre-Revolutionary War days—plays like *The Defeat, The Adulateur,* and *The Group.* She did not intend them to be performed, but to be read and thought about. Her greatest contribution and one that caused considerable controversy was her *Observations on the New Constitution.* In 1788, before the Bill of Rights had been added to the Constitution, she wrote:

> There is no security in the profered system, either for the rights of conscience, or the liberty of the press. . . .
> There are no well defined limits of the judiciary powers, they seem to be left as a boundless ocean. . . .
> The executive and the legislative are so dangerously blended as to give just cause of alarm, and everything relative thereto is couched in such ambiguous terms. . . .

There is no provision for a rotation, nor any thing to prevent the perpetuity of office in the same hands for life; which by a little well-timed bribery will probably be done, to the exclusion of men of the best abilities from their share in the office of government. . . .

There is no provision by a bill of rights to guard against the dangerous encroachments of powers in too many instances to be named. . . .

In her three-volume *History of the Rise, Progress and Termination of the American Revolution* (1805), Mrs. Warren's frank opinions of contemporary political leaders antagonized many former friends, including John Adams. Her writing provoked a temporary rift between the Adamses and the Warrens, and caused John Adams to comment that "History is not the Province of the Ladies."

With the addition of the first Ten Amendments (the Bill of Rights) in 1791, the Constitution spelled out "liberty" in ways that everyone could understand and accept—the right of each person to worship in his own way, the right of free speech, of a free press, of petition for redress of grievances, the right of an individual not to be compelled in any criminal case to be a witness against himself, the right to live without unreasonable searches and seizures, the right of trial by jury.

The Constitution was a remarkable document, written by men whom destiny seemed to have brought together to establish liberty once and for all, not alone for Americans, but as a model for all mankind. But even in its greatness, the Constitution did not apply to all Americans. Women were American citizens only in an oblique sense and black men and women were not citizens at all. Though a woman was a large property owner, a businesswoman, or just a mother seeking a better life for herself and her children, she had no vote to cast in her own behalf. As a property holder she paid taxes without representation, an abuse of power for which the Revolutionary War had been fought, and about which Hannah Lee Corbin of Virginia complained in a letter to her brother, Richard Henry Lee, a signer of the Declaration of Independence and later a member of the United States Senate. A woman could not vote for any of the men who would make the laws she would be obliged to obey, she could not vote on laws that would govern her marriage or her property, and as America's commerce and industry began to grow, she could not participate in the elective process in order to gain equal pay and equal opportunity. The Founding Fathers had forgotten half the United States of America—its women.

CHAPTER EIGHT

The First First Ladies

DURING THE FIRST twenty-eight years of the new republic thousands of brand-new American citizens watched with curiosity mixed with anxiety to see how things were going at the federal capital, which moved from New York (1789) to Philadelphia (1790) and finally to Washington D.C. and the White House (1800). Some wondered apprehensively if the pomp and ritual of the British Court would be introduced in the American capital. The three first ladies—Martha Washington, Abigail Adams, and Dolley Madison—quickly reassured an anxious public by refraining from any pretentious display that might be taken as monarchial ostentation, and by setting high standards for the wives of future presidents. The three first ladies entertained with dignity, adroitly avoided political confrontations, tactfully covered up their husband's faults (and feelings), so-

licitously soothed their husband-presidents who were constantly faced with problems and with precedent-making decisions. Martha Washington, Abigail Adams, and Dolley Madison won the respect, the regard, and the love of American citizens who watched American democracy in action in those first days of the new republic.

Martha Washington (1731–1802) would have liked nothing better than to spend her entire life at Mount Vernon, the Virginia plantation home to which George Washington had taken her after their marriage in 1759. Mrs. Washington thoroughly enjoyed the quiet domesticity of Mount Vernon, and was happy to extend friendly and attentive hospitality to their many friends and guests. The Washingtons spent sixteen years together at Mount Vernon before Washington assumed command of the Revolutionary Army; after the war they were there only five years before Washington accepted the presidency. Less than two years after Washington's eight-year term as president, he died at Mount Vernon.

Martha Washington accepted the changes in her life philosophically, having, she said, "learned from experience that the greater part of our happiness or misery depends on our dispositions and not on our circumstances." She met her sorrows and her joys with serenity. The words most frequently used to describe her were kindness, thoughtfulness, cheerfulness, dignity, nobility, unfailing courtesy, and courage.

Martha Washington was born Martha Dandridge at Chestnut Grove Plantation on the Pamunkey River in Virginia in 1731. The death of her first husband, Daniel Parke Custis, in 1757, left her with two children and considerable wealth. Her marriage to George Washington on January 6, 1759, was a very happy one. She loved her husband deeply, appreciated his ability, and stood by his side during both discouraging and triumphant years.

Every winter during the eight frustrating Revolutionary War years (1775–1782) Martha Washington traveled over rough roads, lived in makeshift frame barracks, and ate army rations to be with her husband in his winter quarters. She was with him at Cambridge, at Morristown, New Jersey, at Valley Forge, Pennsylvania, at Newburgh, New York, and she was always welcome. The troops looked forward to her coming. Her serenity, as she sat day after day knitting socks for the soldiers, was reassuring. She shared cheerfully and uncomplainingly the privations of camp: the lack of privacy, of comforts, even of

good food. Her complete trust in General Washington's ability to bring the long-drawn-out Revolutionary War to a successful conclusion was felt by all around her. She was a silent but effective morale builder during those dark years.

During war summers, when the campaigns were in progress, Mrs. Washington returned to Mount Vernon to supervise the planting, to keep the spinning wheels humming, to keep looms turning out homespun for the war effort, and to carry on the business of the plantation. In 1781 Martha Washington suffered her own private war tragedy, just as peace was near. Her only son, John Custis, died of camp fever on November 5, near Yorktown, shortly after Cornwallis's surrender on October 19, 1781. Her daughter, Martha, had died in 1773 at the age of seventeen.

General and Mrs. Washington looked forward to their return to Mount Vernon to "grow old together in solitude and tranquility." This was not to be. In April 1789 General Washington was elected chief executive of the new republic and took the oath of office on April 30, 1789.

Martha Washington was fifty-eight years of age when she became the first First Lady of the United States. The seat of government was then in New York on Broadway, and it was there that the protocol, the social duties, the ceremony of the office of President were first worked out. Mrs. Washington carried out her social duties with dignity and somewhat formal elegance. Domestic by nature, she found New York life dull and wrote a relative that she felt like a "state prisoner" and that she would much rather be at home.

There were state dinners on Thursdays,

Martha Washington became first lady in 1789. NYPL Picture Collection

a weekly Friday evening reception for which invitations were not required though formal dress was. At these Friday receptions, Mrs. Washington (sometimes called Lady Washington) with the vice presi- dent's wife, Abigail Adams at her side, re- mained seated as she received guests or bade them good-bye.

After only one year the seat of govern- ment was moved, this time to Philadel-

Abigail Adams, in an engraving after a painting by Gilbert Stuart.
NYPL Picture Collection

phia, a very gay city. Its women dressed elegantly and expensively. There were dancing assemblies, theatre parties, balls, and visiting. Mrs. Washington punctiliously returned calls on the third day, escorted by one of the President's secretaries, arriving in a cream-colored chariot deco-

rated with enameled figures, drawn by six horses and driven by coachmen in white liveries.

Martha Washington was delighted to return to Mount Vernon in 1797 after President Washington had completed his second term of office. Now at last she was, as she wrote a friend, "steady as a clock, busy as a bee, and cheerful as a cricket." When George Washington died less than two years later in 1799, she seemed to lose interest in life and spent long periods in an attic room devoting herself to needlework, which she had always enjoyed. She died in 1802 and was buried at Washington's side at Mount Vernon.

Abigail Adams, the first First Lady to live in the White House, and the only First Lady to have both a husband and a son as President, and the first American woman to join her husband at a diplomatic post abroad, was one of the most outstanding women of her era.

When John Adams became minister to The Hague, commissioner at Paris, and finally first American minister to Great Britain, Abigail joined him for a five-year sojourn abroad after brushing up on her self-taught French. During John Adams's eight-year term as vice president (1789–1797) the Adamses lived in New York and Philadelphia, and finally, after John Adams had been inaugurated president in 1797 they lived briefly in the huge, bleak, unfurnished White House where Abigail struggled to make life reasonably comfortable. No room was completely finished; everywhere there was the smell of wet plaster, and the chill of dampness and of approaching winter; there were no logs for the fireplaces, no bells to call servants. Abigail Adams called the White House "great castle, built for ages to come," but there were insufficient funds to run the "great castle," a condition that was to drain the purses of succeeding presidents.

The first New Year's reception on January 1, 1801, was held in the Oval Room,

which Abigail described as a handsome room with crimson furniture. Fires were at last burning, candles were lighted, and government and diplomatic officials appeared in full regalia. But the Adamses did not entertain as frequently or as lavishly as the Washingtons. John Adams's administration was a stormy one, and Abigail grew ill and returned to their home in Braintree in February 1801. Here the Adamses retired and enjoyed seventeen happy years together before Abigail died in 1818.

Dolley Madison "reigned" at the White House for sixteen years, longer than any other First Lady. Thomas Jefferson, a widower, chose Dolley Madison (the ranking cabinet wife) as his official hostess when he became president in 1801. She presided at official dinners and receptions with poise and charm. She became First Lady eight years later when James Madison, her husband, was elected president.

Dolley Madison was one of the most beloved and respected of all First Ladies. She liked people, and always put them at ease. She liked entertaining. She was friendly and warmhearted. She had the gift of bringing together under one roof friends and foes, and of "unruffling ruffled feelings." She was recognized everywhere she went by her exotic clothes—turbans decorated with ostrich feathers, gowns of velvet or satin. She took snuff. She loved to play cards. And she was very well informed about what was going on in politics in Washington. She was alone in the White House when the British set fire to it in 1814 and saved important papers and the well-known Gilbert Stuart painting of George Washington.

Dolley Madison, a warm and generous hostess, was politically well informed during the many years she spent in the White House. NYPL Picture Collection

Dolley Payne Todd Madison (1768–1849) was born of Quaker parents in North Carolina. Her family later moved to Virginia, then to Philadelphia, where, at the age of twenty-two, she married John Payne Todd, a Quaker lawyer who lost his life caring for yellow fever victims during the 1793 epidemic. They had one son. In 1794 she married James Madison, seventeen years her senior, a quiet, scholarly, withdrawn man. Dolley's vivacity and her exuberant love of people complemented her husband's quiet temper.

After Madison had finished two terms of office, they returned to Montpelier, her husband's estate, where they continued to entertain lavishly for twenty years until Madison's death in 1836. Their bountiful hospitality and the improvidence of her son (her only sorrow) left Dolley Madison in financial difficulties. She returned to Washington in 1837 and bought a house on Lafayette Square to which her friends thronged. Eventually she was forced to sell Montpelier in 1844. The purchase by Congress of her husband's papers provided needed funds for her final years. Dolley Madison's last appearance in the White House was in February 1849, when President Polk escorted on his arm the eighty-one-year-old Dolley. Greeting guests, they walked through the crowded rooms of the White House that she knew so well. Washington still loved Dolley. She died in 1849, having survived the terms of the first ten (and almost eleven) American presidents.

During Jefferson's administration, while Dolley Madison was presiding as First Lady at the White House, Sacajawea, an American Indian woman, was establishing herself as the first woman explorer, traveling as a member of the Lewis and Clark Expedition.

The West was an uncharted wilderness, the realm of trappers, Indians, a few intrepid colonists, and mountain men, when Thomas Jefferson became president in 1797. The Mississippi basin and the land that lay westward did not even belong to the United States. For years Jefferson had been fascinated with the idea of western exploration, of knowing exactly what flora, fauna, and terrain lay beyond the Mississippi. The possibility of a navigable river that might unite the East Coast with the West Coast still tantalized men, so Jefferson took action. He asked for, and got, a Congressional appropriation in 1803

to send out an exploring expedition to learn the facts about the West. He went still further. Even before the expedition was organized, he bought from France (with the approval of Congress) the Louisiana province for $12 million. Extending from New Orleans all the way north to the Canadian border, it added a highly strategic block of land to the new republic, and made exploration of the far West doubly important.

Jefferson's exploring expedition got under way on May 14, 1804, headed by Meriwether Lewis and William Clark, both Virginians, both born leaders, both endowed with scientific curiosity. On this long journey, which lasted two years and four months, they took an Indian woman, her husband, and their newborn son.

The exploring party first met Sacajawea and her husband, Touissant Charbonneau, a French-Canadian trapper, while wintering at Fort Mandan on the Missouri River in what is now the state of North Dakota. Charbonneau was hired as an interpreter; he brought along Sacajawea his young wife, who belonged to the Lemhi band of Shoshoni Indians who then inhabited present-day Idaho. Sacajawea had been taken captive, sold as a slave, and eventually had become the property of Charbonneau. She was to prove of inestimable value on the expedition.

Carrying her baby son on her back, Sacajawea made the approximately 8,000-mile trek west and back, the only woman among some forty men. Her presence signaled peace to Indian tribes along the way. She hunted for wild herbs and plants when food became scarce.

"When we halted for dinner the squaw

This statue of Sacajawea by Amercan sculptor Alice Cooper honors the Indian woman whose courage and skill contributed so much to the success of the Lewis and Clark expedition. *NYPL Picture Collection*

THE FIRST FIRST LADIES 67

busied herself in searching for the wild artichokes which the mice collect and deposit in large hoards," Lewis wrote on Tuesday, April 9, 1805. "This operation she performed by penetrating the earth with a sharp stick about some small collection of drift wood, her labour soon proved successful, and she procured a good quantity of these roots. . . ."

Sacajawea's resourcefulness and fortitude were exemplary. Once, when a boat overturned in a storm, her agility saved valuable records and instruments. She persuaded the Lemhi Shoshoni to supply the expedition with horses, to act as a guide over the difficult Lolo Trail, and to direct the group to the navigable waters of the Columbia River. Sacajawea's small son, Jean Baptiste, nicknamed "Pompey" by Clark, became the mascot of the expedition and a great favorite of Lewis and Clark.

Sacajawea had a mind of her own. According to the journals of Lewis and Clark, she wanted very much to see the Pacific Ocean and "that monstrous fish" (the whale). She begged insistently to be included on one of the exploring trips to the Pacific, saying that "she had traveled a long way with us to see the great waters, and that now that monstrous fish was also to be seen, she thought it very hard she could not be permitted to see either." Sacajawea got her wish on January 6, 1806. She and her husband were included in one of two canoes bound for the Pacific.

The Lewis and Clark expedition arrived back at Fort Mandan on August 17, 1806,

leaving Sacajawea and Charbonneau and Pompey in their village. But Clark did not forget Sacajawea. Writing to Charbonneau he said that "your woman who accompanied you that long dangerous and fatigueing rout to the Pacific Ocean and back, deserved a greater reward for her attention and services on that rout than we had in our power to give her at the Mandans. As to your little Son (my boy Pomp) you well know my fondness for him and my anxiety to take and raise him as my own child. I once more tell you if you will bring your son Baptiste to me I will educate him and treat him as my own child. . . ."

Accounts conflict as to the ultimate fate of Sacajawea and her son. Her death was reported by a fur trader as taking place on December 20, 1812. He describes her as "a good and the best woman in the fort." Reportedly Clark became guardian of "my boy Pomp" and of the couple's later child, a little girl.

In June 1905, Susan B. Anthony, who was famous as the leader of the woman suffrage movement in the middle 1800s, spoke at the unveiling of a statue to Sacajawea in Portland, Oregon, the gift of Oregon clubwomen to the Lewis and Clark Exposition. The bronze statue of Sacajawea, her baby strapped to her back, was the work of the American sculptor Alice Cooper. It was the first statue erected to a woman because of her deeds of daring, Miss Anthony pointed out, a fitting recognition to a tireless, resourceful woman who, as Lewis and Clark reported "inspired us all."

CHAPTER NINE

Woman's Sphere

ALREADY, AT THE turn of the 1800s, the clergy had determinedly taken their century-long stand on woman's sphere. Modesty, piety, morality, Christian benevolence were some of the virtues that clergymen assigned to the character of womanhood. As for duty to her husband, a woman was to be "the lovely vine, which now twines itself so gracefully upon the trellis." Women who assumed "the place and tone of man as a public reformer" or who were presumptuous enough to become "public lecturers and teachers" were condemned. And the clergy closed the door emphatically on women discussing things "which ought not to be named" (meaning sex). They stressed over and over again woman's inferior strength, and claimed that her place was rightfully the home and the church "aloof from the bustle and storm of active life."

A few women writers, among the fifty or so whose books were published in the first half of the 1800s, spoke out against a "sphere" for women. Some women read, either delightedly or thoughtfully, Englishwoman Mary Wollstonecraft's *Vindication of the Rights of Women* (1792), which was to become one of the "feminist bibles" of the 1800s. Writing with an energy that caused one Englishman to liken her to a "hyena in petticoats," she addressed her readers:

My own sex, I hope, will excuse me, if I treat them like rational creatures, instead of flattering their *fascinating* graces, and viewing them as if they were in a state of perpetual childhood, unable to stand alone. I earnestly wish to point out in what true dignity and human happiness consists—I wish to persuade women to endeavour to acquire strength both of mind and body, and to convince them that the soft phrases, susceptibility of heart, delicacy of sentiment, and refinement of taste, are almost synonymous with epithets of weakness and that those beings who are only the objects of pity and that kind of love, which has been termed its sister, will soon become objects of contempt. . . .

"It is replete with fine sentiments," Hannah Mather Crocker (1752–1829) said, referring to Mary Wollstonecraft's vindication. In her *Observations on the Real Rights of Women* (1818), written at the age of sixty-five and after bearing ten children, Mrs. Crocker flatly stated that "the wise Author of nature has endowed the female mind with equal powers and faculties, and has given them the same right of judging and acting for themselves as he gave the male sex." Mrs. Crocker's *Observations* did not stir up a feminist tempest in the 1800s, but some contemporary women must have thoughtfully read and pondered Mrs. Crocker's words.

"Yes, ye lordly, ye haughty sex, our souls are by nature *equal* to yours; the same breath of God animates, enlives, and invigorates us; and we are not fallen lower than yourselves . . ." wrote Judith Sargent Murray (1751–1820), the wife of a Massachusetts Universalist minister (Universalists were among the more liberal religious sects), in her *Desultory Thoughts upon the Utility of Encouraging a Degree of Self-Complacency Especially in Female Bosoms,* written in 1784 under the pen name Constantia. Mrs. Murray wrote a column entitled "The Gleaner" for the *Massachusetts Magazine* in the 1790s and urged both the education of girls and the training of girls to earn their own living. She, too, had read Mary Wollstonecraft.

A brief flurry of novels of seduction, rape, abduction, suicide, stirred the turn of the eighteenth century. Their objective, so their authors claimed, was to warn young women to avoid the blandishments of "gay deceivers" whose intentions were far from honorable. English novelist Samuel Richardson's *Clarissa Harlowe* (1747) initiated the "female in distress" novel, which exposed the public to such hitherto unmentioned subjects as sex and seduction.

The post-Revolutionary public, which was becoming a reading public (the first free town libraries date to the 1830s) was of two minds about these female-in-distress novels. Moralists claimed they "crowded out better books," were too romantic, too ardent, that they "melted rigorous minds" and were un-American, and that novel reading was harmful to the female (though apparently not the male) character. The authors of these female-in-distress novels and their supporters claimed that their stories taught the reader a moral lesson, were set in America, and were often true and could be documented, even to a tombstone in New York's Trinity Church graveyard marking the grave of one of the women "victims."

Two female-in-distress novels, both written by women, were best sellers. Susannah Haswell Rowson's *Charlotte Temple* (1791) went into 200 editions, and Hannah Webster Foster's *The Coquette* (1797) was reprinted eight times between 1824 and 1828. The female victims of these novels were innocent young girls who put their trust in handsome rogues who made false promises. The seducer sometimes repented, but the young women usually died giving birth to a fatherless child. These betrayals were supposed to serve as warnings to young women. No warning seemed to be necessary for the seducer. Nor was the existence of a double standard spelled out. Men's philanderings outside marriage were accepted as natural in the 1800s, and men's lives were rarely ruined by their sexual infidelities. However, women who succumbed to men's advances were forever pointed out as "fallen women."

Maine-born Sally S.B.K. Wood (1759–1855) wrote a female-in-distress novel in reverse. Amelia in Mrs. Wood's *Amelia; or the Influence of Virtue* (1802) stood with rockbound firmness for female virtue and humility. She accepted (as her duty to her husband) his unfaithfulness, his illegitimate children, his mistress, his insults. Mrs. Wood wrote: "Amelia was not a disciple of Mary Woolstonecraft [sic], she was not a woman of fashion, nor a woman of spirit. She was an old-fashioned wife, and she meant to obey her husband; she meant to do her duty in the strictest sense of the word." Orthodox New England clergy must have approved Amelia's strong sense of duty and Mrs. Wood's concern for virtue and social stability. Mary Wollstonecraft would not have approved. She denied any fundamental differences in character between the sexes, attributing the weakness she observed in women to their faulty education.

Free public schools for all the children of all Americans did not exist in the United States until well into the 1800s. There were Latin schools that prepared boys for college. There were academies (charging tuition fees) where education was avail-

able to boys and occasionally to girls. But there was no public school system. Thoughtful Americans were urgently aware that something must be done to prepare American children for their role in the new republic, where mushrooming manufacturing industries were demanding new skills, where commerce and trade were rapidly expanding, and where a well-educated public was imperative for political, business, and cultural growth. However, it took time to work out the details of a free educational system, details such as its financing (which meant taxation), teacher training (which meant the opening of normal schools), and the establishment of a curriculum that had progressive continuity from kindergarten through college. In taking the census of 1840 the federal government included a question on the ability of each person to read and write. In each of several states 50,000 persons admitted that they could neither read nor write in any language. Newspapers commented with astonishment on the fact that some 500,000 Americans were illiterate.

Meanwhile education, such as it was, stressed schools for boys with hardly an oblique thought about schools for girls. Five American women, all contemporaries, were so concerned about the quality and availability of education for girls that they devoted the greater part of their lives to doing something about it. As early as 1819, Emma Hart Willard (1787–1870) became the first woman not only to ask for state aid for seminaries for girls, but to present to the New York State Legislature a widely acclaimed Plan for Improving Female Education (1819). It spelled out the need for an endowment or subsidies to help support seminaries for girls, along with a concerned board of trustees, adequate buildings, well-equipped classrooms, laboratories, and libraries. Her plan won the approval of James Monroe, John Adams, Thomas Jefferson, and Governor De Witt Clinton of New York. However, the New York State Legislature turned down Mrs. Willard's proposal. Nearby Troy, a growing factory town on the Hudson River and close to the Erie Canal (which opened in 1825), offered to raise by taxation some $4,000 for Mrs. Willard's school. The Troy Female Seminary opened with a charter from the New York State Legislature in September 1821. Students, many of whom became teachers, were offered a wide range of subjects—science, history, mathematics, French, Italian, Spanish, German, philosophy. Troy Female Seminary attracted more than 100 boarding students and 200 day students, and convincingly demonstrated girls' ability to master an impressive curriculum. Even the most conservative parents were proud to say that their daughters had graduated from the Troy Female Seminary. Mrs. Willard received widespread publicity for her school, moving discreetly and unobtrusively toward her goals for women's education.

Better teacher training for women was one of the many crusades of Catherine Beecher (1800–1878) who had that tireless "do good" drive that characterized the Beecher family. Her father was the Reverend Lyman Beecher; her sister was Harriet Beecher Stowe, the author of *Uncle Tom's Cabin;* one brother was the famous New York divine, the Reverend Henry Ward Beecher; her other brothers numbered seven ministers. After the death of her fiancé in 1822, Catherine Beecher devoted her life to numerous worthy projects, among them education of young women. She opened the Hartford Female Seminary in Hartford, Connecticut, in 1823, with the "principles of teaching" and calisthenics (one of her hobbies) on the school's curriculum. In 1831 she accompanied her father to Cincinnati where he had accepted the presidency of Lane University. Soon she opened another girls' school, the Western Female Institute, which closed in 1837 for lack of funds. Recruiting teachers to teach the West's two million unschooled children became Miss Beecher's next crusade. She lectured, wrote articles, and briefly identified herself with Cleveland's Board of National Popular Education, a teacher recruiting group. Five hundred New England schoolteachers went West as a result of the energetic recruiting campaigns. Miss Beecher evaluated their teaching ability and teaching experience, and teacher training became her next enterprise. She initiated the opening of teacher training schools in Milwaukee, then in Dubuque, Iowa, and Quincy, Illinois. The Milwaukee school alone survived, eventually becoming Milwaukee-Downer College. Teacher training, as Miss Beecher saw it, should prepare schoolgirls for woman's "proper" sphere, homemaking, as well as provide them with educational opportunities equal to those available for boys. Most of her books (she earned her living by writing) focused on the home: *A Treatise on Domestic Economy* (1841), *The Evils Suffered by American Women and American*

Children: The Causes and Remedy (1846), *The American Woman's Home* (1869). These were not feminist books nor books urging women to demand their rights. Miss Beecher had no interest in the women's rights movement, nor in woman suffrage, although those movements had gained considerable momentum before her death. Rather she upgraded woman's role as housewife and mother, stressing such new ideas as the need for adequate exercise, more comfortable clothing, proper hygiene, physical education, and the training of girls for the profession of teaching, should they by chance need to support themselves.

Mary Lyon (1797–1849) wanted to found an endowed seminary with guaran-

Mary Lyon founded Mount Holyoke Female Seminary in 1837. It later became Mt. Holyoke College. Mount Holyoke College

The original seminary building, Mt. Holyoke Female Seminary. Mount Holyoke College

teed continuity and high scholastic standards. She had attended five different teaching institutions, teaching twenty years to pay for her snatches of education, and she wanted "the adult female youth in the common walks of life" to find a less thorny pathway to education. Her goals were very clear: (1) guaranteed seminary continuity, (2) an interested and concerned board of trustees, (3) admission of students of all economic levels on the basis of an entrance examination, (4) tuition as low as possible. She found the trustees. She raised the first $1,000. She found the site—South Hadley, Massachusetts. In 1837 Mt. Holyoke Seminary was chartered, built, and almost finished (not quite) when the first eighty girls moved in, prepared to take a three-year course of study. Twelve years later Mary Lyon died. Mt. Holyoke survived the loss

of its founder. Its endowment was maintained, and it became Mt. Holyoke College in 1893. The practicality of all Mary Lyon's goals had a strong impact on the development of higher education for women.

Elizabeth Peabody (1804–94) was busy with a variety of projects all her life— teaching, writing textbooks, running her famous Boston bookshop (gathering place for Transcendentalists), publishing books, lecturing, writing. It was in 1859 that she discovered the Froebel kindergarten system and promptly organized in Boston in 1860 the first formal kindergarten in the United States. In collaboration with her sister Mary, widow of Horace Mann, who had revolutionized public school teaching and organization, she wrote *Moral Culture of Infancy, and Kindergarten Guide* in 1863.

The most persecuted schoolteacher in the early 1800s was Prudence Crandall (1803–90). She dared to make an experiment that didn't work. In 1833 she opened a school in her home for black girls from educated families in the village of Canterbury, Connecticut. She wanted to train these girls to become teachers, hoping that they, themselves, would open schools for black girls in their hometowns, and that the idea would continue to grow. She was boycotted by resentful villagers, her water supply polluted, her black pupils barred from the local church. She herself was arrested. Upon her acquittal, a local mob attacked her house one dark night in September, 1834, breaking windows, battering down walls, destroying the furnishings. To protect her pupils from further physical harm she closed the school. Although the Connecticut state government did nothing at the time to compensate Miss Crandall for damages, fifty-two years later the legislature granted her a small pension.

Some American fathers in days before a public school system was introduced into the United States took great pains to give their daughters a masculine education. Anne Bradstreet was well educated. Theodosia Burr (1783–1813), daughter of Aaron Burr, was studying Horace, Plutarch, French, mathematics, and science at the age of eleven, her father writing instructions to her tutors, determined that her education should equal that of men and prove that "women have souls." Margaret Fuller (1810–50) was studying Latin and English grammar under her father's supervision, and at the age of seven, she was reading Horace, Ovid, and Virgil.

The encouragement and teaching of her astronomer-father led Maria Mitchell (1818–89) to the discovery of a comet, bringing her world fame and a challenging professorship at Vassar College. Night after night father and daughter climbed to the roof of their Nantucket Island home in Massachusetts to observe the sky and study the stars. At the age of twelve, Maria became expert in recording for her father time passed during solar eclipses. She studied mathematics, a skill essential for an astronomer. Together she and her father made thousands of observations, both of them often so absorbed in sweeping the skies that they hardly noticed the bitter cold of a winter night.

Her first job as librarian at the Nantucket Atheneum gave her spare time to read, to teach herself German, and to prepare for her more cherished career as an astronomer. Fame came to Maria Mitchell at the age of 29. On October 1, 1847, standing alone on the rooftop sweeping the sky with her telescope, she discovered a new comet; her father verified her find. News of the discovery traveled around the world. Maria won the award offered by the King of Denmark for the first telescopic discovery of a new comet, a gold medal, and the honor of having the comet named for her. In 1848 Maria became the first woman elected to the American Academy of Arts and Sciences in Boston. In 1850 she was elected to the American Association for the Advancement of Science; Louis Agassiz nominated her. Maria Mitchell's greatest opportunity was still to come, however. In 1865 Matthew Vassar, founder of Vassar College, offered to build an observatory with a twelve-inch telescope (then the third largest in the United States) at the college, and offered her a professorship at Vassar. Miss Mitchell and her father moved to Poughkeepsie and she began a twenty-three-year teaching career. She was a stimulating and unorthodox professor, demanding that her students "question everything" and learn by observing, not by memorizing. Continuing her own research as she taught, she encouraged students to share her evenings observing the sky and to travel with her to the sites of solar eclipses.

Maria Mitchell's interests were not limited solely to astronomy. She was a founding member of the Association for the Advancement of Women in 1873. She supported women's rights movements. In 1873 she was elected the first woman member of the American Philosophical Society, and in the same year, she served as vice president of the American Social Science Association. She died one year after her retirement in 1888. A bust of her was placed in the Hall of Fame for Great Americans in New York City in 1905.

Determined and ambitious young women who did not have fathers interested in their education, and who had to make their own way or earn their own way, faced hostility and discrimination getting into college, remaining there, and graduating on equal footing with men. It took Lucy Stone (1818–93) nine years to save enough money (seventy dollars) to go to college. She was twenty-five when

Maria Mitchell, who discovered a comet in 1847, shown here (back row, to right of the telescope) *with her astronomy students at Vassar College. Vassar College Library*

she left for Oberlin College in Ohio, the only college in 1843 that awarded women degrees equal to those received by men. Traveling by train, and by boat across Lake Erie, sleeping on deck with the cargo to save money, it cost $16.65 of Lucy's $70 to get to Oberlin from her West Brookfield, Massachusetts, home.

At Oberlin, board cost one dollar a week, so Lucy worked. For doing housework in the women's dormitory she was paid three cents an hour. For teaching two hours a day in the college preparatory school she received twelve and a half cents an hour. She cooked in her room in order to reduce her expenses to fifty cents a week. She got up at two o'clock in the morning to study. Once, when her father (who did not approve of college for women) loaned her forty dollars (on which he charged her interest) she was able to give up one of her jobs and sleep until 5:00 A.M. She did not have enough money to go home for vacations, so during those periods she taught on campus to support herself, and to save for the next semester. When she graduated in 1847, she bought a new dress. It was her second new dress in her four years at college.

Lucy Stone was considered a radical at

Lucy Stone's class picture at Oberlin College, 1847. Oberlin College

Oberlin, partly because she subscribed to *The Liberator*, William Lloyd Garrison's antislavery paper. Blacks were admitted to Oberlin and the college was antislavery, but the faculty disapproved of William Lloyd Garrison's extreme ideas. Lucy had a few other brushes with the faculty, one over the matter of discrimination against women. Lucy liked debating, and women were not allowed to become members of the debating team. When commencement day approached in 1847, she was chosen by her classmates to write a commencement essay, but refused to do so, because, as a woman, she would not be allowed to read it at the commencement exercises. For a time her degree was in jeopardy. Although she steadfastly refused to write the essay because her principles were "more important to her than herself," she finally did receive her bachelor's degree.

Her father thereupon sent her enough money to return home, with the stipulation that he would take it out of the small legacy he planned to leave her. He did not believe in women speaking in public. Lucy Stone was determined, however, and she became one of the most outstanding nineteenth-century public speakers on behalf of both the antislavery and the woman-suffrage causes.

When Elizabeth Blackwell (1821–1910) decided to become a doctor in 1847 she was turned down by twenty-nine medical schools including Yale, Harvard, Bowdoin, and every medical school in New York City and Philadelphia. She was discouraged, but did not give up because the "idea of winning a doctor's degree assumed the aspect of a great moral struggle." She studied medicine privately with

John Dickson, a clergyman-doctor in Ashville, North Carolina, where she was teaching at the time. Later she studied with his doctor-brother in Charleston, South Carolina. In desperation she began applying for admission to rural medical schools. Geneva College in northern New York finally accepted her after male students, who had been polled by the college, jovially agreed to accept a woman as a fellow student. She began her studies at Geneva College (it later became a part of Syracuse University) in 1847.

Although she had finally gained admission to a medical school, her troubles were just beginning. She was ostracized by villagers who considered it brazen behavior for a woman to attend classes with men. The boarders at the village home where she obtained lodgings ignored her. Her fellow students, however, gradually became friendly, admiring her courage and dignity, and her studiousness. Her professor of anatomy became her friend and protector. In 1848 she was admitted for the summer to Philadelphia Hospital where she got her first practical experience with patients. She was there for the outbreak of a typhus epidemic and she later made this epidemic the subject of her thesis. Elizabeth Blackwell graduated from Geneva College with an M.D. January 23, 1849, at the head of her class. She refused to walk in the commencement procession, considering it unladylike.

To give herself more thorough training, she went abroad for advanced study, but on her return she experienced years of frustration in her efforts to build a New York practice. Landlords would not rent her office space. She was not permitted to practice in hospitals. Finally she had to buy a house and start a clinic in a New York slum area. She persevered and, by 1857, with the help of concerned New Yorkers and Quaker acquaintances, she had raised enough money to found the New York Infirmary for Women and Children (today the New York Infirmary).

Her sister, Dr. Emily Blackwell, and a friend, Dr. Marie E. Zakrzewska, joined the infirmary staff to help Dr. Blackwell after their graduation from Western Reserve Medical School. In 1868 a Women's Medical College was added to the New York Infirmary so women could study medicine without the frustrations that

In her efforts to receive professional medical training and to establish a practice, Dr. Elizabeth Blackwell encountered great resistance because she was a woman. New York Infirmary

A class at the Women's Medical College, founded by Dr. Elizabeth Blackwell in 1868 because most medical schools would not admit women. New York Infirmary

prospective women doctors suffered in the mid-1800s.

Many other young women faced similar difficulties in establishing themselves in their chosen careers, among them Lucy B. Hobbs (Taylor) (1833–1910) in becoming one of the first women dentists, Antoinette Brown (Blackwell) (1825–1921) in becoming the first woman ordained minister, Mrs. Myra Bradwell (1831–94) in being admitted to practice before the bar, and Dr. Harriot K. Hunt (1805–75) who, though she had studied medicine with an English couple named Mott and had established a lucrative practice in Boston, was refused admission to Harvard University for further study.

CHAPTER TEN

Women Activists and the Antislavery Movement

BOTH THE VICTORIAN attitudes that shrouded sex, marriage, the home and the family in conventional rigidity and the numerous inequities that women endured were persistently attacked by the few women who dared to stand up and speak out as liberals in the early nineteenth century. Called "freethinkers," advocates of "free love," "bluestockings" or "shockers," these women espoused causes that were considered outrageous at the time. Since they were not considered a threat to the establishment, they escaped the violent public censure that later women speakers incurred. They were tolerated on the public platform and at times attracted considerable followings. Ultimately the new republic would learn to take seriously the many problems that these "radical" women pinpointed in the early 1800s.

Scottish-born Frances Wright (1795–1852) advocated one cause after another with equal conviction and enthusiasm, lecturing on birth control, liberalized divorce laws, free education, legal rights for women, capital punishment, abolition of slavery, equal education for women, and the need for trade schools and for a strong labor movement. Miss Wright was a magnetic speaker with an exceptional gift of eloquence, an unequaled command of words, and a "rich and thrilling voice." "Know why you believe and understand what you believe, and possess a reason for the faith that is in you," she told her audiences.

Frances Wright spent half her own fortune to implement her antislavery views by purchasing slaves, freeing them, and establishing them in a community called Nashoba near present-day Memphis, Tennessee. Circumstances seemed to bode ill for Nashoba from the start. It was located in an inaccessible desolate forest. Its shared work program, and its schools, never really got off the ground. Badly supervised during Miss Wright's long absences, and falling into disrepute for alleged immorality, Nashoba was finally abandoned. Miss Wright found jobs for her forty liberated slaves in Haiti. Another of her projects was a "Hall of Science" in New York—a small church converted into a lecture center. Here she spoke on her favorite subjects, and her lectures were well attended. Ten-year-old Walt Whitman was one spellbound listener.

Auguste Comte, French philosopher and founder of positivism, was her friend and neighbor in Paris where Miss Wright lived briefly after her marriage to a French physician. Lafayette was one of Miss Wright's friends for years. Miss Wright's frequent crossings to and from Europe (which totaled at least ten) left her various projects dangling. Finally she chose Cincinnati for her home, campaigning for the Democratic party in the 1836 presidential elections and for the Democrats in New York in the 1838 mid-term elections, making her probably the first woman political campaigner. Her death in Cincinnati in 1852 brought an end to her provocative career. Many of the causes and crusades that she had so enthusiastically supported were implemented in later years—and found to be not so radical after all.

Mary Grove Nichols (1810–84) believed the key to life was good health, a subject on which she began lecturing in 1838, having secretly studied books on health as a young girl. When Mrs. Nichols mounted the platform to lecture on anat-

omy and hygiene, she faced women who knew very little about their bodies and very little about sex. She recommended to them what seemed in those days a radical regimen of fresh air, exercise, cold baths, wheat bread, a vegetarian diet, no tea, coffee, alcohol, and comfortable clothing. All her life she wrote health articles, edited health magazines, participated in the activities of the American Vegetarian Society, and opened her own (mostly short-lived) water-cure establishments. For a time she endorsed free love and spiritualism, but ultimately was converted to Catholicism. Though Mrs. Nichols was sometimes an extremist in her efforts to liberate women (and men) from Victorian concepts and traditions, she did much to alert American women to aspects of health and hygiene, which, through ignorance and prudery, had long been ignored.

Margaret Fuller's contribution to the elevation of the status of women was in the intellectual field. Her first job—teaching in Bronson Alcott's experimental school in 1836—brought her in close touch with Boston's transcendentalism (1820–60) with its belief in the divinity of human nature and its effort to give mankind new stature in a new republic. Miss Fuller came to know the transcendentalist group —Emerson, Hawthorne, the Alcotts, Thoreau, Longfellow, and others. Elizabeth Peabody, a co-worker at Alcott's school, became her friend. By 1839 she began her famous *Conversations* in Elizabeth Peabody's bookshop, where wives of famous transcendentalists, contemporary women writers, and other notable Bostonians listened to Miss Fuller speak on such topics as ethics, art, education, health, woman and her rights, mythology, faith. Margaret Fuller wrote for and helped edit the *Dial*, a quarterly transcendentalist journal edited by Emerson, wrote her famous feminist book *Woman in the Nineteenth Century* (1845), and accepted a job on Horace Greeley's *New York Tribune* in 1844. Though her assignment was literary criticism, Miss Fuller did a series of reform articles for the *Tribune* based on personal visits to Sing Sing prison, and on the conglomerate of asylums, prisons, and reformatories on New York's Blackwell Island, examining these public institutions with a critical eye.

In 1846, she became foreign correspondent for the *New York Tribune*. Traveling through Europe, she met such European intellectuals as Wordsworth, the Carlyles, De Quincey, George Sand, and others. In April 1847 she arrived in Rome and immediately became involved in the cause of Italian freedom. Giovanni Angelo, Marchese d'Ossoli, her junior by ten years, became her lover. Their child was born on September 1848. Their marriage took place sometime in 1849 while they were working on a history of the Roman revolution, which Margaret at that point considered her lifework. In May 1850, the Ossolis sailed for New York, taking their manuscript with them. When their ship was only an hour or so from New York Harbor, a tremendous storm arose, the

Margaret Fuller was a leading intellectual of her day. NYPL Picture Collection

ship foundered, and the Ossolis were lost. Horace Greeley for whom Margaret Fuller had worked called her "the most remarkable and in some respects the greatest woman whom America has yet known."

Though "radical" women who spoke their views publicly were usually considered by press and public to live in a world of their own, gentlewomen coming out of their homes to state their beliefs from a public platform were bitterly attacked by men who had no intention of allowing women to leave their proper sphere to express an opinion (except their husband's) or to speak from a public platform on behalf of any cause at any time or anywhere. Give them an inch and they'll take a mile was the nineteenth-century man's reaction to women who spoke out. To women with a cause to communicate it was important to speak from a public platform which was a medium for the expression of opinion in the mid-1800s. But it was a real hazard for a woman speaker, standing alone on a public platform, to face an audience that might at any moment assail her.

Throw her out! Drag her out! Sour old maid! were some of the catcalls from the audiences. Sometimes rotten eggs or rotten cabbages were thrown at the speaker. Once Lucy Stone suffered a head injury when a man in the audience hurled a prayer book at her. Once, on the coldest day of winter, a hose was forced through a window near the platform and icy water turned on Lucy Stone as she spoke. Dripping wet and shivering, she continued her speech. Pepper was sometimes thrown about the lecture hall forcing sneezing audiences to leave. The clergy, particularly,

denounced women speakers, quoting the Bible as their justification for putting women down. Newspapers called women speakers "brazen infidels," "female fanatics," "childless women," "foreign incendiaries." But women braved these hardships and humiliations to get their messages across to the American public. The chief crusades they advocated were antislavery, women's rights, and temperance, (the prohibition of the sale and consumption of liquor).

Angelina and Sarah Grimké were pathbreakers for gentlewomen speaking on a public platform. They were daughters of a distinguished and prosperous South Carolina family. Sarah M. Grimké (1792–1873) and Angelina E. Grimké (1805–79) spoke to Northern audiences about the wrongs of slavery, which they personally had witnessed on their family plantations. They had left their family home near Charleston, South Carolina, in the 1820s to settle in Philadelphia, had become Quaker converts, and the antislavery cause became their challenge. Later, after they had been attacked in a pastoral letter distributed by the Congregational Ministers Association of Massachusetts for their unwomanly audacity in speaking from a public platform, the Grimké sisters espoused the cause of women's rights as well.

Two of many tracts that they wrote, Angelina's *An Appeal to the Christian Women of The South* (1836) and Sarah's *Letters on the Equality of the Sexes, and the Condition of Women* (1838), established the sisters as forerunners of women's involvement in both the antislavery and the women's rights movements. For

Angelina Grimké (left) *and Sarah Grimké* (right) *were pioneer lecturers on the antislavery issue.* NYPL Picture Collection

two years Angelina and Sarah lectured in New England, at first in private homes, then in churches (for women only), then to mixed audiences, describing the plight of slave women defenseless against the sexual advances of their masters, of field hands who bore lifetime scars from whippings and beatings, of children forbidden to learn to read or write, and of slave families with no future for themselves or their children. Often audiences were moved to tears by the eloquence of the Grimké appeals. On February 21, 1838, Angelina became the first woman to address members of a Committee of the Legislature of the State of Massachusetts. The hall was so crowded that people had to stand in the aisles and in the lobby as she spoke passionately about the wrongs of slavery and presented a petition bearing the names of 20,000 antislavery women. It was one of

Angelina's last speeches. After two years of lecturing, she was beginning to lose her voice.

The Grimké sisters' courageous public-speaking crusade left an unforgettable impact on the century in which they lived, and it gave courage to other women to follow in their footsteps by speaking out fearlessly, regardless of criticism, in behalf of causes in which they wholeheartedly believed.

Once introduced to the evils of slavery by the Grimké sisters' harrowing accounts of slave life on a southern plantation, women became so deeply concerned that they could no longer be silent. The antislavery movement became their first crusade. By the 1830s women were out ringing doorbells, getting names on antislavery petitions, and sending them to state legislatures and to Congress. They were founding Female Anti-Slavery societies. They were on the move organizing their first national crusade and nothing would stop them.

It took courage for women to go out and ring doorbells in those days, but many women did it, and John Quincy Adams, then a member of Congress, defended their right to do so. Addressing Congress, he stated that, "The mere departure of women from the duties of the domestic circle, far from being a reproach to her, is a virtue of the highest order, when it is done from purity of motive, by appropriate means, and the purpose good." Many of women's yellowed, crumbling, faded antislavery petitions may still be seen in the National Archives in Washington.

Lucretia Mott (1793–1880) organized the first Female Anti-Slavery Society in Philadelphia in 1833. More than sixty women, including several black women attended the first meeting. A call was promptly sent out for a Women's National Anti-Slavery Convention in New York in 1837. It was in these antislavery conventions and meetings that the more courageous women learned to speak in public, address legislatures, present petitions, and lobby.

The women's antislavery movement was not without its harassments. When the National Anti-Slavery Convention of American Women met in Philadelphia in 1838, proslavery elements burned down the newly built Pennsylvania Hall, where the meeting was held. The women escaped the fire, but mobs rampaged for hours throughout Philadelphia demonstrating against blacks and against women's involvement in antislavery activities. The Philadelphia

National Gazette commented that women should stay at home and read instead of "attending useless discussions and listening to itinerant lecturers." Undaunted, the women continued their meetings the following day in Sarah Pugh's schoolhouse. When Abigail Kelley Foster (1810–1887), another woman who spoke against slavery, was elected a member of an American Anti-Slavery Association Committee in 1840, the clergy not only refused to serve on the same committee with a woman, but an antiwomen split took place in antislavery groups. Abby Kelley Foster was sometimes called "that woman Jezebel" and "vile woman" and sometimes refused hotel accommodations as an undesirable.

Eventually women were admitted to full membership with voting rights in the all-male American Anti-Slavery Society, though some male members, who loudly declared themselves for freedom of the slaves, wanted to keep women from becoming voting members.

Black women living in the North spoke out in behalf of their own race as part of the 1830s Anti-Slavery Movement. One of the first black women to speak from a public platform was Maria W. Stewart (1803–79), whose two concerns were the antislavery movement and the apathy of her own people to educate themselves and their children. Mrs. Stewart's audacity in speaking, as a woman, from a public platform was frowned upon by her black audiences. William Lloyd Garrison, however, found Mrs. Stewart's talks and articles interesting enough to publish in *The Liberator*.

The plight of slaves who fled to Canada was the "cause" adopted by Mary Ann

Shadd Cary (1823–93). Her chief concern was how to educate black refugees for their new life of freedom. Mrs. Cary moved to Windsor, Canada, in 1851, and opened a school for blacks there. Later, in 1854, she moved to Chatham, Canada, where she became editor of *The Provincial Freeman*, a weekly newspaper designed to encourage togetherness among the black community who were trying to make a new life in a new country.

Harriet Tubman (c. 1820–1913), herself a fugitive slave who had successfully made her break for freedom in 1849, dedicated her life to leading others to freedom. Over and over again she made trips into Maryland, nineteen altogether, following a route that she herself mapped out, and brought an estimated 60 to 300 slaves to freedom, including her own elderly father and mother. On one occasion she took an entire party all the way to Canada where she had established a home.

Harriet Tubman had extraordinary bravery. A broken skull, which she had suffered when hit by a white overseer, caused Mrs. Tubman to black out at times, but she did not allow this disability to become a handicap. She simply learned how to cope with it. She paid no attention to the fact that a

Harriet Tubman (far left) *with some of the slaves she helped free. Sophia Smith Collection*

Tall, gaunt Sojourner Truth made a powerful impression on her audiences. Sophia Smith Collection

reward of almost $40,000 was offered for her capture, and continued her rescue work unconcernedly. At the end of the Civil War Mrs. Tubman, still indefatigable, opened a Home for Indigent Aged Negroes at her residence in Auburn, New York.

When there was male hostility in an audience or a lag in an antislavery meeting, tall gaunt Sojourner Truth (c. 1797–1883) would frequently stride to the platform. She was always ready to speak out about the sufferings of women and about their strength with a forcefulness and magnetism that silenced even the boldest heckler. She was given the name Isabella by her slave parents who were owned by a wealthy Dutch family in Ulster County, New York. The name Sojourner Truth was given her by "voices," for Sojourner Truth was a mystic, attaching herself to a variety of religious groups in her search for God. As she wandered alone, speaking about her religious beliefs with an earnestness and conviction, Sojourner Truth "discovered" the antislavery movement in 1846, and traveled and spoke, sometimes with other abolitionist leaders, in Ohio, Indiana, Missouri, and Kansas. In 1850 she "discovered" the women's rights movement and began speaking at women's rights meetings in Ohio, New York, and elsewhere, always welcomed and greatly respected by women's rights leaders.

Seven different reforms occupied Frances Ellen Watkins Harper (1825–1911) during her long lifetime—she lived to be eighty-six years old. By 1854 she was lecturing for the antislavery movement. She aided fugitive slaves. She lectured in the South during the Reconstruction period, her special concerns being education, temperance, domestic morality. She headed the Department of Work Among Negroes of the Women's Christian Temperance Union.

The role of the dedicated black women in the antislavery movement should not be underestimated. They were motivated women who saw needs and met them, sometimes working independently, sometimes working with antislavery organizations and the underground railroad. At the end of the war these black women leaders started constructive programs for black women on their own initiative, and cooperated ably and loyally in the women's rights movement.

Eight American women sailed for England in early May 1840 as delegates to the World Anti-Slavery Convention in London. They had heard, even before they left the United States, the rumor that their credentials as delegates might not be honored. But the women confidently headed toward London, in spite of the rumor. Lucretia Mott represented the American Anti-Slavery Association. The other women represented auxiliary Anti-Slavery societies in Boston, New York, and Philadelphia. All were highly respected women and had been active leaders in antislavery programs in their communities. All were well educated and from well-established families.

On the bright and sunny June morning in 1840 when the women delegates arrived at Freemason's Hall, London, they found that seeds of dissension had already been liberally sown by groups of male delegates regarding the presence of women. Instead of discussing the problem of slavery, the entire first day was devoted to discussing the propriety of admitting women delegates. Some men said that it would "lower the dignity" of the convention. Some said that women were "constitutionally unfit for public or business meetings." Some of the English clergy, "dancing around with Bible in hand," quoted the Scriptures and stated that admitting women delegates was against the will of God and that women should keep within their proper sphere. A few men made speeches in behalf of the women delegates, one man going so far as to say that it was "one of the most encouraging and most delightful symptoms of the time."

Meanwhile the American women delegates sat and listened quietly to humiliating accusations and to the surprising vacil-

Lucretia Mott was an inspiring speaker for the causes of antislavery, women's rights, and peace.

lation of some of their American male colleagues. The women were never offered a chance to defend themselves, an opportunity that Lucretia Mott could have handled with wisdom and dignity.

When admission of the women delegates came to a vote, not all, but almost all of the male delegates voted no. Thereupon the men began deliberations on slavery, at a World Anti-Slavery Convention which seemed content to "secure freedom for the slave while denying equality to women."

The women delegates were led to a railed-in balcony where they listened silently day after day to the convention deliberations. Sitting with them, in protest, was William Lloyd Garrison, publisher of *The Liberator*, and Charles Remond, a black delegate. With them also sat a young bride, Elizabeth Cady Stanton (1815–1902), whose husband was a delegate to the convention. The meeting of Lucretia Mott and Elizabeth Cady Stanton under these humiliating circumstances was eventually to trigger the women's rights movement in the United States. Their long and serious conversations in London were concluded by their firm resolution to form a society advocating the rights of women upon their return home.

Lucretia Mott's involvement in social reform spanned almost the entire nineteenth century. She was one of the most highly respected women of the 1800s for her vigilance, for her inspired talks, her measured decisions, her impartiality, her imperturbability under all circumstances and for her wholehearted commitment to those causes in which she truly believed.

In 1821, at the age of twenty-eight, Lucretia Mott was inaugurated into the ministry of the Society of Friends. The variety of her interests is breathtaking. Her opposition to slavery was implemented by deeds as well as words. Preaching against slavery as early as 1829, she refused to buy any products produced by slave labor, including such staples as cotton and sugar. She organized the Philadelphia Female Anti-Slavery Society in 1833 and was an organizer, in 1837, of the Anti-Slavery Convention of American Women. Her home was always ready to receive slaves who came via the Underground Railroad. She traveled thousands of miles speaking for the antislavery cause, and held meetings in slave states, even when mobs and violence threatened. She was one of the instigators, in 1848, of the Seneca Falls Women's Rights Convention.

After the Emancipation Proclamation Mrs. Mott was a supporter of suffrage for freed slaves. She was active in the women's rights movement. She was the first president of the Equal Rights Convention, held in 1866 to press for equal rights for all Americans regardless of race, color, or sex. Mrs. Mott was a pacifist, and was vice president of the Pennsylvania Peace Society. She supported the Whole World's Temperance Society Program. She was the only woman speaker at the organization of the Free Religious Association in Boston during May 1867, other speakers including Ralph Waldo Emerson.

Lucretia Mott and her husband had a happy and intellectually congenial marriage for fifty-seven years. The Motts shared the same concerns and had the same goals. James Mott often accompanied his wife on her speaking engagements. The Motts had six children, one of whom died in infancy. Their home was a hospitable one with writers, reformers, royalty, politicians, scholars dining at their table. The Motts welcomed guests from many states, the conversation occasionally making "merry over the bigotry of the church, popular prejudices, conservative fears, absurd laws, and customs hoary with age." In 1857 the Motts retired to a country house, called Roadside, north of Philadelphia.

Mrs. Mott continued her activities after her husband's death, speaking and working for her many causes until just before her own death in 1880 at the age of eighty-seven.

The 1800s were to produce many memorable women but none more respected, none with greater dedication to the causes in which she so profoundly believed, none whose presence on all occasions radiated such serenity, than Lucretia Mott. She looked, when she spoke, "as though she had seen a vision," someone once said, and her words were not a speech but a "psalm of life." Lucretia Mott was one of the great women of the 1800s.

CHAPTER ELEVEN

Changing Conditions Change Women's Lives

CHANGING CONDITIONS IN the United States opened up new horizons for women during the 1830s and the 1840s. Industrialization brought some women into the factory. Opportunities opened up for women in the West, where there was both land and gold for the taking. Wives who went with their husbands and families often suffered hardships in the long weary journey in Conestoga wagons.

In the early 1800s the South was building a profitable cotton-producing industry with unpaid slave labor. (A woman, Catherine Greene, had encouraged Eli Whitney to invent the miraculous cotton gin which speeded up the cleaning of cotton.) The North was building a profitable textile manufacturing industry with young women operators who worked long hours for low wages. Samuel Slater's introduction of English cotton-spinning machinery

in the 1790s had triggered New England's mushrooming textile industry. Already by the late 1790s Alexander Hamilton had presented his Report on Manufactures, asking Congress for tariff protection for infant industries. The South did not favor tariffs, so Hamilton's report was rejected.

Meanwhile "infant industries" were making rapid and profitable progress with the help of their low-paid women workers. From the remote farmhouses and small villages of New England thousands of girls came to take jobs in the textile mills of Lowell, Lawrence, Fall River, Waltham, and other New England factory towns. They worked twelve or more hours a day, six days a week, for an average wage of $2.00 a week plus room and board in company-owned boardinghouses. Some girls worked to help their impoverished families, some to put their brothers through

LOWELL
OFFERING

August, 1845.

"Is Saul also among the prophets?"

A REPOSITORY
OF ORIGINAL ARTICLES, WRITTEN BY
"FACTORY GIRLS."

LOWELL: MISSES CURTIS & FARLEY.
BOSTON: JORDAN & WILEY, 121
Washington street.
1845.

A cover from the **Lowell Offering.** *Lowell Historical Society*

college, some wanted money to try to continue their own education. By 1833 some 3,800 women and girls were tending looms and spindles in Lowell, Massachusetts, and Lowell had become the showcase town of industrial America. Foreign celebrities such as Charles Dickens, Harriet Martineau, and others visited Lowell, admired its neat-looking blocks of boardinghouses, its five-story mills fronting the Merrimack River, its banks where employees thriftily deposited whatever money they could save from their weekly two-dollar wages. Visitors particularly praised the factory girls, who were pretty in a wholesome way, dressed neatly, were well mannered and self-reliant.

For many Lowell girls a job in the mill opened new horizons. They subscribed to Lyceum Lecture courses (twenty-five lectures for fifty cents) at which Edward Everett, John Greenleaf Whittier, Daniel Webster, Ralph Waldo Emerson, and John Quincy Adams were among the speakers. The girls wrote poems, essays, stories for the *Operatives Magazine* or the *Lowell Offering*, which local clergymen helped edit and which the girls published themselves. Some girls ultimately made careers for themselves. Lucy Larcom (1824–1893), who started working in the mills at the age of eleven, later managed to attend school,

become a teacher, and publish an informative book entitled *A New England Girlhood* in 1852 as well as volumes of verse. Margaret Foley became a cameo cutter. Harriet Hanson Robinson was active in the antislavery and women's rights movements.

In 1845 about 90 percent of the Lowell girls were native Americans. By 1850 50 percent of the Lowell girls were Irish immigrants. And by the 1850s Lowell itself was no longer the showcase of industrial America. The much-admired flower beds no longer fronted the mills. The open spaces between mills with a view of the Merrimack River had been filled in with more five-story mill buildings. The original Lowell girls were slowly drifting away.

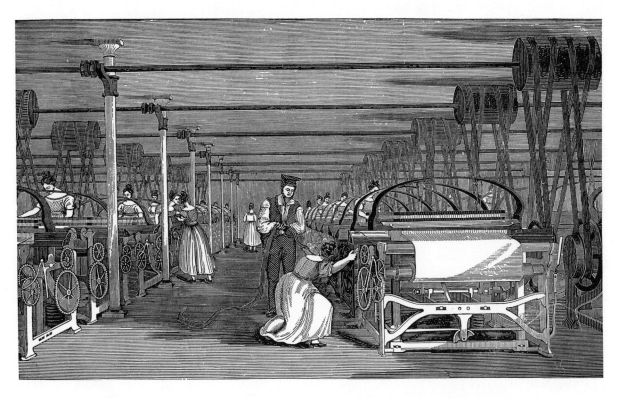

Women tending power looms in a New England cotton factory about 1840. Each woman had charge of only one or two looms. Merrimack Valley Textile Museum

But before this happened an attempt was made by some of the veteran Lowell girls to improve working conditions by organizing labor unions.

After eight years in Lowell mills, Sarah Bagley the first woman trade unionist, started to question the "privileges" and "pleasures" of Lowell mill girls so praised by admiring visitors and so exploited by management. Orestes Brownson's series of articles on the laboring classes in the *Boston Quarterly Review* had helped open her eyes to conditions that she had previously accepted as tolerable. She had originally written articles for the *Lowell Offering* on "The Pleasures of Factory Life," but by 1844 those "pleasures" were subject to doubts.

Sarah Bagley's discontent led her to invite five mill girls to join her for a grievance session on a December evening in 1844. The girls' complaints were many— the long tiring twelve-hour (and sometimes thirteen-hour) day, the ceaseless noise and clatter of looms and shuttles, the discomfort of flying lint, the stifling stale air of mill rooms on account of windows that were nailed down, the lack of bathing facilities at the end of a long dirty mill day, the nineteen-minute break allowed for breakfast, and then only after two hours of breakfastless work, the discomfort of sleeping six girls to a room and two to a bed, the speed-up system with no increase in wages, no paid vacations and only four annual holidays.

The Female Labor Reform Association was the result of this meeting, with Sarah Bagley as president, and with the motto "Try Again" as a rallying cry. The first and most immediate goal, the girls agreed, would be to obtain a ten-hour working day.

The totally inexperienced Sarah Bagley proved to be a good "labor leader" during the two years that followed. She signed up 300 members within three months and 600 within a year. News of the association reached other mill towns. Sarah went to Manchester, Nashua, and Dover, New Hampshire, to Waltham and Fall River, Massachusetts, to form branch unions. She spoke out boldly about grievances and called the mill owners "driveling cotton lords who arrogantly aspire to lord it over God's heritage." She wrote pamphlets. She attended the first convention of the New England Workingmen's Association in Boston—trade unionists totaled some 300,-000 by the late 1830s. She got signatures on a petition to be presented to the Massachusetts House of Representatives demanding the ten-hour working day.

In these efforts the New England Working Men's Association supported her. Finally, after repeated postponements, a legislative hearing was called for February 13, 1845 at which both men and women were asked to testify. Sarah Bagley testified and so did Eliza Heminway and Judith Payne, stating that long working hours had been detrimental to their health. Though these women spoke convincingly, the cards were stacked against the petitioners. Cotton textile magnates of Boston dominated the Massachusetts legislatures. The petition was turned down by the Massachusetts House and later by the Senate. Thwarted by management and by the government, the women's labor movement struggled on for a while, but by 1848 it collapsed. Sarah Bagley had already left the movement and the mills. But ground had been broken for a woman's labor movement, and woman had played a daring role and built a partly successful organization.

January 24, 1848, changed the lives of many Americans. On that day gold was discovered in Sutter's millrace in the Sacramento Valley, California. At first nobody believed it. But when men began to arrive in San Francisco carrying nuggets of pure gold, the trek to the goldfields started. "The blacksmith dropped his hammer, the carpenter his plane, the mason his trowel, the farmer his sickle, the baker his loaf, and the tapster his bottle," one contemporary wrote. San Francisco, a dismal, shoddy village in January 1848, within months grew to a metropolis of some 25,000. People came by the thousands from all parts of the United States—

around Cape Horn in any old tub of a ship they could find, across the Isthmus of Panama, hoping they would connect with a ship on the Pacific coast, across the Great Plains. And California, without permission of Congress, voted itself a state, did not allow slavery, drew up a constitution, and chose a governor and a legislature. Somewhat reluctantly (because of the prohibition of slavery) Congress admitted California to the Union in 1850.

Women followed the fortune-hunting Forty-Niners west to the gold fields. Fifty-thousand unattached women, by one estimate, moved into grubby gold-rush towns between Independence, Missouri, and San Francisco, California, between 1850 and 1870. The notorious Barbary Coast of San Francisco attracted about 10,000 adventuresses—some fortune hunters, some of dubious character, some gamblers, some

Farm couple on the Nebraska plains in front of the house they built out of sod, 1888.
Solomon D. Butcher Collection, Nebraska State Historical Society

Skilled with a rifle and a pistol, this western cowgirl
rode the range when her rancher-father was short of help.
Solomon D. Butcher Collection, Nebraska State Historical Society

shrewd madams. There were women in the gold-rush shack villages of the Sierra Nevadas, at Pikes Peak, at Alder Gulch and Last Chance, and in the Black Hills of Dakota. Some women made fortunes, one way or another, some found themselves on the street, and some married and settled down respectably.

Lola Montez (1818–61) brought to the rough-and-ready male population of San Francisco and California mining towns her glamorous past and her provocative Spider Dance. She was the former mistress of a king, Ludwig I of Bavaria, and she had the unattainable aloofness that suggested "class" to the crude prospectors.

Martha Cannary Burk (1852–1903) was a teen-age orphan on her own at the age of fifteen. She has come down to us in history as Calamity Jane because her life was fictionalized in 1877 by newspaper writers and dime novel editors looking for a colorful western heroine. She was glad to embellish stories about herself whenever the occasion offered. She was, however, an excellent horsewoman, often wore men's clothes, and probably hired out as a bullwhacker. She was a heavy drinker, frequented mining town bars, and occasionally settled down for a while here and there with a "husband" though the only man she apparently married was Clinton Burk, a Texan, in 1885.

CHAPTER TWELVE

The Seneca Falls Convention and the Women's Rights Movement

IN JULY 1848, fate seems to have brought together five women in the right place to start the women's rights movement. Elizabeth Cady Stanton was living in Seneca Falls, New York at the time. Lucretia Mott was visiting her sister, Martha Wright (1806–1875), in a nearby town. The solemn compact that Mrs. Stanton and Mrs. Mott had made eight years before at the World Anti-Slavery Convention in London, to take action regarding women's lowly status, was about to be implemented. However, none of the five women who met for a social afternoon around the tea table in the Waterloo home of Jane Hunt on July 14 was aware that their meeting would have momentous results. Bored and frustrated, Mrs. Stanton unexpectedly began to pour out a "torrent of long-accumulating discontent" about the numerous grievances suffered

by women. Then and there the five women present decided to do something. Before they parted a notice had been sent to the *Seneca Falls Courier* announcing to women of surrounding towns that the first Women's Rights Convention would take place on July 19 and 20 in the Methodist Church in Seneca Falls.

In the five days following Mrs. Mott, Mrs. Stanton, Mrs. Wright, Mrs. Mary Ann McClintock, and Mrs. Jane Hunt drew up, with moments of doubt and moments of near panic, a Declaration of Women's Rights in the format of the Declaration of Independence. It boldly stated that all men and women are created equal. Its Declaration of Sentiments pointed out that a woman had never been permitted to "exercise her inalienable right to the elective franchise," that, if single, she must pay taxes without representation, that, if married, she is "civilly dead," with no right to her wages or her property, that, if divorced or separated, the law gives the husband a "false supposition of supremacy," that a woman is discriminated against in employment and in the professions, that the most remunerative jobs and professions are not open to her, that colleges are closed against her, that she is excluded from the ministry, that a double standard of morals prevails.

On the beautiful July 19th morning of the Seneca Falls Convention, some three

Elizabeth C. Stanton a rebellious thinker and a fluent writer for the women's rights movement, raised seven children, and said that motherhood required "more knowledge than any other department in human affairs." NYPL Picture Collection

hundred people appeared for the first day's meeting, including, unexpectedly, forty men. Some women drove in by farm wagon from the surrounding countryside, bringing friends and neighbors along. James Mott, husband of Lucretia Mott, presided at the meeting. No woman dared to do so. A few women made speeches. For Mrs. Stanton, who was to become a forceful and eloquent public speaker, the speech she read at this first Women's Rights Convention was her first. One by one the fourteen resolutions submitted to the convention were discussed and passed unanimously—all except one. Even Lucretia Mott quailed before the resolution that read "Resolved, that it is the duty of the women of this country to secure to themselves their sacred right to the elective franchise." This resolution was carried by a small majority headed by Mrs. Stanton. Frederick Douglass, a black man, was one of the few men voting for the resolution.

The press for the most part ridiculed the Seneca Falls Women's Rights Convention, with headlines such as "Bolting Among the Ladies," "Women Out Of Their Latitude," and "Insurrection Among the Women." Some of the more timid signers of the Seneca Falls Declaration withdrew their signatures. But word got around far and wide to women that action had been started in their behalf, and the movement gained momentum.

Two weeks after the Seneca Falls Women's Rights Convention a follow-up convention was held in Rochester, New York (July 1848), with many of the same people attending. No national organization was formed. No headquarters were established. No officers were elected. But the idea of women's rights and the possibility of the vote for women spread from these meetings to the north, to the south, and to the west.

One thousand people attended a Women's Rights Convention held in Worcester, Massachusetts, on October 23, 1850, including delegates from as far away as California, and men and women from ten other states. The idea of women's rights was established in women's minds from then on. National conventions were held every year from 1850 to 1860 (with the exception of 1857) and there were meetings in Pennsylvania, Ohio, Indiana, and Massachusetts. Individual women also publicly took a stand for women's rights. Pauline Wright Davis's magazine, *The Una,* announced that it was "Devoted to the Elevation of Women," and became the first women's rights magazine. Lucy Stone, the silver-tongued orator of the antislavery movement, began lecturing throughout the country on women's rights, and Susan B. Anthony, the "mother of woman suffrage" joined the cause.

Four women kept the women's rights movement alive—Lucretia Mott, Lucy Stone, Elizabeth Cady Stanton, and Susan B. Anthony. Miss Anthony, though a latecomer to the cause, had such executive ability, such indefatigable energy and determination, that she would hold the suffrage movement together for the coming fifty-five years.

Susan B. Anthony did not attend the Seneca Falls Convention of 1848 nor the Rochester, New York follow-up convention. She read newspaper accounts of the meetings, listened to her father, mother, and sister enthusiastically talk about the Rochester Women's Rights Convention but she remained unconvinced. Teaching was Miss Anthony's profession and chief interest. She was also sympathetic to the temperance movement, and the antislavery movement. It was when she discovered that all three of these movements were dominated by men that she began to consider woman's role in the 1800s.

Susan B. Anthony (1820–1906) came from a liberal-minded well-to-do Quaker family. At nineteen she was teaching school. Her first grievance was the fact that her salary was only one-fourth the amount paid male teachers for the same work. When she tried to speak in behalf of higher salaries for female teachers at the New York State Teachers' Convention in Rochester, New York (where two-thirds of the 500 teacher-delegates were women) she was forced to wait until the male teachers took a vote on the advisability of allowing a woman the privilege of speaking. The same thing happened in the temperance movement. When Miss Anthony tried to speak at the Sons of Temperance Convention in Albany, New York, in 1852, she was told (even though she was a delegate of the Rochester Daughters of Temperance) that women were invited to listen and learn but not to express their opinions. These rebuffs made her aware that there was a need to liberate women from the control men exercised over what women considered was their right to be heard.

The chance meeting, in 1850, of Susan B. Anthony and Elizabeth Cady Stanton, marked a turning point in Miss Anthony's life. The two women immediately became

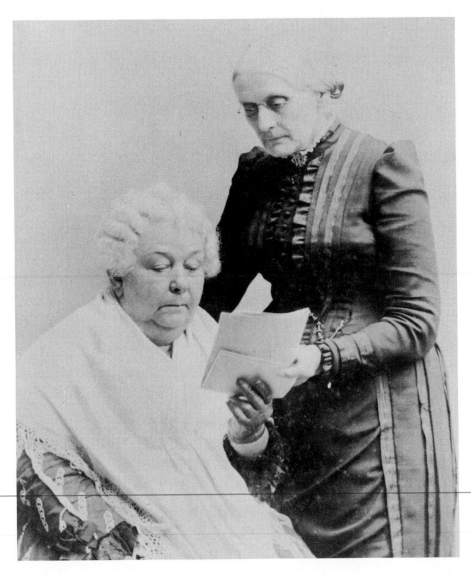

Susan B. Anthony (standing) *and Elizabeth Cady Stanton, two great leaders of the women's rights movement. Library of Congress*

friends and soon discovered that their talents complemented each other. Mrs. Stanton was a fluent writer and public speaker. Miss Anthony was a fact collector, an indefatigable organizer, but a diffident speaker though she spoke whenever called upon to do so. Working together, these two women steered the women's rights movement through the nineteenth century.

Miss Anthony began with a series of campaigns by petition for redress. From 1850 to 1920 (with the exception of war years) literally millions of women's signatures on a variety of petitions would bombard state legislatures, and members of Congress would not be allowed to forget that women wanted their rights and the vote. For the first time, many women faced the fact that they were second-class citizens with no right to secure guardianship of their children in case of divorce, with no right to keep their own earnings, with no right to draw up a will without their husbands' signatures, without recourse to the law, and without the vote.

One bride was brave enough to write a marriage contract in which many of these grievances were spelled out. Mrs. Henry Blackwell had been married a year before she decided that she absolutely must take back her maiden name, Lucy Stone, and Lucy Stone she remained the rest of her life. The wedding itself had been more conventional than her friends had expected from so rebellious a feminist. She had worn an ashes-of-roses-colored wedding dress instead of her usual Bloomer Costume; her fiancé, Henry Blackwell, dressed quite properly in a white waistcoat. There had been roses decorating the living room, but there had also been a "marriage contract" read at the wedding, written jointly by bride and bridegroom. It was not the first such "contract." Robert Dale Owen and Mary Jane Robinson had a "marriage contract" at their wedding in 1832. But because Lucy Stone was a nationally known public speaker and feminist, her "contract" made news and so did the fact that the presiding clergyman, Thomas Wentworth Higginson, omitted the word "obey" from the ceremony at the request of the bride and bridegroom.

On May 1, 1855, Lucy and Henry declared:

> While acknowledging our mutual affection by publicly assuming the relationship of husband and wife, yet in justice to ourselves and a great principle, we deem it a duty to declare that this act on our part implies no sanction of, nor promise of voluntary obedience to such of the present laws of marriage as refuse to recognize the wife as an independent, rational being, while they confer upon the husband an injurious and unnatural superiority, investing him with legal powers which no honorable man would exercise, and which no man should possess. . . . We believe that personal independence and equal human rights can never be forfeited, except for crime; that marriage should be an equal and permanent partnership, and so recognized by law; that until it is recognized, married partners should provide against the radical injustice of present laws, by every means in their power.

Many capable women were ready to help the cause of women's rights, among them the Grimké sisters, Jane Swisshelm who published the *Pittsburgh Visiter,* Amelia Bloomer, Matilda Joslyn Gage, and others. On the lecture platform in addition to Lucy Stone were Abby Kelley Foster and Ernestine Rose (1810–1892). Mrs. Rose, known as the Queen of the Platform, was one of the most eloquent, witty, liberal speakers of the mid-1800s, her lecture career lasting thirty-seven years. Born in Piotrkow, Poland, the daughter of a rabbi, she came to the United States with her husband, William Rose, in 1836. Starting out alone, and paying her own way, she lectured in twenty or more states on the abolition of slavery, women's rights, human rights, and the free-thought movement. From 1837 on she worked for the passage of a married women's property bill in New York State, sending the first petition to the New York legislature, and addressing the legislature five or more times until a law was enacted in 1848.

Women now had two crusades—their own women's rights crusade and the antislavery crusade. The women's rights movement grew slowly during the next twenty years, partly because of the demands their

A picture of men and women active in both women's rights and the antislavery movements, taken at Lucy Stone Blackwell's house. Lucy Stone sits on the porch (second woman from right), Abbey Kelley Foster is next to her (at left); at far right is Theodore Weld, who married Angelina Grimké in 1838; next to him stands Henry Blackwell; William Lloyd Garrison sits second from left, against porch pillar. Sophia Smith Collection

male antislavery colleagues made on women in behalf of the antislavery cause. (Miss Anthony organized the collection of 400,000 signatures—a truly amazing achievement in those days—urging the passage of the Thirteenth Amendment abolishing slavery.) Again and again women selflessly deserted their own women's rights movement temporarily in order to collect names on petitions to be sent to Congress urging the abolition of slavery.

After a while the newspapers toned down their ridiculing of women, though when there was an opportunity to help the women's cause they were often silent, and when there was something to criticize,

they were ruthless in their condemnation. In 1852, commenting on the Women's Rights Syracuse Convention held on September 10, the *Syracuse Daily Star* wrote, "Perhaps we owe an apology for having given publicity to the mass of corruption, heresies, ridiculous nonsense, and reeking vulgarities which these bad women have vomited forth for the past three days . . ." And the *New York Herald* writing about the same convention, called the women "mannish . . . like hens that crow," and said that "they would not be guilty of such vulgarity as to live with their husbands . . . They want to be lawyers, doctors, captains of vessels, and generals in the field."

CHAPTER THIRTEEN

The Civil War Years

THE 72-YEAR-OLD Union was falling apart even as Abraham Lincoln took the oath of office as sixteenth President of the United States on March 4, 1861. Only a month later war broke out. Lincoln had been conciliatory in his inaugural address, pointing out that "there needs to be no bloodshed or violence; and there shall be none, unless it be forced upon the national authority," and, in measured words, he reiterated his objective: "to save the Union."

With the daylong Confederate bombing of Fort Sumter at Charleston, South Carolina, on April 12, 1861, the Civil War began, and it polarized loyalties and caused anguished decisions on both sides. Southern wives married to Northern husbands, and vice versa, had to make a choice whether to support the North or the South; citizens in many states found that their consciences separated them from those they loved. The South stood for state sovereignty and for slavery, its "peculiar institution." Its pride had long suffered from Northern antislavery invective. It was apprehensive of growing Northern industrial and financial power. The North, patriotically indignant that the flag had been fired upon, its antislavery feeling running high, rallied to the support of the Union. In the end twenty-three Union states and eleven Confederate states faced each other, all emotionally outraged and all forgetting the words Lincoln had used to conclude his inaugural address: "We are not enemies, but friends."

Northern minds had been stirred by Harriet Beecher Stowe's *Uncle Tom's Cabin*. "Is this the little woman who made this great war?" was Abraham Lincoln's greeting to her when she visited the president in the White House in 1862. *Uncle Tom's Cabin* had at that time become a world best seller. People who had been indifferent to slavery, or lukewarm about it, were aroused to action by this book. It sold 300,000 copies within a year, and made Mrs. Stowe a celebrity almost overnight. She was a Beecher by birth, a member of the famous family that produced Henry Ward Beecher, Catherine Beecher, and six minister sons in all. Harriet Beecher Stowe (1811–1896) wrote *Uncle Tom's Cabin* chapter by chapter as a serial story for *The National Era,* an antislavery publication, while caring for children and running her house in Brunswick, Maine, where her husband was a professor at

Daguerreotype portrait of Harriet Beecher Stowe, author of Uncle Tom's Cabin. *Metropolitan Museum of Art, New York*

Bowdoin College. Mrs. Stowe had no room of her own to write in. The words "tumbled forth" from her pen on scraps of paper wherever she was and whenever she had time to write. She wrote the last chapter first in February 1851, and had expected to write only three or four installments. There were forty before she finished. And within three months after the story's publication in book form, her royalties were $10,000. "How she [Mrs. Stowe] is shaking the world with her *Uncle Tom's Cabin,*" wrote Henry Wadsworth Longfellow.

Ten years had passed after the publication of *Uncle Tom's Cabin* before war actually broke out. Neither the Union nor the Confederacy was ready for war. Women on both sides immediately started to organize their own war programs. Within two weeks some 20,000 women's societies had sprung up in the North and South. Women knitted, rolled bandages, scraped lint, made clothing, collected donations. New York had its Women's Central Relief Association with Louisa Lee Schuyler as president and Dr. Elizabeth Blackwell as a member of the board. Northern women's war efforts were uncoordinated nationally until the Secretary of War was pressured into taking action and the Sanitary Commission was established on June 9, 1861, under the authority of the government, but generously supported by women of the nation. Auxiliary Aid Societies, formed throughout the country to assist the commission's work, raised some $92 million to aid the sick and wounded. Mrs. Annie T. Wittenmyer (1827–1900) of Iowa was appointed superintendent of all army diet kitchens.

Women members of the Sanitary Commission at Fredericksburg, Virginia, 1864. Women cared for the sick and wounded, collected and distributed tents, food and medical supplies. Library of Congress

Cordelia Harvey, widow of Governor Louis Harvey of Wisconsin, established convalescent hospitals and worked with war orphans. Mrs. Eliza Howland, her sister, Georgeanne Woolsey, Katherine Prescott Wormeley, and Helen Gilson were assigned to floating evacuation hospitals.

Though it is appalling to contemplate, the United States had no adequately trained nurses in the mid-1800s. "Born nurses" cared for the sick. The first American nursing schools date to the 1870s. When the War Department looked about for a superintendent of army nurses, they chose Dorothea Dix (1802–1887) who, though not a nurse, had been highly successful in arousing the country to hospital needs for mental patients who were miserably confined to dank cellars or poor houses and inadequately clothed and fed. Miss Dix's ability to get state and federal action (thirty-two state mental hospitals had been initiated by her efforts) made her a logical choice when she offered her services to the government at the outbreak of the Civil War. Miss Dix's standards were strict. She insisted on plain women over thirty, strong enough to turn a soldier lying wounded in a hospital bed, and "no hoopskirts," please. Meanwhile, in New York, Dr. Elizabeth Blackwell began training New York women as nurses. In Chicago, Mary Livermore, Jane Hoge, and Eliza Porter organized a mammoth Sani-

A Sanitary Commission nurse cares for a group of wounded soldiers at Fredericksburg.
NYPL Picture Collection

tary Commission Fair that lasted two weeks, netted $100,000 and sparked similar fairs and bazaars throughout the country.

Churches and homes became workshops where women met to sew for the army. Wealthy women sometimes provided material to outfit an entire regiment or a hospital. Farm women worked to plant and harvest the crops in place of absent fathers and sons. Poor women worked in mills and factories, taking the places of men who had gone to war.

In the South, women collected funds for gunboats, opened refreshment centers for soldiers and wayside homes for refugees. There were active war relief societies in Alabama and South Carolina. Sally Thompkins supported a twenty-two-bed hospital in a rented house in Richmond, Virginia, one of the first Southern women to support a hospital. Mrs. Ella King Newsom was appointed superintendent of an army hospital in Kentucky. Mrs. Rose Rooney of New Orleans was "mother" to the Fifteenth Louisiana Regiment and Mrs. Betsy Sullivan "mother" to the First Tennessee Regiment. "Mothering" included sewing, cooking, nursing and counseling the men. Kate Cumming (c. 1828–

1901) though untrained, soon taught herself to work on the battlefields and in hospitals, serving from 1863 to the war's end. She once "chased" her hospital through four states. She defended the respectability of women working in army hospitals and eventually became a "matron" (hospital supervisor). *Women's Work in the Civil War,* published in 1867, contains sketches of some five hundred Southern women who were active in the war effort.

One woman wrote the marching song sung by Union soldiers during the Civil War. It was printed in hymnbooks and sung in churches. It was translated into Italian, Spanish, and Armenian soon after

its appearance. Again and again its author, Julia Ward Howe (1819–1910), copied the verses for admirers and autograph hunters. No song so moved soldiers and civilians of the Union to great deeds and great courage as did the "Battle Hymn of the Republic."

Julia Ward Howe wrote the hymn in Washington on November 18, 1861. The previous day she had been reviewing the troops with a party of friends and was greatly moved by the sight of fathers, brothers, and young sons going off to war. The words came to her in the "gray dawn of the next morning," line after line, stanza after stanza. She lay quietly wait-

Julia Ward Howe, author of **The Battle Hymn of the Republic** *and later an ardent suffragist.* Library of Congress

Clara Barton, who ministered to soldiers on the battlefields of the Civil War, later founded the American Red Cross. American Red Cross

ing "till the voice was silent and the last line was ended." Then she crept quietly out of bed, groped for a piece of paper and "the stump of a pen which I remembered to have used the day before," and scribbled down the words of the hymn in the dark, as she often did when inspiration came to her at night. She went back to bed and fell asleep, saying to herself, "I like this better than most things I have written." The poem was published by the *Atlantic Monthy* in its February 1862 issue; Mrs. Howe was paid $4.00 for it. It was "somewhat praised," but made no stir. Then, all at once, everyone was singing "The Battle Hymn of the Republic." Soldiers were marching to it. Almost anytime anywhere people's spirits would lift,

and people's courage would be renewed when someone began to sing it.

The North had some unique "lone wolves" among its women volunteers. Mother Mary Ann Bickerdyke (1817–1901), an experienced nurse, made her own way for four years, moving to whatever battle area she felt needed her. She would walk in suddenly, unannounced, and turn an army hospital upside down—cleaning out the filth, dismissing inefficient employees, opening diet kitchens and setting up working systems for patient care. No one dared stop her, for as General Grant once observed, "Mother Bickerdyke outranks everybody, even Lincoln." She was loved, respected, and obeyed. Clara Barton (1821–1912), as strong willed as

Dorothea Dix, cut red tape and worked directly on the battlefields. "I went in while the battle raged," she said. At the battle of Antietam a soldier was shot to death in her arms as she was giving him a drink of water.

These two women continued in their Civil War roles to the bitter end. Mother Bickerdyke refused to leave battlefields until all her boys had been discharged, and then went to Kansas and opened Bickerdyke House at Salina to help veterans resettle in the West. Clara Barton spent four years after the war tracing missing soldiers; she worked without a salary and often used her own money when the Congressional appropriation of $15,000 proved insufficient. Miss Barton wrote 63,000 letters to families seeking fathers, sons, or brothers. She had to leave some 40,000 men unaccounted for at the end of her indefatigable search. Later Clara Barton organized the American Red Cross.

Few women doctors served in the war —none on the Confederate side. Male army doctors resented women doctors in those days. It took Dr. Mary Walker (1832–1919) three years to get her commission as contract surgeon in 1864. Her habit of always wearing male clothes alienated many people, who considered her a freak. She reported for battlefield duty, but was almost immediately taken prisoner, to the astonishment of Confederate physicians when they encountered her.

There was one woman chaplain—Mrs. Ella F. Hobart who served the First Wisconsin Artillery. She was refused a commission because she was a woman.

Four hundred women, more or less, enlisted as soldiers in the Civil War, some on the Union side, some on the Confederate side, escaping detection because there were no thorough army preinduction physical examinations in Civil War times. Some women died undiscovered. When they were wounded or ill, women soldiers deserted, rather than risk detection. If they were hospitalized and discovered, they were promptly discharged upon recovery. Many reenlisted under another name.

Women soldiers gave various reasons for their enlistments, according to fragmentary records which have survived the years. Some were rebellious teen-agers, looking for escape or for adventure. Some young girls had dreams of becoming another Joan of Arc, leading an army to a glorious victory. Lizzie Compton claimed she had enlisted as a Union soldier at the age of fourteen and served in seven different regiments, changing her regiment whenever she feared detection. Fanny Wilson of New Jersey managed to serve eighteen months before she was detected. On the Confederate side, Mrs. Amy Clarke enlisted to be with her husband, and remained in his regiment after he was killed at Shiloh. Mrs. Malinda Blalock of North Carolina posed as her husband's brother, enlisting as Sam Blalock.

The Union Army's most famous woman soldier was Sarah Emma Edmonds (1841–1898). Even before she enlisted she had posed as a man, selling Bibles for a Hartford, Connecticut, publishing firm. When war broke out she was living in Michigan and enlisted in the Second Michigan Infantry under the assumed name of "Franklin Thompson." During the two years that she served, she was assigned to hospital duty, served as mail carrier, as aide to a colonel, and volunteered to spy behind the Confederate lines. She deserted when she contracted a fever requiring hospitalization. Her book entitled *Nurse and Spy in the Union Army* appeared in 1865 and sold 175,000 copies.

Following the army, or making intermittent visits, was a variety of women—mothers seeking wounded sons, wives seeking wounded husbands, wives of officers, many of whom accompanied their husbands to war, would-be nurses, adventure seekers, other camp followers.

Spying attracted a few women during the Civil War, either because they found its dangers exciting and challenging, or because they were loyal to the cause with which they identified. Women's clothes —hoopskirts, petticoats, parasols—and braided and puffed hair were excellent hiding places for military drawings, messages, dispatches.

Mrs. Rose O'Neal Greenhow (1815–1864) was one of the most adroit and sophisticated of Confederate spies. She lived in Washington where she was a popular political hostess and had many prominent and influential friends. As early as 1861 she began sending dispatches to the Confederates, with information, it is claimed, enabling them to prepare in advance for the Battle of Bull Run and thereby defeat the Union Army. Counterespionage agents eventually arrested Mrs. Greenhow on the steps of her Washington home, and put her under house arrest, but not before she swallowed the ciphered message she had in her possession. Her home became known as Fort Greenhow and several other suspected women spies were con-

fined there. All were under constant surveillance. Later Mrs. Greenhow was confined to Old Capitol prison, but managed, somehow or other, to smuggle out messages. Eventually she was sent across Confederate lines, went to England as an unofficial Confederate agent, wrote a book about her spying career, and sailed for home in 1864. Her ship was chased by a Union gunboat as it foundered during a storm off North Carolina. Mrs. Greenhow tried to escape in a small rowboat but it overturned and she was drowned, weighted down, the story goes, by a money belt filled with gold sovereigns.

Teen-ager Belle Boyd had thrilling adventures as a Confederate spy. She eavesdropped on Union war councils, rode horseback through the darkness of Virginia nights (sometimes as far as thirty miles) to report Union plans to Confederate leaders.

One of the most elusive and effective spies was Elizabeth Van Lew (1818–1900). She spied for the Union from her home in Richmond, Virginia, posing as an eccentric woman and convincing people that her craziness was harmless. Miss Van Lew helped Union prisoners escape from Richmond's Libby prison. She supplied General Grant with information, some of which she obtained by placing a domestic (Mary Elizabeth Bowser) in the Confederate White House where she could overhear the conversations of Confederate officials.

Only one woman, Mrs. Mary Surratt (c. 1820–1865) was executed, but not for war spying. She was convicted as a conspirator in the assassination of Abraham Lincoln. Her son had been a friend of John

Daring spy for the Confederacy, Belle Boyd. *Library of Congress*

Wilkes Booth but Mrs. Surratt, at whose house one of the assassination conspirators had boarded, was apparently unaware of the plot. Mrs. Surratt was hanged on July 7, 1865. Historians consider that she was the victim of assassination hysteria that swept the country following Lincoln's death.

The Civil War continued, and took its toll on the women of the South. Prices went up exorbitantly. Confederate dollars were worthless paper. There was a shortage of food, a shortage of clothing. There were no shoes to be had. Women were making dresses out of bedspreads. Cities and towns were under fire. Homes were destroyed. Livestock and hoarded supplies had long ago been commandeered. Exploding shells forced women to take refuge in cellars or to flee burning houses with nowhere to go. These and countless other Civil War experiences filled the diaries, journals, and letters of Southern women as the war came nearer and nearer.

"I was hungry, very hungry," wrote Mary Ann Harris Gay after Sherman's departure from devastated Atlanta in September 1864. "There was nothing left in the country to eat. Yea, a crow flying over it would have failed to discover a morsel with which to appease its hunger . . . Every larder was empty, and those with thousands and tens of thousands of dollars were as poor as the poorest, and as hungry, too. What was I to do? Sit down and wait for the inevitable starvation?" Mary Ann Harris Gay did not sit down and wait. She went to the battlefields to hunt for lead to exchange, hopefully, for food "to keep us from starving." The day was bitter cold as she and her servant, Telitha, scratched with stiff, bleeding hands the rubble of the battlefield looking for bullets and Minie balls. Then carrying bags heavy with lead they had found, they began their long walk to the commissary through a desolate city. The "courteous gentleman in a faded grey uniform" who weighed their heavy baskets gave them more food than they had dreamed of—sugar and meal, lard, flour, and meat. "I can never describe the satisfaction I experienced as I lifted two of those baskets and saw Telitha grasp the other one, and turned my face homeward," Mrs. Gay wrote.

Emma Le Conte in Columbia, South Carolina, wrote about the horrors of bombing and burning. "We ran to the front door just in time to hear a shell go whirring past," she wrote. "It fell and exploded not far off. This was so unexpected. I do not know why, but in all my list of anticipated horrors I had not thought of a bombardment." That night the wind "blew a fearful gale, wafting flames from house to house with frightful rapidity. By midnight the town (except the outskirts) was wrapped in one huge blaze . . . I have seen it all . . . O I have seen the 'Abomination of Desolation.' It is worse than I thought . . . The entire city is in ashes—only the outer edges remain."

"Everything me and children's got is patched," wrote a soldier's wife in Nansemond City, Virginia, to her husband. "Both of them is in bed now covered up with comforters and old pieces of karpet to keep them warm, while I went 'long out to try and get some wood . . . We haven't got nothing in the house to eat but a bit o' meal! . . . We can't none of us hold out much longer down here."

Writing seemed to alleviate some of the pain Southern women felt when there was no place to go and nothing to eat. Diaries, journals, reminiscences, and novels have come down to us relating days of anguish and of courage in the South.

One of the most informative women writers of the Civil War period was South Carolina-born Mary Boykin Miller Chesnut (1823–1886), Confederate wife of James Chesnut, Jr., who served in the U.S. Senate from 1859 to 1860. Her daily diary of conversations, observations, and comment provides a perceptive background to the Civil War as viewed from the South. Mrs. Chesnut was an abolitionist, but she steadfastly supported the Confederacy in which her husband was active. She wrote on spying, on Confederate "government girls," on postwar dilemmas of young women over whether or not to marry a crippled soldier; she told of having to exchange her clothes for food when she was a refugee in North Carolina. After the war Mrs. Chesnut revised her 400,000-word diary, which ultimately was published after her death as *A Diary from Dixie*.

After the Civil War many Southern women were without money, sometimes without homes or possessions, and often without menfolk to work the land or earn a living for the family. Plantations lay in waste. Cities had been burned to the ground. Food supplies had long since run out. Refugees wandered helpless and penniless, seeking a place to resettle. Southern women were often too proud to ask for charity or to admit their desperate condition. Some hired themselves out as domestic servants, some tried to plow their devastated fields. Some women had to sell their land acre by acre to pay taxes and survive. Some took in sewing, opened schools, or were lucky enough to get a job.

In 1866 two New Yorkers, Mrs. Algernon S. Sullivan and Mrs. James Roosevelt, became so concerned about Southern women that they organized the New York Ladies Southern Relief Association. Through benefits, balls, dinners, and theatrical performances some $71,000 was raised and sent to Southern clergymen for distribution to needy women in Virginia, North and South Carolina, Mississippi, Alabama, and Georgia.

In the North, federal and state aid was available for veterans and their widows and children, but getting a pension or getting relief was often a long difficult process. The government had employed women during the war as stenographers, clerks, bookkeepers. Many continued their government jobs in postwar days. By 1875 the number of "government girls" employed in Washington had doubled. They held jobs as typists, operators of business machines, secretaries, receptionists, their jobs later protected by the passage of the Civil Service Acts of the 1880s. Sometimes prominent women made penniless by the war took government jobs. Even Confederate women found employment in Washington, among them Mrs. George Pickett, wife of General Pickett, and Mrs. Emma Richardson Moses, daughter of a prominent South Carolina lawyer. Southern women were sometimes appointed to jobs as postmaster.

Women who had worked in factories at war jobs and still needed them were often replaced by veterans. A few voices were heard in behalf of the plight of women factory workers "living by sufferance" in postwar days on their low wages. Helen Campbell exposed their pitiful status in a series of articles in the *New York Times* in 1889 entitled "Prisoners of Poverty." By 1890 some 17,000 Southern women were also working in Southern factories, often financed by Northern capital. Few people gave thought to working women's problems or seemed sensitive to their dilemma. Susan B. Anthony did. In her New York Working Women's Society she endeavored to organize New York's working women and to bring them into unions. The New York Workingwomen's Protective Union (1868) tried to protect women against unscrupulous employers and unfair practices by offering legal aid and other kinds of help.

CHAPTER FOURTEEN

Encountering the Difficulties of Campaigning

THE FIRST POST-CIVIL WAR woman suffrage challenge came in Kansas where, for the first time in any state, a woman suffrage amendment was up for a vote in the November 1867 elections. Lucy Stone and Henry Blackwell went to Kansas to campaign for woman suffrage, as did the Reverend Olympia Brown of Michigan, an 1860 graduate of Antioch College, and an ordained Universalist minister. Mrs. Stanton and Miss Anthony joined the group later for a two weeks' speaking tour. The suffrage campaigners made their way from town to town by horse-drawn wagon, by stage, by mule team, sleeping in vermin-infested hotels, and eating food "floating in grease." They spoke in schoolhouses, in churches, and out of doors. Their opponents were the liquor interests, who feared women would vote for a temperance amendment, and the conservative German

and Irish settlers who were particularly emphatic about woman's place being in the home. Neither the Kansas Republican Party nor the Democrats supported the Kansas Woman Suffrage Amendment, though at the last minute (and too late) the Republicans gave the amendment a lukewarm blessing.

To boost the women's cause George Francis Train was suggested to Miss Anthony as a campaign speaker. Eager to accept any help, Miss Anthony agreed, and found herself with an unexpectedly flamboyant traveling companion. George Francis Train was a wealthy, but eccentric, railroad developer and a Democrat. He wore gaudy clothes—a blue coat with brass buttons, a white waistcoat, patent leather shoes, lavender kid gloves. He willingly joined the woman suffrage lecture circuit, paying his own way. He was an entertaining speaker, cajoling his audiences into supporting the vote for women. He also had causes of his own to advocate, which included paying the national debt by greenbacks, an eight-hour working day, and freedom for Ireland. He opposed giving Negro men the vote before women got it and was considered a Copperhead (a Northerner who sympathized with the South). Though she did not always agree with his views, Miss Anthony found Train a courteous, good-natured, and kindly traveling companion as they stumped the state of Kansas. And when Mr. Train offered to finance a woman suffrage weekly newspaper to be called *The Revolution,* with Miss Anthony as publisher, she accepted eagerly. Such a publication had always been her dream.

When the election was over and the Kansas Woman Suffrage Amendment had been defeated, friends in Kansas advised Miss Anthony to end her association with Train. Friends in the East were equally insistent that she drop this "unbalanced charlatan" pointing out that he would hurt, rather than help, the woman suffrage cause. But Train offered to lecture all the way east with Mrs. Stanton and Miss Anthony, paying all their expenses, and both women agreed that they could not turn down the opportunity to speak out on woman suffrage in such important cities as St. Louis, Louisville, Chicago, Cincinnati, Buffalo, Rochester, Boston. Because of this decision many old friends turned against the two women, including such active supporters as Lucy Stone, Henry Blackwell, William Lloyd Garrison, and Stephen Foster.

Train soon walked out of Miss Anthony's

life. He was jailed in England for his Irish revolutionary activities. Left with *The Revolution* to finance as best she could (Train's contribution lasted only a short time) and with the ill will of many friends, Miss Anthony went doggedly ahead. Neither this obstacle nor future obstacles caused her to waver from her woman suffrage goal. She was particularly proud when the first issue of *The Revolution* (a 16-page, smaller-than-tabloid size paper) came off the press on January 8, 1868, with its masthead bearing the motto Men, Their Rights And Nothing More; Women, Their Rights And Nothing Less. It was the first woman suffrage paper, and it carried a variety of news about women —their clubs, their professions, their labor problems, their need for the vote. It also carried Mrs. Stanton's "radical" views on divorce and marriage, and for a while Mr. Train's views on currency and the eight-hour workday—views that conservative women frowned upon. *The Revolution* lasted two and a half years, until May 1870. It left Miss Anthony $10,000 in debt. She eventually paid off every penny, by lecturing and by her own personal austerity.

The woman suffrage movement was temporarily at a standstill after the Fifteenth Amendment to the Constitution was ratified in 1870. It stated that "the right of citizens of the United States to vote shall not be denied or abridged by the United States or by any State on account of race, color, or previous condition of servitude." Black men had been given the vote, but not black or white women. Miss Anthony and Mrs. Stanton felt let down particularly by their former male

The second class status of women (as well as other groups) is dramatized in this poster titled American Woman and Her Political Peers, *showing Frances Willard surrounded by an idiot, a convict, an Indian, and an insane man. Sophia Smith Collection*

supporters who had insisted that it was the "Negroes' Hour" and that black men deserved the vote for their years of servitude. When women suggested that it was also "Women's Hour," prominent men who had supported the women's rights movement —such as Ralph Waldo Emerson, William Lloyd Garrison, Horace Greeley—were silent.

Everyone in the movement seemed to

have a grievance. Miss Anthony was dissatisfied with the Equal Rights Association because it had given priority to votes for blacks over votes for women. Lucy Stone was annoyed by Miss Anthony's lecture tour with George Francis Train; and, she was not sympathetic to Mrs. Stanton's liberal theories on marriage and divorce; and she leaned toward working for a state by state rather than a solely federally focused woman suffrage amendment. Miss Anthony became impatient about inaction, wanted to get on with the job, and she thought that a federal woman suffrage amendment would be the most expedient way to get the vote.

Two new woman suffrage organizations rose out of the different philosophies of the leaders of the movement. Miss Anthony and Mrs. Stanton took the first step. In 1869, following the annual meeting of the about-to-be-defunct Equal Rights Association in New York, they called a meeting of like-minded women and formed the National Woman Suffrage Association. Mrs. Elizabeth Cady Stanton was elected President. Its goal was to work for a federal woman suffrage amendment. Women from nineteen states were present for the organization meeting, including Lucretia Mott and Ernestine Rose.

Within months Lucy Stone and a Boston suffragist group retaliated by forming their own "more conservative" American Woman Suffrage Association in Cleveland, Ohio, on November 24, 1869. It admitted men, and its membership was set up on the basis of accredited delegates, their number based on state populations. Its annual conventions were to be held in representative American cities. Its goal was to work for municipal, state, and national suffrage. Its founding members included Lucy Stone, Julia Ward Howe, Henry Blackwell, Antoinette Brown Blackwell, among others. Its home base was Boston.

To Miss Anthony's envy (for lack of money she was about to suspend publication of her woman suffrage weekly *The Revolution*), the new association also had a soundly financed eight-page weekly, *The Woman's Journal*, its first issue appearing on January 8, 1870. *The Woman's Journal* described itself as devoted to the "interests of woman, to her educational, industrial, legal and political equality, and especially to her right of suffrage."

The two woman suffrage organizations existed side by side for twenty years, each working in its own way for woman suffrage. In 1890, with merger negotiations having dragged on for three years, the two suffrage groups became the National American Woman Suffrage Association with Mrs. Elizabeth Cady Stanton as first president of the reunited groups.

Meanwhile, in 1878, Senator A. A. Sargent of California, a close friend of Susan B. Anthony, had introduced into Congress a woman suffrage amendment known as the Susan B. Anthony Amendment. It lingered in the desks of Congressmen for forty-two succeeding years.

Another splinter group, far more militant than any that had yet appeared, would enter the suffrage scene after the turn of the century and help move the Anthony Amendment along. It was led by rebellious young American women activists who had trained in London under woman suffragist Emmeline Pankhurst, and who were aggressively determined to

Leaders of the suffrage movement meet in 1888 to plan an international suffrage meeting. Susan B. Anthony sits in the front row, second from left; Elizabeth Cady Stanton is third from right. Library of Congress

have the vote and to have their rights. But before that, some conventional old-timers turned rebellious themselves.

Some women suffragists asserted that they, too, were citizens, and that the Fourteenth Amendment asserted positively that "no State shall make or enforce any law which shall abridge the privileges or immunities of *citizens* of the United States." This statement, they claimed, gave *women citizens* also the right to vote. Demonstrations by women voting "illegally" took place from time to time all over the country and publicized women's determination to have the vote.

The first women to attempt to vote under the Fourteenth Amendment were New Jersey suffragists. New Jersey women had had the vote from 1776 to 1807, but lost it when the New Jersey legislature passed a new constitution in 1807. Some 172 women cast "ballots" on November 19, 1868, in a presidential election. The women boldly entered the election center, attempted to vote in the legal ballot box, and when they were refused, "voted" in a women's ballot box, manned by 84-year-old Margaret Pryer, who looked strong-willed and dignified in her sober Quaker garb. Four of the women voting were black.

This unflattering caricature of Susan B. Anthony, from an 1873 newspaper, suggests that women have stepped out of place in demanding the vote. NYPL Picture Collection

In 1870 the Grimké sisters, Sarah nearing eighty years of age, walked through driving snow on a blustery winter day to cast ballots, in a separate ballot box, at Hyde Park, Massachusetts.

Not to be outdone Susan B. Anthony voted in the presidential election of 1872 and received the widest publicity of all "illegal" voters. Though aware that she could be fined $500 and sentenced to prison for a maximum of three years, Miss Anthony boldly led sixteen Rochester women to the polls to register and to vote. She was arrested, charged with "knowingly, wrongfully and unlawfully" voting for a representative to the Congress of the United States. At the trial Miss Anthony was refused the right to be her own witness on grounds that she was "incompetent to testify," and the presiding justice, Ward Hunt, ordered the jury to find a verdict of guilty. Miss Anthony sat in silence until Justice Hunt asked her if she had anything to say about the verdict of guilty before he sentenced her. She certainly had—she spoke at length on the conduct of the trial and on women's right to the vote. Her sentence was a fine of $100 and the costs of the prosecution. She declared she would never pay a penny of it and she never did. When she found that she could not carry the verdict to the Supreme Court by a writ of habeas corpus because the justice would not jail her, it was a great disappointment to Susan B. Anthony.

One illegal voting case did get to the Supreme Court—that of *Minor* vs. *Happersett* in which Virginia Minor of St. Louis brought suit in 1872 against an election inspector for his refusal to register her as a voter. The case reached the Supreme Court in 1874, and Chief Justice Morrison R. Waite wrote the unanimous decision that "suffrage was not co-extensive with citizenship."

It was not suffragist Susan B. Anthony, nor suffragist Elizabeth Cady Stanton, nor suffragist Lucy Stone who won the first state (then a territory) to woman suffrage, but a six-foot-tall, craggy-faced, 180-pound pioneer woman named Esther Hobart McQuigg Slack Morris (1814–1902).

Born in Tioga County, New York, Esther Morris, a widow, headed toward Illinois where her deceased husband, Artemus Slack, had owned some property. She married John Morris while in Illinois and, in 1869, moved to the gold rush town of South Pass City, Wyoming, its population 460, its saloons numbering seven. There are several versions of why and how Mrs. Morris managed her woman suffrage coup in Wyoming. Some say she lost her rights to property belonging to her deceased husband in Illinois because of her sex and thereupon became converted to woman suffrage. Some say that she heard Susan B. Anthony speak on woman suffrage and embraced the cause of women's rights. In any event she lost no time after her move to Wyoming in inviting candidates in an upcoming Wyoming election to her house for tea (so the story goes). She convinced William H. Bright, a rising politician, to introduce a woman suffrage amendment in the Wyoming Territory's legislature if he won the election. Bright did win, and he introduced the woman suffrage amendment. The amendment passed the 21-member legislature on December 10, 1869, and the governor signed it into law. The legislature at the same time passed laws providing equal pay to women teachers and giving women control of their own property, perhaps to attract women to this developing territory.

Since they were qualified voters, Wyoming women were soon called to jury duty, and though some men objected, women served on juries so conscientiously that, one story goes, evildoers fled the state. Mrs. Esther Morris was appointed

Justice of the Peace in South Pass City on February 14, 1870. She settled seventy cases during her term of office, and there were no reversals.

Mrs. Morris was still living when Wyoming applied for admission to the Union in 1880 as a woman suffrage state, though she was not in Wyoming at the time. When Congress hesitated over Wyoming's woman suffrage law, Wyoming officials sent this ultimatum: "We will remain out of the Union a hundred years rather than come in without woman suffrage." Congress capitulated, and Wyoming became the first woman suffrage state to enter the Union (1890).

Abigail Scott Duniway (1834–1915) knew from personal experience western pioneer women's need for "rights" and for the vote. She had traveled westward by ox-drawn wagon at seventeen, losing her ailing mother and one brother before the family reached Oregon. She had taught school briefly, married at nineteen, borne five sons and one daughter by the age of thirty-five, and had, like other pioneer women, made thousands of pounds of butter a year for market "with never a penny of my own," sewed, cooked, washed, ironed, baked, cleaned, and canned. "I was," she said, "a general pioneer drudge." At twenty-eight she was supporting the entire Duniway family. Her husband had lost their prosperous Clackamas County farm by unwisely endorsing notes for a friend who defaulted, and shortly thereafter he had an accident that left him a semi-invalid. To earn money Abigail Duniway started a boarding school, then opened a millinery and notions store in Albany, Oregon, where the family had moved.

The vigor and determination that helped Wyoming women win the vote is evident in this photograph of Esther Morris.
NYPL Picture Collection

While she was teaching and running her millinery store Mrs. Duniway listened to many heartbreaking stories. There was a woman who was not allowed to administer her husband's estate even though she had helped earn some of the money involved by selling butter, eggs, and poultry. There were many women who had to "steal" money secretly from their husband's pockets to pay for a new hat, a ribbon, a veil, or clothes for the children. There was a woman who had no recourse when her husband deserted her and her five small children after selling all the household furniture and pocketing the money.

From then on Abigail Duniway was in the thick of the fight for the franchise for women. Moving to Portland, Oregon in 1871, she started a weekly newspaper called *The New Northwest*, dedicated to the cause of pioneer women's rights in the states of Oregon, Washington, and Idaho. With the help of her growing sons, she began lecturing as well as writing about women's rights and women's need for the vote. When Susan B. Anthony visited the Pacific Northwest in 1871, Mrs. Duniway accompanied her on a 1,000 mile speaking tour. By 1873 she had organized the Oregon Equal Suffrage Association and was traveling by horse, by stage, by coastal steamer, by rail, by riverboat through Washington, Oregon, and Idaho, speaking on woman suffrage, sending back news to *The New Northwest*.

Getting the vote for Northwestern women was not easy. It took Mrs. Duniway and her colleagues a lifetime of hard work to put woman suffrage through the legislatures of the Northwest states. Idaho adopted a constitutional amendment granting woman suffrage in 1896. Washington women did not get the vote until 1910. Oregon, Abigail Duniway's own state, held out the longest. A woman suffrage constitutional amendment was defeated in 1884, in 1900, in 1906, in 1908, and in 1910. Finally in 1912, when the seventy-eight-year-old Abigail Duniway was confined to a wheelchair but still an ardent campaigner, Oregon women received the vote. In recognition of her years of effort to bring women suffrage to Oregon, Mrs. Duniway was asked to write the Oregon suffrage proclamation, and to sign it jointly with Governor Oswald West. Mrs. Duniway also became the first registered woman voter, symbolic of a goal toward which she had worked for forty-one years.

CHAPTER FIFTEEN

New Challenges, New Opportunities

MORE RAPIDLY THAN ever before, the post–Civil War generation of women began to move toward emancipation. Life was a little easier in the home, with the advent of food canning (1804), the telephone (1876) the carpet sweeper (1876), the electric fan (1882), and gas illumination (1885). The typewriter (1868), shorthand (which reached the United States in 1852), the fountain pen (1884), and the Linotype machine for printing (1885) made women's office work easier. And the bicycle (1884) began to open the door for the adoption of more comfortable clothes. The railroads made travel from place to place easier. Getting to know the country and its people by this easy means of locomotion shortened the distance between East and West, North and South. There were 35,000 miles of railroads by 1865 and by 1869 the East was joined with the West by rail.

These new inventions and new means of communication gave women more time to crusade for a cause if they felt so inclined, more time to expand their minds by reading. Across the country women began to make their voices felt. With amazing rapidity the domestic arts and the creative arts developed new dimensions. Educational and professional training proliferated. The nursing profession made its debut. A consciousness of the dilemmas of American Indians led women to take action. Two women founded new religions. Two women announced their candidacy for president of the United States.

Women's magazines brought news of these developments and of what women were thinking and doing as persons, not always just as housewives and homemakers. They reached a potential audience of some eleven million women from Maine

Many inventions, including the typewriter, made office work more efficient. This 1873 model had no shift key and only capital letters. Sperry Remington

to Georgia and westward to California. More women could now read and write as public schools were funded and developed:

The woman's magazine of the century was *Godey's Lady's Book*, edited for forty years by Mrs. Sarah Josepha Hale (1788–1879). It was a conventional magazine for the most part, but often diverged discreetly from its "woman's sphere" focus.

It was read by society leaders, housewives, and mill girls. Its circulation reached 150,000, a record for its day. The Godey color prints of contemporary fashions were so beautiful and disarming that husbands overlooked the "in-between" articles, which sometimes mentioned the need for women doctors, higher education for women, trained nurses, equal property rights, representation on school boards, exercise, dieting, and a plea for more comfortable clothes. Neither Frank Leslie's *Lady's Magazine* nor his later *Lady's Journal* competed with *Godey's Lady's Book*. Another publisher of fashion magazines, Ellen L. C. Demorest (1824–1898), introduced American women to the first paper patterns for home dressmaking. They were stapled to her magazine, *Mirror of Fashions,* which employed 200 women in its pattern department. Feminist magazines had been under way since 1849, and *Harper's* started publication in 1850, the *Atlantic* in 1857.

A few cookbooks had been written in the early years of the nineteenth century, and prior to that date cookbooks—English "bookes of cookery" were treasured American colonial heirlooms, sometimes mentioned in wills, and passed down from mother to daughter. By the latter half of the nineteenth century, more and more cookbooks were appearing. Mrs. Sarah T. H. Rorer was prompted by the illness of her first son to study nutrition hoping to learn diets that might be helpful to her son's recovery. She found the subject so interesting that she attended supplementary lectures at Philadelphia medical

A page of fashion from Godey's Lady's Book, 1867. *NYPL Picture Collection*

schools in 1883 and opened her own Philadelphia Cooking School in the same year. Mrs. Rorer's *The Philadelphia Cook Book* appeared in 1886 and made her nationally famous.

Scientist Ellen H. S. Richards (1842–1911), the first woman admitted to the Massachusetts Institute of Technology, and the first woman to be admitted to membership in the American Institute of Mining and Metallurgical Engineers, and an instructor in sanitary chemistry at M.I.T. by 1884, seems an unlikely person to interest herself in home economics, but she believed science should work for women. In her spare time she appraised the American home scientifically, and conducted an investigation on the adulteration of staple groceries. With the financial help of Pauline Agassiz Shaw, Mrs. Richards opened the New England Kitchen to study food and nutrition and later started a school lunch program and a school of housekeeping. By 1895 Domestic Science had made its way to the University of Chicago, with Miss Marion Talbot (1858–1948) heading the first Department of Household Administration, and Sophronisba P. Breckinridge (1866–1948) who had a law degree from the university giving courses in the economic and legal aspects of family life. It was not long before home economics was recognized by public schools, colleges, by the United States government and by the American public as a necessary, intelligently oriented, and scientifically based educational discipline.

Women were often too modest to consult male doctors about female diseases even late in the 1800s, and had little confidence in the few available women doctors.

Instead they read books for ideas on treating female diseases, such books as Dr. Frederick Hollick's *The Matron's Manual of Midwifery and the Diseases of Women during Pregnancy and in Child Bed*, or Samuel Jennings's *The Married Lady's Companion*. On birth control they consulted Robert Dale Owen's *Moral Physiology* (1831), the first birth control book to be published in America, or Charles Knowlton's *Fruits of Philosophy*. But for cramps, and for nerves, vapors, anxieties, fainting spells, headaches, chills, and similar vagaries that beset nineteenth-century women, they turned to Lydia Pinkham's Vegetable Compound, which appeared on the store shelves in 1875 and has remained there ever since. As the mother of five, Lydia Pinkham concocted from her researches her own remedies, among them a special brew particularly for women. Her women neighbors were delighted with this "medicine," which made them feel good when they had cramps or other female complaints. It contained unicorn root, pleurisy root, liferoot, black cohosh, fenugreek seed, water, and alcohol. When the Pinkham family fell into hard times during the financial panic of 1873, Mrs. Pinkham's sons suggested that she sell her brew. Lydia Pinkham's Vegetable Compound became a very profitable 96-year-long Pinkham family project. It made the user feel good—the first bottles contained 18 percent alcohol, although most women were unaware of this. Testimonials were used to advertise the product, including one from a state W.C.T.U. official who highly recommended the medicine, unaware, obviously, that it contained alcohol.

Women in the late nineteenth century

helped to break down the prejudices against female doctors, and to establish once and for all that women physicians' achievements could equal and in fact surpass those of men. Dr. Mary C. Putnam-Jacobi (1842–1906) wavered at first between medical practice and medical research, but ultimately chose medical practice. She received her M.D. in 1864 from the Woman's Medical College of Pennsylvania, interned briefly in Boston's New England Hospital for Women and Children, volunteered her services in soldiers' hospitals in New York during the Civil War, and left for advanced study in Europe in 1866, remaining there five years until she felt that she had perfected her medical education. Upon her return to the United States in 1871, Dr. Putnam-Jacobi became the country's leading woman physician.

Very few male physicians could equal her training or her published articles (more than one hundred) on physiology,

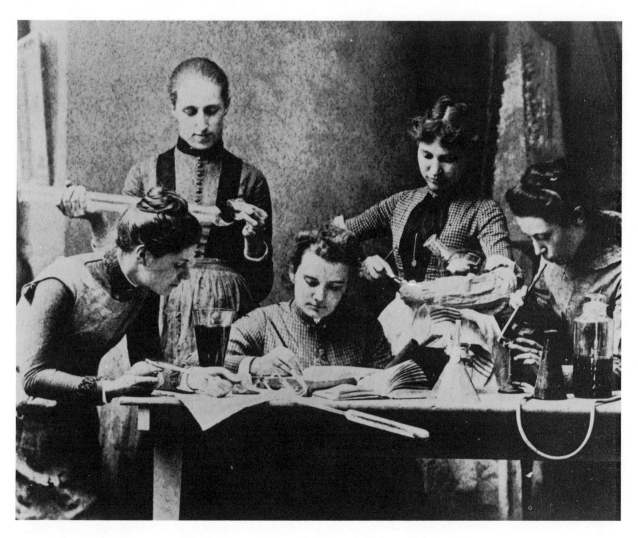

Chemistry students at Smith College in 1889. Smith College Archives

neurology, pediatrics, pathology, and medical education. Gradually she broke down medical prejudice against women. She was admitted to several medical societies and the hitherto impregnable New York Academy of Medicine. She organized in 1872 the Association for Advancement of Medical Education for Women. She lectured and held a professorship at the Woman's Medical College of the New York Infirmary for Women and Children, gave clinical lectures on children's diseases at the New York Post Graduate Medical School (1882–85). She was consulting and attending physician at the New York Infirmary, and initiated and opened a children's dispensary at Mt. Sinai (1873). She married Dr. Abraham Jacobi, a leading American pediatrician, in 1873. Dr. Putnam-Jacobi was an active suffragist and author of *Common Sense Applied to Woman Suffrage* (1894). Her great contribution, aside from her medical skills, was to demonstrate that women were intellectually, physically, emotionally, and creatively capable of assuming major responsibilities as physicians, and in her insistence in maintaining the highest standards in medical training for women as well as for men.

Although more and more colleges were accepting women as the century progressed, very few of the more than five million women gainfully employed by 1900 were college graduates. The earliest women's colleges were Georgia Female College (1836), Mary Sharp College (1851), Elmira College (1855), and the coeducational Oberlin (1833)·and Antioch (1852). The first Midwest state university to accept women was Iowa State in 1858. Sage College, a woman's branch of Cornell, was opened in 1874. The University of Michigan admitted women in 1870, as did the University of Illinois and Ohio State. Boston University became coeducational in 1869. All of these schools had to accept students unprepared in Latin, Greek, and other basic subjects and found it necessary to function partly as preparatory schools. It was not until the organization of the Society for the Collegiate Instruction of Women in 1882 (which later became Radcliffe College) that a standard of education for women was set comparable to that for men. Harvard professors agreed to instruct qualified women students, and Harvard examinations were required for admission. Shortly thereafter Bryn Mawr was founded, with standards of scholarship comparable to those at Harvard, and with a dynamic twenty-six-year-old dean, M. Cary Thomas (1857–1935). Smith College was opened in 1875.

Religious books and history books found their way into public libraries sooner than novels did, and women who could not buy or borrow the novel they wanted to read might find them serialized in the magazines of the day; or, with a dime to spend, novels could be bought in Irwin P. Beadles' Dime Novel Series. Women wrote eighteen best sellers between 1800 and 1875, and beginning in the last quarter of the century, many novels appeared that are still popular today. Louisa May Alcott (1832–88) was well rewarded for the many years that she spent supporting her improvident but brilliant family (her father was educator Bronson Alcott) when *Little Women* (1868) sold 38,000 copies, and by 1870, 50,000 copies were in print.

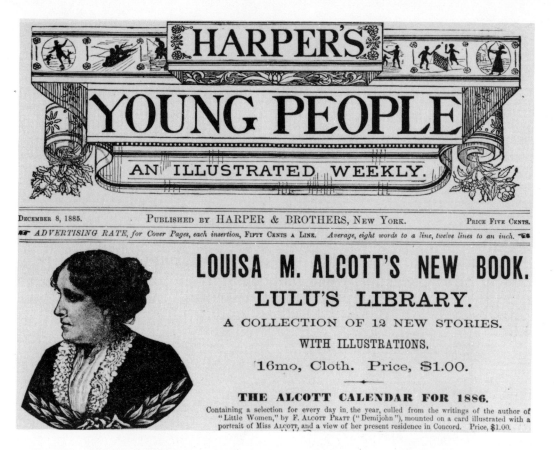

The success and popularity of Louisa May Alcott's work is obvious in this 1885 advertisement for one of her books. NYPL Picture Collection

Both her *Little Women* and *Little Men* were best sellers. Mary Mapes Dodge wrote *Hans Brinker, or the Silver Skates* in 1865. Gene Stratton Porter (1863–1924) earned an estimated two million dollars in royalties from her nineteen books, the most famous of which is *Laddie* (1913). Kate Douglas S. Wiggin (1856–1923), whose best known book is *Rebecca of Sunnybrook Farm* (1903), wrote her first book, *The Story of Patsy* (1883), to raise money for the Silver Street Kindergarten in San Francisco where she had taught. Eleanor H. Porter (1868–1920) made a deep impression not only on the American public but also on foreign readers. *Pollyanna* (1913), the story of the "glad" girl, was translated into eight languages, and its impact was so strong that the word "polly-anna" came to mean "an excessively or blindly optimistic person." British-born Frances Hodgson Burnett (1849–1924) came to the United States in 1865 with her widowed mother and began writing to support her family during the South's financially difficult post–Civil War days. Her *Little Lord Fauntleroy* (1886) and *The Secret Garden* (1911) are still popular classics. Harriett Mulford Lothrop (1844–1924) used a pen name, Margaret Sidney, for her popular *Five Little Peppers and How They Grew* (1881), because her father disapproved of women writing for publication. The *Little Pepper* series was reprinted year after year, selling more than two million copies.

American settings, American dilemmas, and American romances were popular and

Emily Dickinson at the age of seventeen.
NYPL Picture Collection

profitable subjects, but American women also wrote books of protest. Inhuman factory conditions were the subject of Elizabeth S. Phelps Ward's (1844–1911) *The Silent Partner* (1871). Helen Hunt Jackson (1830–85) wrote *A Century of Dishonor* (1881) and *Ramona* (1884) to call attention to the Indian problem. Edith Wharton's *Ethan Frome* (1911) depicted the life of the poor in a New England farm community.

And in 1886, the work of a great American poet, Emily Dickinson, was discovered posthumously. Emily Dickinson (1830–86) had written poems all her life in the solitude of her room in the spacious Dickin-

son family home in Amherst, Massachusetts, though few people knew she was writing. Her sister found 1,775 of Emily's poems in neat packets, hidden away in a dresser drawer after Emily's death. There were poems about life, about nature, about love, about death, about eternity, all of them infused with a penetrating perception of the cycles of life and a desire to express both the simplicity and the immense power of nature.

Nature is what we see,
The Hill, the afternoon—
Squirrel, Eclipse, the Bumble-bee,
Nay—Nature is heaven.

Nature is what we hear,
The Bobolink, the Sea—
Thunder, the Cricket—
Nay—Nature is Harmony.

Nature is what we know
But have no art to say,
So impotent our wisdom is
To her simplicity.

The search for truth or for an understanding of life's deeper meaning also found expression in several religious movements which had world-wide scope, and which were founded by women at the end of the 1800s.

Mary Baker Eddy (1821–1910) had some thirty years of illness, of loneliness, and of wandering from place to place searching for healing and for peace before her religious enlightenment crystallized. She claimed that the turning point in her life came when, in 1866, after a bad fall on the ice and a serious injury to her back, she arose from her bed healed after reading a Scripture verse. With this healing came the awareness of her mission to carry to all the world her message of mental healing, Christian Science. She began writing *Science and Health,* which ultimately would go through 382 editions and would by 1910 sell 400,000 copies. Then she began teaching others the principles of mental healing. She opened the Christian Scientists' Home in Lynn, Massachusetts, in 1875 for meetings and classes. She held the first public Christian Science service in 1875. The Church of Christ, Scientist, was chartered in 1879. Mrs. Eddy had trained some six hundred students by 1889. By 1890 twenty churches had been opened, 250 practitioners had been trained, ninety societies had been

formed, thirty-three teaching centers established. The *Christian Science Monitor* began publication in 1908. Christian Science commentary on the Lord's Prayer has a "feminist" touch that most religions do not have. Every Sunday throughout the world when the Lord's Prayer is read in many languages, Mrs. Eddy's accompanying commentary begins "Our Father-Mother God."

Ellen G. H. White (1827–1915), co-founder with her husband, James S. White, of the Seventh-day Adventists traveled throughout the country during her lifetime guiding, supervising, preaching, and explaining the goals of the Seventh-Day Adventist Church. These goals included the belief in the second coming of Christ, observance of the seventh-day Sabbath (Saturday) and strong emphasis on education. She was opposed to tea, coffee, flesh food, and stressed the importance of exercise and fresh air. Mrs. White was a prolific writer, contributing to Adventist magazines, writing 50 books, and some 4,000 articles during her lifetime. She lived to be eighty-eight years old and to see the Seventh-Day Adventist Church spread throughout the world.

Though women were accepted as religious leaders, as writers, as poets, and increasingly as public speakers in the late 1800s, when it came to women running for president, that was a different matter. Nevertheless, two women made the attempt. Victoria Woodhull (1838–1927) was the first woman to announce her candidacy for president. In her brief meteoric New York career as the first woman broker on Wall Street, the first woman to publish her own "house organ," and the first

Belva Lockwood fought for the right to practice law before the Supreme Court of the United States and was a presidential candidate as well. NYPL Picture Collection

woman to address a congressional committee on woman suffrage, she managed to do more than most contemporary women's rights leaders would have dreamed possible. But she was a daring opportunist who in the long run lost the trust of Susan B. Anthony and the National Woman Suffrage Association. When she held her own convention in 1872 and announced her candidacy for president, with Frederick Douglass as her running mate, Mr. Douglass ignored the nomination, and her self-instigated candidacy quickly ended.

Belva Lockwood (1830–1917), a woman dedicated to social reform, twice received the presidential nomination, once from a small California-based wom-

en's party, the National Equal Rights Party. She was a self-made woman. Married at eighteen, she was a widow with a daughter to support at twenty-three. Unhesitatingly, she sold her husband's business and began attending college supporting herself and her daughter by teaching as she studied. By 1866 she decided that Washington, D.C., would offer her greater opportunity, so she moved, opened a boarding school, and, in 1868, married Dr. Ezekiel Lockwood, a dentist. He helped run her school while Belva studied law at the only Washington law school that would admit a woman, the National University Law School. She completed the course in 1873, but she had to write President Grant who was the law school's ex-officio president before she was given her diploma. She was admitted to the bar of the District of Columbia in 1873 and soon had a very lucrative law practice.

When it became necessary to plead cases before the Court of Claims, Mrs. Lockwood was refused because she was not only a woman, but a married woman. Thereupon she started, in 1876, her own crusade to open up the higher courts of the land to women lawyers. It was a three-year struggle, but Belva Lockwood persisted and won, in 1879, passage of the bill that she had drafted opening up to women the right to practice before the Supreme Court of the United States. She became the first woman admitted to such practice. She was fifty-nine years old at the time.

Belva Lockwood favored a woman's party as a means of focusing attention on the idea of a woman president. In this spirit she accepted the nomination for president by the small and obscure National Equal Rights Party, and campaigned with buttons and banners for equal property rights and equal voting rights for women, for a temperance amendment, for uniform marriage and divorce laws, for the end of corruption in high places. She stressed the fact that women "in this free Republic contrary to the Bill of Rights" were governed "without their own consent." She received 4,149 votes in the 1884 election.

In 1906, Belva Lockwood was one of the attorneys for the Eastern Cherokee Indians in a case against the United States. Her argument before the Supreme Court resulted in the tribe being awarded five million dollars. Women had started the first crusade in behalf of the plight of American Indians in the 1880s, bombarding Congress with petitions, making investigative surveys, writing articles and books, lobbying in Washington, and organizing the first associations to speak out for the interests of American Indians.

A 300-foot-long roll of 13,000 names was presented to President Rutherford B. Hayes (and later to the House) in February 1880 through the efforts of the two instigators of the Indian crusade, Mary L. Bonney (1816–1900) and Mrs. Amelia S. Quinton (1833–1926). Mrs. Bonney and Mrs. Quinton organized the Central Indian Committee, which eventually became the Women's National Indian Association in 1883. Its members worked tirelessly toward the honoring of Indian treaties and ending encroachment on Indian territory. Mrs. Quinton lobbied in Washington for an educational program for Indians, for prohibition of liquor on the reservations, for individual apportionment of land, and American citizenship for Indians.

Meanwhile other outstanding women joined the movement. Ethnologist Alice Cunningham Fletcher (1838–1923) drafted and lobbied into passage a bill providing apportionment of land to Omahas, made surveys and prepared exhibits for the Interior Department and the Indian Bureau, and collected relics and artifacts for the Peabody Museum where she held a life fellowship. She wrote a *Handbook of American Indians* in 1907. Helen Hunt Jackson's *A Century of Dishonor* (1881) documented the government's mishandling of Indian affairs. Although the Interior Department asked her to make a survey of Mission Indians on the West Coast, the public remained so indifferent to the Indian question that Miss Jackson decided to do for the Indians what Harriet Beecher Stowe had done for the slaves. *Ramona*, published in 1884, aimed to be the *Uncle Tom's Cabin* for the Indians. The novel went into three hundred printings and was made into three motion pictures.

Little was done about the appalling lack of trained nurses in the United States after the Civil War, though women who had worked for the Civil War's Sanitary Commission were well aware of the acute need for trained nurses. Finally, in 1873, a number of women in a number of different places became concerned about the nursing situation. Mrs. Elizabeth C. K. Hobson reported, after a visit to New York City's Bellevue Hospital, the horrifying tale of so-called nurses who were actually vagrants or prisoners, without

A University of Nebraska pole-vaulter wears a uniform adapted from the bloomer costume. University of Nebraska photo

training, completely incompetent, and who terrorized acutely ill patients in Bellevue wards. By May 1873 the United States's first Nurses Training School based on the Florence Nightingale system (which provided systematic supervised instruction by qualified teachers and observation of a variety of patients) was founded at Bellevue with Mrs. Hobson helping to draft the original plan.

From the year 1873, nursing schools spread rapidly throughout the United States attracting as students some of the great pioneer women of the nursing profession: Lillian Wald (1867–1940) whose Henry Street Nurses Settlement House became world famous; Mary Adelaide Nutting (1858–1948) and Isabel Robb (1860–1910), both of whom worked to raise professional standards. Linda Richards (1841–1930), the first graduate nurse, was a unique pioneer. After a trip to England where she studied with Florence Nightingale, and a trip to Japan where she opened Japan's first training school for nurses, she traveled throughout the United States founding nursing schools or improving their standards as she went. She was one of the first women to try to set standards for proper nursing care for the mentally disturbed.

Still, still, in spite of this burgeoning activity, even the most dedicated feminists failed to emancipate themselves from whalebone corsets, an assortment of drawers, petticoats, chemises for underwear, and long unsanitary skirts—clothing that totaled altogether some twelve to fifteen pounds in weight. There was a brief interlude during which time Amelia Bloomer promoted the Bloomer costume in her magazine *The Lily* and inadvertently gave it her name. It consisted of a belted tunic and knee–length loose pantaloons reaching to the ankle, (later bloomers were worn in high-school and college gymnasiums). Although it was not an immodest costume, it took courage to wear the Bloomer outfit on the street, to say nothing of appearing in it on the public platform. Invariably it called forth whistles, catcalls, and lewd remarks.

Although unconventional women's righters wore the Bloomer costume for a while ("What incredible freedom I enjoyed for two years," wrote Mrs. Stanton, "like a captive set free from his ball and chain . . ."), reluctantly, one by one, they gave it up. "The cup of ridicule is greater than you can bear," said Mrs. Stanton to Miss Anthony, who held out the longest. Finally Miss Anthony too packed her Bloomer costume away, disgruntled that her friends had succumbed to the ridicule it had called forth, and commenting that she could "see no business avocation in which woman in her present dress *can possibly earn equal wages with man.*"

CHAPTER SIXTEEN

Frances Willard and the W.C.T.U.

SURPRISINGLY ENOUGH, WOMEN who had set up hospital units in the Civil War and had organized huge Civil War benefit bazaars, had never organized a club for themselves until the year 1868, when Jennie C. Croly called some New York women together to organize the country's first woman's club. "No one of those connected with the undertaking had ever heard of a woman's club, or of a secular organization composed entirely of women, for the purpose of bringing all kinds of women together to work at their own objects in their own way," she wrote. Women who attended the meeting considered themselves very bold. One woman's husband disapproved so vehemently that he forbade his wife joining. Another woman, on being invited to join a Midwest woman's club, wrote: "The offer of a seat in the Cabinet of the United States would have

surprised me less . . . I remember regretting that I should happen to be wearing an apron at such a momentous hour . . ."

Soon women's clubs were springing up all over the country, and women members were getting to know each other as persons. College women began to organize; black women in Washington, D.C., had the Colored Women's League (1896), its ambitious program including courses in English literature, a model kindergarten, a nursery for children of working mothers, sewing, cooking, and gardening courses; farm women had the Grange; in the South there was the United Daughters of the Confederacy, and patriotic and historic organizations included the Colonial Dames of America (1890) and the National Society of the Daughters of the Revolution (1891); Jewish women founded the National Council of Jewish

Women of Black River Falls, Wisconsin, at one of their regular get-togethers for tea, crocheting, and discussion. State Historical Society of Wisconsin at Madison

Women in 1893. As time passed, specific groups of women would have their own organizations, among them women lawyers, doctors, deans of women, sculptors, musicians, writers; and the National Council of Women of the United States, an "umbrella organization" suggested by Elizabeth Cady Stanton, would come to have an international counterpart. But no single woman's club or federation of clubs in the 1800s had as many members, or was as active as Frances Willard's Woman's Christian Temperance Union, organized in November 1874. Its membership, totaling some 200,000 women, spanned the country.

Frances Willard was one of the most influential women in the United States in the late 1800s. She was president of the Woman's Christian Temperance Union for nineteen years, from 1879 to 1898. Some women supported temperance because

their legal status as married women offered them no protection under the law against either physical abuse or abandonment by a drunken husband. Reform-minded women felt that the liquor traffic was the great enemy of reform and the chief foundation of corruption in the country. But Frances Willard was no grim-faced and resolute old maid, wearing a white ribbon and waging a self-righteous battle against alcohol. On the contrary, she was a vivid, magnetic person, with a flair for publicity that was unique in her day, and with a self-appointed mission to open up new vistas for American women. Temperance was only one of the W.C.T.U. crusades.

Frances Willard (1839–1898) had organizing genius. She built the W.C.T.U. into the largest woman's organization in the United States by administering its program on both the state and local levels. Altogether there were 10,000 local unions, supervised by state unions, and 57 state unions supervised by the national union. For ten years Miss Willard toured the United States from end to end speaking in every state and every territory, in cities and in small towns, covering between fifteen and twenty thousand miles annually. During these trips to the far corners of the country she stirred women into action, encouraging them to participate by calling her program Home Protection, a title innocuous enough to forestall criticism from husbands or from the clergy.

To Frances Willard the W.C.T.U. meant more than merely a "temperance movement." It meant an opportunity to expand the thinking of women all over the country by introducing them to the some thirty-nine Home Protection activities. Do Everything, was Miss Willard's motto. "Everything" meant kindergartens, legislation to improve the status of women, physical culture, health programs, hygiene, woman suffrage, welfare work in prisons, programs for Indians, blacks, and immigrants, peace programs, mothers' problem circles, school savings banks, a police matron program. These were a few of the activities that the W.C.T.U. members worked on For God, for Home and Native Land—the W.C.T.U. motto. Miss

Frances Willard tries out a bicycle. Women's Christian Temperance Union, Evanston, Illiniois

Willard had extraordinary persuasive ability and tact. She knew how to make every new program sound like a necessary and challenging part of a woman's life.

The well-attended national conventions over which Miss Willard presided were always exciting. The hall was decorated with flags, flowers, and bunting. There was stirring music, as sense of belonging to a "going thing." There were some dissenters, but the loyalty and love the W.C.T.U. membership had for their leader silenced most of them.

When Frances Willard died, she was so beloved and respected that her funeral service was attended by 2,000 people in New York. Chauncy M. Depew, then president of the New York Central Railroad, provided a special funeral car to take her body to Chicago, and there some 20,000 people, many of whom had waited hours in blustering cold winter weather, filed past her bier.

Frances Willard and other women were not uninvolved in the organization of political reform parties that arose to correct the economic inequities that beset many Americans in the last decades of the 1800s. Giant industries—steel, oil, the railroad—towered impersonally over men and women who trudged wearily to the mills or the mines each day, dinner pail in hand, to work twelve hours at a monotonous and sometimes dangerous job for meager pay. By the end of the 1800s, as Theodore Roosevelt once aptly put it, "the old familiar relations between employer and employee were passing. A few generations before, the boss had known every man in his shop; he called his men Bill, Tom, Dick, John. . . . There was no such relation between the great railway magnates, who controlled the anthracite industry, and the one hundred and fifty thousand men who worked in their mines." The rich were growing richer, and the poor were growing poorer, as wave after wave of depressions swept the country. Even farmers were involved. They too felt the crunch of big business, particularly the railroads' high freight rates and the loan companies' high interest rates.

The Republican and the Democratic parties, the two major political parties in the United States, were challenged toward the end of the 1800s by a veritable maze of small parties that came into power to protest these and other grievances. By 1892 farmers and industrial workers united at an Omaha convention to form the Populist Party, which accused the Republican and Democratic parties of corruption, of dominating the ballot box, of impoverishing labor, of muzzling the press, of denying labor the right to organize, of building massive fortunes. The Populist Party demanded a long list of changes in the economy, in government, and in laws. Times were bad in Kansas in the 1890s: wheat was fifty cents a bushel, corn had fallen to eight cents, oats to ten cents a bushel, and some farms were mortgaged at 8 to 10 percent. Freight rates were prohibitive. It was cheaper to burn corn for fuel than to market it. Farmers were ready to listen to anyone who believed in their cause—even a woman.

As many as 5,000 farmers and their wives drove for hours in farm wagons to hear Mary Ellen Lease (1850–1933) attack the railroads, the Republican Party, the loan companies, and Wall Street. Mary

A portrait of Frances Willard. Women's Christian Temperance Union, Evanston, Illinois

Ellen Lease knew whereof she spoke. She and her husband had given up farming in 1882 after years of frustration on the Kansas Plains. Tall, gaunt, and stately in her long black dress, a large emerald pin at the neck, Mary Ellen Lease walked back and forth on the platform, her eyes never leaving her farmer audience, whipping them up into a fury over their "blighted hopes" and "blasted fortunes." When she told farmers to "raise less corn and more hell" in her compelling voice, the crowds cheered and shouted. "She could recite the multiplication table and set the crowd hooting or hurrahing at her will," a contemporary once remarked. Her supporters called her "Our Queen Mary." Political opponents called her the "Kansas Pythoness." She put forth a mighty effort for the Populist Party during the years 1890–94. In 1892 she stumped the far West and South with Populist candidate James B. Weaver, exhorting, condemning, and challenging "silk-hatted Easterners," and the "specially privileged."

For the election of 1892, Frances Willard's political ambitions led her to try to form one powerful coalition of reform parties that would embody the best idealism in the West and South, including woman suffrage and prohibition, and sweep the country. She called a conference of political reformers in Chicago prior to the big nominating convention in St. Louis. Six political leaders were there, and all together they represented some one million votes, including 250,000 for the Prohibition party, and 500,000 for the Knights of Labor. Miss Willard represented 200,000 W.C.T.U. members, who though without the vote could be a source of powerful social pressure in support of a platform that would "protect the home." There was complete agreement in Chicago on a platform for a new party, and the platform was signed by those present.

With nearly a million votes in her pocket and a party platform providing something for farmers, for workers, and the vote for women, Frances Willard went confidently to the St. Louis Convention expecting that the convention could be adroitly steered toward the coalition party of her dreams. But on the very first day, Miss Willard found her well-laid plan completely thwarted. Helen Gougar (1843–1907) of Indiana had quietly convinced the Prohibition Party that their interests lay in meeting and working separately; she claimed that the prohibition plank put forward by Frances Willard was not strong enough. Some say Mrs. Gougar was jealous of Frances Willard. Whatever the reason, Mrs. Gougar was willing to sacrifice political expediency and allow personal enmity to isolate the Prohibition Party with its 250,000 votes.

Without the Prohibition Party's votes, Miss Willard had lost the opportunity that she hoped would be her greatest reform triumph. Though the St. Louis Convention honored and cheered her, they knew, and she knew, that she had lost her political power.

"Next to becoming a saint some day," Miss Willard once said, "I would like to be a politician." She had been a politician, but in a way that she had not envisioned by that statement. She had shown political leaders the power that a woman could command.

CHAPTER SEVENTEEN

The Century Turns

PEOPLE'S MINDS TURNED with the turn of the century to subjects and proposals that had previously been ignored or glossed over. At least some of the nation's 76 million men and women began criticizing trusts being built up by big business, reading Edward Bellamy's *Looking Backward* (1888), talking about immigration and immigrant problems, and reading what the muckrakers such as Ida M. Tarbell had to say in books and magazine articles about industry and industrialists. The phrases "cheap labor," "high profits," "ethical justice," "social consciousness" were heard frequently in conversation, not just at Populist rallies. One of the most widely read and influential feminist books at the turn of the century was *Women* and *Economics* (1898) by Charlotte Perkins Gilman (1860–1935) which advocated economic independence for women as a means of liberation.

Women could vote in four states—Wyoming (1869), Colorado (1893), Utah (1896), and Idaho (1896), but women's voting power in these four states was not powerful enough to make an impact on Congress. Women quietly worked on for woman suffrage, which the dynamic leadership of determined and sometimes militant women would bring to victory in the first quarter of the new century. Women worked hard for social reform, and sometimes found support from women philanthropists. Mrs. Phoebe A. Hearst (1842–1919) whose only son, William Randolph Hearst, rose to fame as a newspaper publisher, established scholarships for women and a center for women students at the University of California, Berkeley. Mrs. Russell Sage (1828–1918) gave a dormitory to the Emma Willard School and founded in Troy, New York, Russell Sage College to provide vocational training for women.

Mrs. Jane E. Stanford (1828–1905) was cofounder with her husband of Stanford University in California. Women became aware of crowded slums, of children working long hours in hazardous factories, of sweatshop women working for a mere pittance, of the lack of labor unions for women. Women saw these needs and women did something about them.

Labor unions were feeling their way to solidarity and encountering innumerable frustrations. A major problem was the thousands of immigrants pouring into the United States, most of whom worked for low wages, a fact that kept everybody's wages down. Rich and powerful trusts had negotiating power that labor did not have. And there were, also, the sweatshop workers, both men and women, who worked under intolerable conditions for a mere pittance because they had to earn a living. They could not afford to pay union dues, so the unions ignored them.

A few enterprising working women had begun to organize small trade unions in the 1860s. Miss Augusta Lewis organized the New York Typographical Union No. 1. Miss Kate Mullaney was the driving force behind one of the most successful of women's unions, the Troy (N.Y.) Laundry Workers Union. This union struck for higher wages in 1863 and 1868 and won increases each time. The success of the Knights of Labor in winning a railroad strike against Jay Gould encouraged some women workers to turn for help to the Knights, and to form Woman's Assemblies that the Knights welcomed, the first one dating to 1881. Statistics began to be compiled on working women. Miss Mary Hanafin, a salesclerk, reported to an Assembly

in 1886 that the average woman factory employee was working a ten-hour day for five dollars a week. Mrs. Leonora M. Barry interviewed working women for a three-and-a-half-year period, reporting back that most working women were afraid to join an organization, afraid to take a stand against their employers in favor of better working conditions and increased wages, afraid to speak up for fear of being fired. What women needed was powerful support that would allow them to win shorter hours, better wages and working conditions, and ultimately, equal opportunity, and equal pay for equal work. It was a long time coming, but women made some valiant efforts along the way.

Grace Dodge (1856–1914) was one of the first dedicated wealthy women to work with ("not for" she clearly stated) working girls. Her Working Girls Clubs, started in 1884, provided an opportunity for working girls to get out of the slums at least for a few hours a week, meet other working girls, and develop self-confidence and self-respect. When, in 1906, Miss Dodge became president of the National Board of Young Women's Christian Associations, she helped provide an expanding program of cultural, recreational, and social activities for young working women.

Josephine Shaw Lowell (1843–1905) became aware of the plight of New York department store girl clerks in 1886 when Alice Woodbridge, a former store clerk herself, called the attention of Mrs. Lowell and Dr. Mary Putnam-Jacobi and others to the intolerable working conditions of many department store girls. The girls worked for two dollars a week from 7:45 A.M. to midnight, with only a few minutes for

Carrying work home for the family to sew. From **A Pictorial History of American Labor** *by William Cahn*

Mother Jones marching with children who worked in the textile mills of Pennsylvania. United Electrical, Radio and Machine Workers of America

lunch, on a six-day-week schedule, and sometimes on Sunday (without pay) in order to take stock. They had no place to sit down during the day, no lockers, no paid vacations. Mrs. Lowell decided that a consumer boycott would get the quickest action. She organized the New York Consumers' League in 1890 to call attention to department store women's plight and to urge a boycott of all stores not okayed by the League. The idea of a boycott and of consumer action to right labor wrongs caught on, and has been utilized over and over again in the course of social reform.

When Florence Kelley (1859–1932) became general secretary of the National Consumers League in 1899, she worked indefatigably for legislation in behalf of working women and children. There were moments of triumph when states did pass protective labor legislation, and moments of defeat when courts struck down the legislation as unconstitutional. *Muller* vs. *Oregon* (1908) a case that involved a ten-hour day for working women, argued by Louis D. Brandeis, resulted in the Supreme Court upholding a ten-hour day for Oregon working women. Mrs. Kelley did not live to see all her goals achieved, but she and others of her decade had initiated attitudes and action that would crystallize in the labor reforms of the Franklin D. Roosevelt administration.

At the age of fifty, Mother Jones (Mary Harris Jones, 1830–1930) began her long struggle to better workers' bleak, cheerless and seemingly hopeless lives. From 1877 to 1921 she was on the scene at Pittsburgh helping striking railroad employees, in the coal mines of West Virginia and Colorado, and in the copper pits of Arizona. Once, in Pennsylvania, she organized a mop-and-bucket brigade of miners' wives to drive off scabs. Carrying mops, pails of water, and brooms, and beating on dishpans, the women arrived, yelling and hollering and frightening the mules and the scabs alike as they tried to enter the mines. The plight of small children working in mills and mines particularly concerned Mother Jones. In 1903 she led a march of working children from the textile mills of Pennsylvania to the Oyster Bay home of President Theodore Roosevelt to dramatize their plight. Roosevelt refused to see them, but people all along the march became aware of the sad life of working children, and fed and clothed them and gave them shelter. Mother Jones was a devoted labor agitator, capturing the imagination of labor as no other women had yet done.

But more than imagination was needed. Many women realized that the prestige and power of a trade union was imperative.

And so, in 1903, while the American Federation of Labor was holding its annual convention in Boston, a group of women—labor organizers as well as socially prominent and financially independent women—were also meeting. As a result of this meeting, the National Women's Trade Union League was formed.

The National Women's Trade Union League backed striking women, provided training courses for potential women labor leaders (some forty women took these courses), conducted wage-and-hour surveys, and kept the women's labor movement intact until it could stand on its own feet or become integrated into the American Federation of Labor.

When working women's first major New

Headquarters of the Women's Trade Union League of New York, January, 1910, during the shirtwaist workers' strike. Museum of the City of New York, The Bryon Collection

This fire escape was of little use to Triangle Shirtwaist workers trapped inside their building. Employers often kept doors locked to prevent workers from leaving early or to maintain the proper temperature for handling fabrics. Brown Brothers

York strike (shirtwaist workers against Leiserson & Co. and the Triangle Waist Company) occurred in 1909–10, the New York branch of the National Women's Trade Union League provided bail for strikers, raised strike funds, opened relief kitchens, publicized the women's cause, and kept the strikers morale high during thirteen bitter cold winter weeks. Wealthy New York women raised money for the strikers. Newspaper reporter Ida M. Tarbell (1857–1944), who was known as a "literary bushwhacker" and "terror of the trusts" for her scathing report on Rockefeller's oil monopoly, and who once received a letter addressed to "Ida M. Tarbell, Rockefeller Station, Hades," used her power to protest treatment of the women strikers by law enforcement officials. Their attitude was summed up by one man who accused the women of participating in a "strike against God and nature."

By 1911 the National Women's Trade Union League had eleven branches in major cities. Wherever there were women striking, the Women's Trade Union League was there, with bail, with relief kitchens, and with publicity.

The horror of New York's March 25, 1911 fire when a loft building occupied by the Triangle Waist Company trapped girl shirtwaist operatives on the eighth, ninth, and tenth floors with stairway exits barred, tragically pinpointed the American working woman's hopeless plight. There was no escape at all for the trapped women. They could either burn to death or to leap to death. One young woman, holding her weekly pay envelope in her hand, scattered its pitifully small contents, six one-dollar bills, one by one out the window before she jumped. One-hundred -and forty-six working women burned to death or leaped to death, some holding hands to give each other courage as they jumped. The employers were acquitted. Help for the American working women still had a long, long road to travel.

Settlement houses, which began to spring up in the United States in the late 1800s, also called attention to the city slum problem and neglected working women and children. Residents at settlement houses were usually young women just out of college who were seeking an opportunity to serve humanity. Usually they stayed for a few years working on settlement house programs, then moved on to a job or to marriage.

Jane Addams (1860–1935), who attained worldwide renown during her lifetime not only for her settlement work but for her peace activities, bought Hull House in Chicago's crowded slum area in 1889. Hull House (and most other settlement houses) did not start off with a set program, but slowly responded to the needs of the slum community, encouraging slum neighbors to discuss community problems and participate in decision-making. Whatever the cause, it was given a hearing at Hull House. Within four years, activities numbered forty, and included a day nursery, a gymnasium, cooking and sewing classes, a playground, a dispensary.

Illinois's first factory inspection act, which passed the state legislature in 1893, had the active backing of Hull House. Hull House battled for the establishment of Chicago's (and the nation's) first juvenile court (1899), for child labor laws, for recognition of labor unions, for the elimination of health hazards in dangerous trades, and of course for better pay, shorter working hours, and better working conditions for women. Miss Addams's presence at Hull House gave it dignity, prestige, and skillful guidance during forty-six years.

Lillian D. Wald and Mary Brewster, both nurses, and both concerned with the misery of the slums, came face to face with appalling instances of disease, poverty, and hopelessness when they took an apartment on the top floor of a slum tenement on New York's Lower East Side in 1893. With funds supplied by generous donors, Miss Wald was able to purchase the House on Henry Street in 1895, and establish it as a Nurses Settlement House. The first staff numbered eleven persons, nine of them trained nurses. Less than ten years later there were ninety-two nurses, their annual visits totaling 200,000, and branches had been opened in upper Manhattan and

Jane Addams during the early years at Hull House. Sophia Smith Collection

the Bronx. The House on Henry Street grew into a neighborhood center, occupying seven houses, with two uptown branches, a neighborhood playhouse, and a music school. Miss Wald remained active until 1933, retiring after a forty-year career as one of the most influential, widely known, and beloved public health workers of her day. She was elected to the Hall of Fame for Great Americans in 1970.

A Henry Street visiting nurse takes a shortcut over apartment roofs as she makes her rounds in 1908. Visiting Nurse Service of New York

Miss Mary E. McDowell (1854–1936) was appointed director of Chicago's second settlement house, the University of Chicago Settlement House, when it opened its doors in 1894. It was located in the "back of the yards," a dismal area near the Chicago stockyards and meat packing plants, where the air was filled with the stench of butchered cattle, of a nearby garbage dump, and of an inadequate sewage system. Miss McDowell's first crusades were for better garbage disposal, for a community park, for a branch library, for a

municipal bathhouse and for manual training in the public schools. She worked for the appointment of a City Waste Commission. She founded a day nursery, a club for children. She supported strikers in the 1904 stockyard strike. She helped found the National Women's Trade Union League in 1903. She was appointed Chicago's Commissioner of Public Welfare in 1923. For forty years she was in the forefront of social reform.

One indominable woman addressed herself to another vital problem that women faced at the turn of the century. The right of every woman to become pregnant by choice became the crusade of Margaret Sanger (1883–1966), who coined the phrase "birth control," went to jail for distributing contraceptive information, faced the hostility of the clergy, risked heavy fines, and court action. As a visiting nurse, in 1912, she stood at the bedside of Sadie Sachs, a slum woman dying of an attempted abortion because the doctor had told her she would not survive another baby but had not told her how she could avoid pregnancy. Margaret Sanger decided then and there that she would discover the "secret" of birth control and make it available to all women everywhere. She left Sadie Sachs' bedside and walked until dawn, thinking about women's plight (her own mother had given birth to eleven children) and of American women down the centuries who had not only faced the threat of Indian attacks, the loneliness of western plains, the drudgery of housework, but the inevitability of giving birth to more children than they perhaps wanted or could afford.

For months Margaret Sanger researched, unsuccessfully, the "secret" of preventing conception, studying medical texts and interviewing physicians. She went to Paris and interviewed doctors, housewives, druggists, midwives. She collected formulas, techniques, and devices until she felt ready to help women become "biologically emancipated." She returned to New York, and prepared a booklet called *Family Limitation*, which gave a complete description of contraceptive devices and techniques. Distribution of such information was illegal, and Anthony Comstock, head of the New York Society for the Suppression of Vice, was a vigilant man. Nevertheless, Mrs. Sanger found a printer willing to risk running off 100,000 copies, which she wrapped in small bundles and

Margaret Sanger (left) *in court with her sister, 1916. NYPL Picture Collection*

mailed to key cities where friends would distribute them. She knew this would give her a test court case. In August 1914 she returned to Europe to continue her research. It was during this trip that she became aware of the profound impact birth control would have on a nation's health and economy, and she began to focus her attention on the international aspects of birth control.

Facing arrest upon her return to the United States, in October 1915, she discovered that her husband had already been sentenced to jail for giving a copy of *Family Limitation* to one of Anthony Comstock's undercover men. The charges against Mrs. Sanger were dismissed, however, leaving the law still untested.

She opened a birth control clinic (also against the law) in the Brownsville section of Brooklyn, basing its operation on a clinic she had seen in Amsterdam. At 7:00 A.M. on the clinic's first morning, a line of women stretched around the block. Margaret, her sister Ethel, who was a nurse, and Fania Mindell of Chicago manned the clinic, which survived about ten days before it was closed. Ethel was jailed and went on a hunger strike. Margaret served thirty days in jail. Her case was appealed and conviction upheld, but the judge interpreted the law to mean that a physician could give contraceptive information to a married woman if he felt it was beneficial to her health.

Largely through the efforts of Margaret Sanger, by the 1920s the attitudes of physicians and of the courts and of the public were slowly changing. The American Birth Control League (later known as the Planned Parenthood Federation of America) was formed. Physicians were supporting the birth control movement, and so was the American Medical Association. World governments were becoming aware of the danger of a population explosion. Margaret Sanger's life was devoted to making birth control information available and legal, and its importance recognized. She lived to see every one of her goals achieved, a rare and rewarding experience for a reformer.

Europe offered certain Americans at the turn of the century an environment of freedom, or knowledge—or ambience—that they could not find in their own states. It was not only Margaret Sanger who was led to Europe to accomplish study that she could not do in the U.S.; many creative and performing artists were living or studying abroad, and that trend would continue on into the 1930s, until it would be possible for Americans to refer to an expatriate community in Europe. American women singers had to go to Europe to study, to gain experience, and sometimes to obtain contracts. Opera singers of the late 1800s had to have "compelling ambition, dauntless determination, and assertive elbows" to gain recognition and an opportunity to perform. Rome was the mecca of American sculptors at the turn of the century, as was Paris the fertile ground for inspired painters.

When the new Metropolitan Opera House opened in New York for its first season in 1883, its "Golden Horseshoe" boxes were occupied by the fashionably gowned wives of New York millionaires. The total wealth of the Golden Horseshoe patrons was estimated at $500 million. Patrons and patronesses listened decor-

Olive Fremstad as Salome (holding the head of John the Baptist) startled audiences with her Dance of the Veils. Metropolitan Opera Archives

ously (or eyed one another), and the balconies shouted bravos as American prima donnas of the golden age of opera sang roles for which they were already world famous. It was quite a change from the behavior that characterized an American theatre audience just sixty years earlier. Mrs. Frances Trollope, visiting America between 1827 and 1830, thought audience decorum less than satisfactory. "All gentlemen wore their hats, and the spitting was unceasing," she wrote. By the late 1800s theatres were among the first public places willing to experiment with Thomas Edison's dangerous new electric "lighting plant." Times had changed.

The two most glamorous and beloved prima donnas of the golden age of opera were Mary Garden (1874–1967) and Geraldine Farrar (1882–1967). During her sixteen years at the Metropolitan Opera

House Geraldine Farrar packed the house at every performance at which she sang. She was a beautiful woman, had a magnificent voice, and was a great actress. She made her debut in 1901 at the age of nineteen in Berlin. Caruso was frequently her partner, the two stars forming an unsurpassed duo in the golden age of opera. Mary Garden made her debut in Paris in 1900. Claude Debussy created the role of Mélisande for her, and called her the "only Mélisande." She never took a curtain call after the death of Mélisande because, she said, "it was I who really died," so closely did she identify with the character she was portraying.

Sitting in front of a stage (and later, in front of a movie screen) the public was willing to relax its Victorian principles—a bit. Olive Fremstad (1872–1951), an opera singer whose beauty was described as "Botticellian," made somewhat of a sensation as Salome, a role which she created at the Metropolitan Opera in 1907. The Dance of the Veils aroused protests—and raised eyebrows, but she retained the role, and a large following. Perhaps dance more than any other theatre form challenged the audience to loosen its Puritanism and Victorianism in order to appreciate the movement of the human body on the stage. However, two of the most gifted American dancers at the turn of the century found that they had a more receptive and sympathetic audience in Europe.

Loie Fuller (1862–1928) made her debut as a dancer in 1891 in New York wearing a pale green skirt of thin China silk, its voluminous folds following the movement of her body as she danced a hypnotism scene. The spontaneous enthusiasm of the audience at this performance inspired her to experiment with gauzy fabrics and with light. She danced on a pane of glass lighted from below. She used phosphorescent material, dancing in darkness. Isadora Duncan, who traveled briefly with Loie Fuller in Germany, described a Fuller performance ecstatically. "Before our very eyes she turned to many coloured, shining orchids, to a wavering, flowing sea flower, and at length to a spiral-like lily. . . ." Loie Fuller performed on tour in America several times, but she preferred the audiences in Europe, where the sculptor Rodin, and the painter Toulouse-Lautrec were her friends.

Isadora Duncan (1878–1927) rebelled against the stiltedness of ballet forms, and worked out her own understanding of the solar plexus as the center of the body's movement, and of free-form dance as a means of expressing the natural beauty of the body. Although she was at eighteen giving solo performances of her free-form dancing in New York society homes, she, like Loie Fuller, found a more sympathetic audience in Europe. She performed in Britain, then moved to Paris, danced in Greece and Hungary; in Berlin audiences refused to leave the theatre, demanding encores, and students unhitched the horses from her carriage, which they then pulled through the streets "in triumph." Isadora Duncan searched constantly and fruitlessly for a sponsor and a country where she could establish a school to train young girls in her art. None of her schools survived, but the concepts of her art remained—her perceptive dedication to the beauty of the human body, her constant endeavor to express its ideals and human passions, her devotion to exploring the "nature of movement with respect to the nature of man." These aspects of her art survived as her legacy, and other great founders of American modern dance would develop and extend her work.

Four of the first successful American women artists had worked or studied abroad by the turn of the century. Mary Cassatt (1844–1926) was settled permanently in Paris by the 1870s. She identified with the Impressionist school and had a lasting friendship with Degas, who admired her work and invited her to become one of the Impressionist group. She introduced the United States to some of the first Impressionist paintings when she exhibited at the 1879 Society of American Artists' show. Three women sculptors, Harriet Hosmer (1830–1908), Edmonia Lewis (1845–1909?), and Anne Whitney

Isadora Duncan combined strength and grace in her movement. Library of Congress

Mary Cassatt's self portrait, painted in 1878. From the collection of Mr. and Mrs. Richman Proskauer, photograph by Brenwasser

(1821–1915), all of whose work stands in major American cities had lived and worked in Rome. Edmonia Lewis' *Hager in the Wilderness* was inspired by her sympathy "for all women who have struggled and suffered." She was part Indian and part black. Anne Whitney did busts of such famous contemporaries as Lucy Stone, Harriet Beecher Stowe, Frances Willard.

Some of the great American actresses of all time appeared on the stage at the turn of the century. Minnie Maddern Fiske (1865–1932) had a sixty-year-long career on the American stage. She was Becky Sharp in Thackeray's *Vanity Fair* (1899) and in 1903 she starred in *Hedda Gabler*. Her talent was so exceptional that she received honorary degrees from Smith College and from the University of Wisconsin. Julia Marlowe (1866–1950) whose speaking voice was considered by many as second only to Sarah Bernhardt's was an excellent Shakespearean actress. She too received honorary degrees, as well as a gold medal from the Academy of Arts and Letters in 1929. Lillian Russell (1861–1922), who symbolized the typical beautiful woman at the turn of the century, aspired to be an operatic singer, but ended up instead the first great lady of musical comedy. Miss Russell was also a strong supporter of woman suffrage.

One of the great American theatre families was coming into view at the turn of the century. Louisa Lane Drew (1820–97), who is sometimes called the "Queen Mother of the American Theatre," spent her entire life on the stage, as an actress, as a director, as a manager. She had a daughter, Georgianna Emma Drew, who

made her stage debut at the age of seventeen, and five years later married British-born Maurice Barrymore. The couple had three children—Ethel (1879), Lionel (1878), and John (1882), all three of whom became famous for their acting. The three Barrymores, Ethel, Lionel, and John, appeared in the motion picture *Rasputin and the Empress* in 1932. In 1944 Ethel Barrymore won an Oscar for

Lillian Russell displays the figure considered desirable at the turn of the century. Photoworld

*In a spirit of freedom and apparent fearlessness, two
women cavort atop Overhanging Rock in Yosemite National
Park, about 1895. National Park Service*

her role as Ma Mott in the film, *None but the Lonely Heart*. In 1955, at the age of seventy-five, she made a motion picture called *Young at Heart*.

One of the great triumphs of women at the end of the century was their role at the Chicago World's Columbian Exposition of 1893 celebrating the 400th anniversary of the discovery of America by Columbus. Women had their own Board of Lady Managers Committee, their own Woman's Building. Some 1,400 women spoke at the various congresses held during the exposition; in fact, they spoke at all of them except three, those on electricity, engineering, and real estate. Frances E. Willard was a speaker at the Temperance Congress, and Mrs. Charles Henrotin of Chicago (1847–1922) read a paper on "Women as Investors" before the Bankers Congress. All of the women who spoke did so before large audiences in "perfect equality with men both as specialists and as orators." The award-winning Woman's Building was designed by Sophia Hayden of Boston, a professional architect who had won the contract in a competition of women architects. She also supervised the construction of the 400-by-200-foot building. Mary Cassatt sent a mural from her Paris studio, and Anne Whitney sent a remolded plaster of *Leif Ericson* and of her *Roma* and some marble busts.

Lucy Stone, that peerless speaker for the woman suffrage movement, gave a talk at the exposition. She said, "I think with never-ending gratitude that the young women of today do not and can never know at what price their right to free speech and to speak at all in public has been earned." It was one of the last speeches she made. Lucy Stone died at her home in Dorchester, Massachusetts, on October 18, 1893.

The leaders of the nineteenth century woman suffrage movement were growing old. Elizabeth Cady Stanton, who alone of all the women present at the Seneca Falls Convention of 1848 had stood out fearlessly and steadfastly for the vote, retired in 1892 as president of the National American Woman Suffrage Association. Ten years later she died at her home at the age of eighty-six. Miss Anthony was stunned at the death of her lifelong friend and collaborator. "I cannot believe," she wrote a friend, "that the voice is still which I have loved to hear for fifty years."

Susan B. Anthony carried on alone for four more years. She traveled internationally, continuing to speak and write on woman suffrage. At the Berlin meeting of the International Council of Women, the entire audience rose whenever Miss Anthony entered the conference hall. Miss Anthony went to Washington for her last congressional hearing in 1906, and also to celebrate her eighty-sixth birthday with the young suffragists she had been training. She assured them that with courage and determination, "failure is impossible." She died two months later on March 13, 1906, at her home in Rochester, New York. At her bedside was Dr. Anna Howard Shaw, who was to carry on the suffrage cause as president of the National American Woman Suffrage Association from 1904–1915.

CHAPTER EIGHTEEN

The Push Toward Victory

HARRIOT STANTON BLATCH, Alice Paul, and Lucy Burns, all of whom had been involved in the militant British woman suffrage movement, returned to the United States from England in the first decade of the 1900s to accuse the American woman suffrage movement of being in the doldrums, stagnant, and "lacking in political know-how."

Harriot Stanton Blatch (1856–1940), daughter of Elizabeth Cady Stanton, arrived in New York in 1902 with her British husband and her daughter and immediately became disillusioned with the old-timers of the National American Woman Suffrage Association. She criticized their unwillingness to take forceful action, their "enmeshed" rigidity, their bogged-down apathy. By 1907 Mrs. Blatch had formed and become president of the Equality League of Self-Supporting Women.

Attention-getting demonstrations, distribution of literature at the polls, and new tactics were the immediate goals, financed by money "dug up from their own pockets." One new tactic was to send industrial women (Mary Duffy of the Overall Workers Union and Clara Silver of the Buttonhole Workers) to Albany to speak to the New York State Legislature in behalf of woman suffrage. Membership in the League grew rapidly and soon totaled 19,000. League members drove to the polls in Model T cars filled with suffrage literature. They made trolley-car campaign tours throughout New York State. They held mass meetings. They helped bring the militant British suffragist Emmeline Pankhurst to the United States and sponsored a mass meeting that filled Carnegie Hall on October 25, 1909. They supplied poll watchers on election day. But the most

New York suffrage parade banners quote two great leaders of the fight for the vote. Elizabeth Blackwell, aged 91, is at far side of carriage. Brown Brothers

dramatic publicity stunt of all was their woman suffrage parade (one of many) on Fifth Avenue in New York on May 21, 1910. It was the first time women had ever marched in a parade. Their protest was against the New York State Legislature's indifference to their demand for the vote. The old guard was shocked at such unladylike behavior. When the National American Woman Suffrage Association and the New York State Suffrage Association were invited to join the march, the claim was made that such a demonstration would "set women suffrage back fifty years," although there was some capitulation in the end.

This first woman suffrage parade in New York (and perhaps in the United States) started at 59th Street with a procession of automobiles carrying officers of woman suffrage organizations, followed by the Collegiate Equal Suffrage League members in caps and gowns, 200 altogether, then by members of the Equality League of Self-Supporting Women, carrying banners. There were speeches at Union Square.

The Women's Political Union (the new name adopted in 1910 for the Equality League of Self-Supporting Women) would hold many more Fifth Avenue parades during the coming years. Parades would no longer be considered "audacious," and pictures and favorable stories would appear in the press. Ultimately Mrs. Blatch became an expert parade or-

Children join in a suffrage march. Photoworld

ganizer, a valuable talent in the days without radio and television.

Alice Paul and Lucy Burns, both young intellectuals who had been studying and working abroad, had trained under the militant British suffragist, Emmeline Pankhurst, before their return to the United States in 1912. Both women, then in their twenties, found the National American Woman Suffrage Association "enmeshed" and "moribund" but offered to work for, and raise money to support, the Congressional Committee in Washington—an offer that was accepted. In Washington the two women soon gathered around them other eager young activists—Mrs. Lawrence Lewis, Crystal Eastman, Mary Ritter Beard, among them.

The Congressional Committee's public debut in Washington was the largest woman suffrage parade ever undertaken in the United States, astutely staged on March 3, 1913, the day before Woodrow Wilson was to be inaugurated. Washington was filled to overflowing with inauguration visitors, including newspaper reporters from all over the United States. The 5,000 (or 8,000) women who marched in this parade had been organized by the five women Congressional Committee members within two months' time. They had provided banners, coined slogans, decorated floats, hired bands, and procured permits. For a while it was a peaceful, impressive parade. Unexpectedly, it turned into a near riot.

The women marchers walked quietly along Washington's broad avenues, while people watched curiously. Then some people in the crowd began jeering and heckling the marchers. The women were shoved, spit upon, struck in the face, insulted with ribald remarks, pelted with burning cigar stubs. Police stood by making no effort to stop the onslaught, as the women literally fought their way through hostile crowds. Harriot Stanton Blatch appealed to a policeman to keep the "hoodlums" away and was told to "go home." Students from Maryland Agricultural College finally rushed to the aid of the marchers, forming rows through which the women could pass, and eventually Secretary of War Stimson agreed to send soldiers from Fort Myer to restore order.

Newspapers throughout the country carried the story of the Washington march and the permissive lawlessness that accompanied it. Outraged public opinion demanded an explanation. The Washington Chief of Police lost his job and Mrs. Blatch summed up the official attitude of the times by saying, "When women were sponsors of a project, that project immediately became a matter of small account in the eyes of the official class."

After the parade, the Congressional Committee was to undertake an intensive seven-year-long campaign for woman suffrage at the Capitol, attracting activist women from all over the country. The Congressional Committee became the Congressional Union, and then in 1917 it became the Woman's Party, which broke with the National American Woman Suffrage Association. As had happened before in the past, each organization adopted its own methods for winning the vote for women.

By 1915 only thirteen states had granted the vote to women, some by constitutional amendment, some by legislative enactment. Women suffrage states did not total up enough presidential electors to make an impact on political parties or on Congress. There was not a single eastern state among them. They were Wyoming (1869), Colorado (1893), Idaho (1896), Utah (1896), Washington (1910), California (1911), Oregon (1912), Kansas (1912), Arizona (1912), Illinois (1913), Alaska Territory (1913), Montana (1914), and Nevada (1914).

Faced with sixty-seven years of failure, the National American Woman Suffrage Association finally shook off its lethargy at the 1915 convention and called back to the presidency Mrs. Carrie Chapman Catt, the only woman whom they believed could lead them to victory.

Carrie Chapman Catt, (1859–1947), a dynamic woman from the West, had been president of the National American Woman Suffrage Association once before, in 1900. She had been Susan B. Anthony's choice for the position. But in 1904 her husband (who had encouraged her in her suffrage work) was close to death, and Mrs. Catt had to resign as president. In the interim years she played an active role in the international woman suffrage movement, as well as organizing a tremendous campaign for woman suffrage in New York State. The National American Woman Suffrage Association was ready to accept Mrs. Catt on any terms, because they so desperately needed her talents as a dynamic, diplomatic leader, an imaginative organizer, and an indefatigable administrator. Mrs. Catt's terms were that she be allowed to pick her own board—a working board—its members agreeing to devote full-time and single-minded effort toward the passage of a federal woman suffrage amendment. Her terms also included statements of cooperation and loyalty from each state's woman suffrage association and the promise to carry out whatever task Mrs. Catt assigned them in the "red-hot never-ceasing campaign" she promised to run. She predicted victory in six years. It took four.

The details of Mrs. Catt's famous Winning Plan were kept secret, because militant antisuffragists (the "Unholy Alliance," Mrs. Catt called them—the liquor interests, political machines, clergymen, big business, and apprehensive Southerners) would have delighted in putting obstacles in Mrs. Catt's path. A $2 million legacy willed to Mrs. Catt by newspaper publisher Mrs. Frank Leslie "to further the cause of woman suffrage" helped finance national headquarters, and pay for traveling expenses, pamphlets, and the publication of a woman suffrage maga-

In overalls and work shoes, two girls load heavy chunks of ice. Thousands of women went to work at new and unusual jobs during World War I. National Archives

Women in Newark, New Jersey, take over the jobs of men who have gone off to war.
National Archives

zine. Mrs. Catt sent Mrs. Maud Wood Park and Mrs. Helen Gardener to Washington to work on Congress and to lobby. And she began building her national staff of dedicated professional organizers, holding them together as a working unit despite a forthcoming war.

The United States formally entered World War I on April 16, 1917, and it affected women's lives in a variety of ways. Women suffragists continued their efforts to win the vote. Some women gave their energy to the attainment of peace. Some women delightedly found war jobs in fields usually denied to them, at wages they were unaccustomed to receiving. Housewives dutifully cooperated in observing wheatless and meatless days, in serving simple meals, and, when possible, in cultivating war vegetable gardens.

The public soon got used to seeing women acting as traffic cops, letter carriers, messengers, elevator operators, and streetcar conductors. Schoolgirls worked on farms (and were often called farmerettes). Their mothers frequently worked in war plants manufacturing high explosives, or armaments, or in fertilizer plants, chemical plants, or automobile factories. To cope with needs of an unexpected influx of women workers into industry the government established a Woman in Industry Service in June of 1918, within the Labor Department. Outstanding women leaders were invited by the government to serve on the Women's Committee of the United States Council of Defense, headed by Dr. Anna Howard Shaw.

Mary Pickford helped sell Liberty Bonds, and so did Miss Helen Taft, a niece of former President Taft. Miss Taft volunteered to climb one rung of a fire extension ladder every time someone in the crowd bought a Liberty Bond. She reached a height of ninety feet in the air four times, and offered to jump into a fire net for a $5,000 purchase. The purchase was made with the stipulation that she refrain from jumping. Mrs. Vincent Astor and other New York society leaders busied themselves raising money for overseas projects for American soldiers. The Y.W.C.A. sent Y girls to run canteens near the firing lines. The Salvation Army sent Salvation Army lassies to serve doughnuts and coffee to American soldiers. Commander Evangeline Booth of the Salvation Army was presented with the Distinguished Service Medal by President Wilson in recognition of the Salvation Army's war services.

Woman pacifists considered the war a reversion to barbarism, a calamity, a horror, and continued to work for peace.

Peace was the primary concern of Jeannette Rankin (1880–1973), the first woman elected to Congress (one woman among 421 men), who took her seat in the House of Representatives on April 2, 1917, as a representative from Montana. Three days later Miss Rankin committed what some people called "political suicide." She voted against entry of the United States into World War I. Miss Rankin could not have done otherwise. She believed in peace, not war. Though she was one of fifty House members voting no, because she was a woman she took the brunt of the public criticism. Twenty-four years later, while she was serving her second term (1941–43), Miss Rankin cast the only vote against the entry of the United States into World War II on December 8, 1941, receiving boos and hisses as she courageously took her stand.

During her first term of office, Miss Rankin, always an active suffragist, introduced the first bill to grant full citizenship to women independent of their husbands, and worked for a woman suffrage amendment, pointing out that, if Congress is supporting a war in behalf of democracy, it should grant a "small measure of democracy to the women of the country." In the twenty-year interim between Miss Rankin's two terms of office, she worked for peace as a member of the International League for Peace and Freedom, Another Mother for Peace, and the War Resisters League. At the age of eighty-seven she led the Jeannette Rankin Brigade of 5,000 women to Capitol Hill in Washington in a protest against the war in Vietnam, which she denounced as "ruthless slaughter."

Jeannette Rankin, first woman elected to Congress, an ardent suffragist, and an equally ardent pacifist. Wide World Photos

Miss Rankin once said that she believed peace could come to the world in as short a time as one year if women organized and truly worked for it with single-minded determination. A good many women in the past had had similar ideas. Lucretia Mott, Frances Willard, Lucy Ames Mead (1856–1936), all had worked toward peace. Now, pacifist women of New York, led by Crystal Eastman lobbied against universal military training, published a pacifist journal, *Four Lights*, and organized classes on world politics, conducted by Emily Green Balch. Miss Balch, a pro-

fessor at Wellesley College, lost her job because of her pacifist activities.

The Woman's Peace Party (later called the Women's International League for Peace and Freedom) ultimately became the most important American women's peace organization. Founded in Washington, D.C., in January 1915, through the efforts of Jane Addams and Carrie Chapman Catt, 3,000 American women attended this convocation, which was addressed by two overseas visitors—Rosika Schwimmer (1877–1948), a Hungarian peace activist (she later became a U.S.

resident but was refused citizenship because she would not take the arms-bearing oath), and Mrs. Emmeline Pethick-Lawrence, a British peace activist.

Jane Addams was elected national chairman of the Woman's Peace Party. Miss Addams's peace position in World War I came near jeopardizing her status at Hull House, and caused her to be expelled by the Daughters of the American Revolution, attacked by the American Legion, and criticized by the American public. She was one of the forty-seven distinguished women aboard the S.S. *Noordam* in April 1915 to sail for Holland through submarine-infested waters on a peace mission. They were on their way to The Hague to participate in an International Congress of Women called to protest World War I, to stop the war if possible, and to discuss ways of preventing future wars.

The Hague Congress of Women had opened on April 28, 1915, with some 1,000 voting women members present, representing twelve countries. At the end of long deliberations the Congress of Women recommended, among other proposals, continuous mediation without waiting for fighting to cease (a plan discussed by American women on shipboard prior to the meeting), a society of nations, a permanent international court and a permanent international disarmament conference, freedom of the seas, education of children in peace objectives. An International Committee of Women for Permanent Peace was established.

To make sure their proposals actually reached the hands of leaders of both warring and neutral countries, the Hague Congress of Women voted that these proposals be delivered in person. Two groups of women carried the Hague plan to European heads of state. Americans included Jane Addams and Dr. Alice Hamilton who visited warring nations, and Emily Balch and Julia Grace Wales who visited neutral nations. Upon her return to the United States Jane Addams personally delivered to President Wilson the conclusions of the Hague Congress of Women, hoping that he would start immediate peace efforts. He was unwilling to take such a step, but his later peace recommendations reflected some of those put forward at the Hague Congress of Women.

Jane Addams received the Nobel Peace Prize in 1931, sharing it with Nicholas Murray Butler, president of Columbia University. Miss Addams contributed her share of the Peace Prize, $16,000, to the Women's International League for Peace and Freedom.

Without the right to vote, American women had once again been asked to sacrifice their sons and husbands on the battlefield, and to work wholeheartedly for the war effort. Their suffrage campaigns had been shrugged off, requests buried in congressional committees, and they had constantly been advised to "be patient." Despite the fact that a war was on, the militant Woman's Party believed the time had come to be impatient.

Approximately three months before war was declared, twelve Woman's Party members had taken their stand before the White House, six at the East Gate with a banner reading "Mr. President, What Will You Do for Woman Suffrage?" and six at the West Gate with a banner reading

"How Long Must Women Wait for Liberty?" The picketing was peaceful, and no laws were broken. Day after day the women stood there, silently, in rain, wind, sleet, bitter cold, and burning sun, holding banners, their slogans changing from time to time. On March 4, 1917, Inauguration Day, a special delegation of 1,000 women marched slowly four times around the White House, buffeted by a windy, bitter-cold rainstorm. As time passed women came from all over the country to join the picket lines. There was a New York Day, a Maryland Day, a Pennsylvania Day, a Susan B. Anthony Day, a College Day.

Little harassment of the pickets occurred until war was declared on April 6, 1917, perhaps because slogans on the banners read "Democracy Should Begin at Home" and "Kaiser Wilson." The police stood by and watched, as "hoodlums" pushed the picketing women about, tore their banners, and shoved them off the sidewalk. At first picketers were merely arrested, then released. Jailings followed, and before the horror had ended 218 women from twenty-six states had been arrested, 97 had been sent to jail. The picketers were peaceful women—some were Quakers, some were in their late seventies and had worked for years to get the vote, some were socially prominent women, some working girls. The fact that the women simply stood there, day after day, silently holding their banners seemed to incense hangers-on and the police, and it was always the women—not the attacking rowdies—who were arrested. The District Courts soon began to sentence the women for obstructing sidewalk traffic, consigning them from a few days to six months in filthy, rat-infested jails, manned by attendants and wardens who shoved the women about, dragged them up stairs, threw them across iron benches, handcuffed them to cell doors. When some of the women went on hunger strikes they were force-fed. Some women were transferred across the border into Virginia for incarceration in the Occoquan Workhouse, a particularly obnoxious prison.

During Woman's Party picketing, Mrs. Carrie Chapman Catt and the National American Woman Suffrage Association kept aloof, periodically declaring that the organization was not in any way connected with the Woman's Party or with the picketing. But its members were actively working for suffrage all over the country.

Meanwhile, members of the Woman's Party were publicizing their arrests and jailings across the country. Senator Jones of New Mexico, chairman of the Senate Committee on Woman Suffrage, visited Occoquan Workhouse on September 24, 1917. On November 27–28 all imprisoned pickets were unconditionally released, and by March 4, 1918, every prison sentence and every arrest had been invalidated.

The Woman's Party claimed that their picketing and their jailings had produced favorable action by Congress. A favorable report on woman suffrage was issued by the Senate Committee on Woman Suffrage on September 15, 1917. A House Committee on Woman Suffrage was appointed on September 24, 1917, with the date (January 10, 1918) set for a vote. And President Wilson had finally yielded. He made his declaration in behalf of the Woman Suffrage Amendment on January 9, 1918.

CHAPTER NINETEEN

Victory and Ratification

ALTHOUGH JEANNETTE RANKIN, the first woman in Congress, was a real "coup" for the suffrage movement, and although Carrie Chapman Catt's "Winning Plan" was making progress and eighteen states had joined the woman suffrage roster by 1918, the first real good news from Washington was President Wilson's announcement in favor of the Anthony Amendment on January 9, 1918. And there was excitement in Washington on the following day when the Anthony Amendment came up for a vote in the House of Representatives. Women packed the balconies, tallies in hand, watching a touching demonstration in their behalf unfold below on the floor of the House. They saw Congressman Sims of Tennessee, suffering from a still unset broken arm and shoulder, come in to cast his yea vote, then Republican leader James R. Mann of Illinois, just released from a

six-month hospital stay, and Senator Branhart of Indiana carried in on a stretcher and finally Representative Hicks of New York, who left the deathbed of his wife, keeping his promise to her to vote for the Suffrage Amendment. And when the roll was called, the Anthony Amendment had won 274 to 136, the required two-thirds majority. There was cheering on the floor and in the balconies, and women left the House of Representatives that day singing the well-known hymn "Praise God From Whom All Blessings Flow." Their joy and gratitude was a little premature. The Senate was another matter.

Both Carrie Chapman Catt and Alice Paul threw their best organizers into the battle for the passage of the Anthony Amendment in the Senate. But the "antis" were equally aggressive. By bringing up the states' rights issue (that states should

Mrs. Carrie Chapman Catt (center) *in white and Dr. Anna Howard Shaw, in academic robes lead suffragists in a New York City parade during the final push toward victory.* The League of Women Voters

have the right to decide on who should get the vote, not the federal government), they helped defeat the Anthony Amendment in the Senate on October 1, 1918, by just two votes.

President Wilson strongly recommended passage of the Anthony Amend-

ment when he called a special session of Congress in May 1919, cabling his message from Paris. The House of Representatives quickly repassed the amendment on May 20 by a wide majority—304 to 89. But the Senate delayed action, and when the amendment did come up on

June 3, 1919, the debate dragged on and on for two long days, with antisuffrage senators making interminable antisuffrage speeches. The final vote on June 4, 1919, was favorable. But it was not the end of the road for either the Woman's Party or the National American Woman Suffrage Association. Fourteen months of hard ratification campaigning lay ahead.

In spite of referendum worries, the National American Woman Suffrage Association held its last convention, its Victory Convention, in a mood of joy in Chicago on February 12-18, 1920. There was cheering, marching, singing. A Ratification Banquet was held commemorating both the victory and the 100th anniversary of the birthday of Susan B. Anthony. There was a Pioneers' Luncheon at which old-timers told tales of their triumphs and defeats. Finally there was the transfer of the National American Woman Suffrage Association into the National League of Women Voters, which Mrs. Catt had helped found as a continuing organization to educate new women voters on their rights as citizens, and to recommend legislation in behalf of women and children. At the close of the last Woman Suffrage Convention, women who had worked together for decades to get the vote separated reluctantly. But the old officers turned to the urgent business of accelerating ratification of the Anthony Amendment by the needed thirty-six states.

There was a rush by pro-women suffrage states to be the first of the thirty-six states needed to ratify the Woman Suffrage Amendment after its passage by Congress on June 4, 1919. Wisconsin and Illinois ran neck and neck for first place.

Then came Michigan, Kansas, Ohio, New York, Pennsylvania, Massachusetts, Texas, all ratifying in the victory month of June 1919. And then came a lull. Some governors refused to call special legislative sessions to ratify the amendment because of the expense involved. Some governors were hostile to woman suffrage. Mrs. Carrie Chapman Catt had anticipated these eventualities and had warned state suffrage organizations not to disband before their state had ratified the suffrage amendment. Women's help would be needed, she pointed out, to put pressure on governors to call special sessions of their legislatures and also to lobby for passage of the amendment.

On the whole, state ratification of the Anthony Amendment went rather well. By March 22, 1920, Washington became the thirty-fifth state to ratify, leaving one more state needed for the necessary three-fourths majority. Vote was pending in several states. But woman suffragists who had waited so long for the vote were impatient. They wanted to vote in the 1920 fall elections. And they were also afraid that anti-suffragists would win over the thirteen states needed to block the amendment.

Tennessee was chosen as the most promising state in which to get the governor to call a special session of the state legislature and as a state well organized to lobby for passage. Tennessee also had an active woman suffrage group—Mrs. Guilford Dudley, Mrs. Leslie Warner, members of the National American Woman Suffrage Association, and Sue White, an energetic young lawyer representing the Woman's Party. Mrs. Carrie Chapman

Carrie Chapman Catt on her return from Washington from the signing of the Nineteenth Amendment giving women the right to vote. The League of Women Voters

Catt and Harriet Taylor Upton of the National American Woman Suffrage Association both went to Nashville from New York to help organize and lobby. Betty Gram and Anita Pollitzer came as representatives of the Woman's Party from Washington. Tennessee Governor Roberts, under pressure from Washington, had no sooner called a special session of the Tennessee State Legislature to consider the Nineteenth Amendment than anti-suffragists appeared in sizable numbers, set up their own lobby, and began an insidious anti-suffrage campaign. They represented the brewers, manufacturing industries, and "undefinable strangers," all of whom opposed woman suffrage as a threat to their own interests. The liquor interests and the satellite "antis" which they attracted eyed the prospect of woman suffrage with hostility, believing that women's votes would be "dry" votes, prohibiting liquor in their states and communities. While women lobbied day after day for two hot summer months, keeping lists of the "yeas" and the "nays" among the Senate and the House, the "antis" set up bars in hotel rooms (Tennessee was a prohibition state) and invited legislators to partake abundantly of their hospitality and to listen to their arguments against woman suffrage.

Finally the Nineteenth Amendment came up for a vote in the Tennessee State Senate on August 13, 1920. It passed 25 to 4. It was then that suffragists realized that the "antis" had been concentrating their efforts on the House. Its vote was considered more dubious. Suffragist lists showed the House vote about evenly divided. Discussion in the House dragged on and on, the "antis" in the House dwelling on the "tender flowerlike nature of woman," on her "inherent weak-mindedness" and on the question of states' rights. All kinds of skullduggery appeared to be going on as the "anti" lobby waged an all-out battle to win the House vote. Suffragists had anxious moments as the amendment at last came up for a House vote on August 18, after repeated postponements. Victory, they calculated, hinged on two votes: the vote of Representative Banks Turner and the vote of Representative Harry Burn—the still hesitating youngest member of the House, whose constituency was against suffrage but whose mother, an ardent suffragist, had urged him to "help Mrs. Catt put 'Rat' in Ratification."

Representative Burns and Representative Turner did vote YES, and, at long last, seventy-two years after the first woman suffrage meeting in Seneca Falls, New York, women had the vote.

On August 26, 1920, early in the morning, Bainbridge Colby, secretary of state, signed the proclamation certifying final adoption of the Nineteenth Amendment, making it possible for millions of American women of voting age to vote in the November 1920 elections.

To achieve this final victory and get the word "male" out of the Constitution, Mrs. Carrie Chapman Catt, president of the National American Woman Suffrage Association, calculated that it had taken

. . . the women of this country fifty-two years of pauseless campaign . . . Hundreds of women gave the accumulated possibilities of an entire lifetime, thousands gave years of their lives, hundreds of thousands gave constant interest and such aid as they could. It was a continuous, seemingly endless, chain of activity. Young suffragists who helped forge the last links of that chain were not born when it began. Old suffragists who forged the first links were dead when it ended.

Nationwide celebrations marked this victory . . . the ringing of bells, flag raisings, victory meetings, processions. A draped flag hung over the tablet that marked the chapel in Seneca Falls, New York, where the first woman's convention had been held in 1848. Wreaths adorned the old building in Cheyenne, Wyoming, where the first women's jury had sat in 1870.

CHAPTER TWENTY

The Innovative Twenties

THE 1920S WAS a decade of revolt, a revolt that was clear from the changed pages of the Sears, Roebuck catalog to the finely toned rhythms of the jazz age in F. Scott Fitzgerald's novels. World War I had brought a change in women's clothes. It was impossible to work in a war plant wearing voluminous skirts, so women wore overalls and knickers and bobbed their hair for convenience. Teen-age girls wore dresses up to their knees, danced the bunny hug and Charleston, and necked in the back seat of their dates' borrowed family cars. The public grew familiar with popularizations of Freud's theory and practice of psychoanalysis, and shared the idea of emancipation in still another form, at the movies. Record crowds were lining up to see Edith Day play the shop-girl in *Irene*, and humming "Tea for Two"

from the hit *No, No, Nanette,* as musical comedy flourished. New Yorkers were traveling uptown to hear concerts by the great musical artists of the day for only twenty-five cents, concerts arranged by a beloved woman named Minnie Guggenheimer. The public was chuckling over *Gentlemen Prefer Blondes* by Anita Loos and the bewildered but well-intentioned dowagers of Helen Hokinson's cartoons. Respectable women were tentatively sipping bootleg liquor in violation of the Eighteenth Amendment for which their grandmothers had worked so righteously and vigorously in the 1800s. Women were even daringly taking an occasional puff at a cigarette. And women had won the vote. Things were so uneventful in Coolidge's Washington that the public basked placidly in an era of "normalcy," enjoying their nine mil-

Two women enjoy the newly installed smoking compartment on the Pennsylvania Railroad. This smoking compartment was exclusively for the use of women passengers. Photoworld

lion or so automobiles and their electrified lives and their liberation from the Victorian Age.

Writers and artists revolting against the domination of "goods" over "ideas" found their way to New York's Greenwich Village; or, like Gertrude Stein, they went to Paris. More and more women would write award-winning plays, novels, poetry, and short stories, and devise new forms in dance and painting. Theatre production would develop with an energy that did not stop in the twenties, or the thirties, or the sixties, for that matter.

Radios brought the big events of the decade into the home—Henry Ford's new Model T. at the low low price of $250, Charles A. Lindbergh's nonstop flight to Paris (1927), the St. Valentine Day massacre in Chicago (1929) when Al Capone and the "Bugs" Moran gangs clashed, Richard E. Byrd's daring flight over the

North Pole (1926) and his South Pole Expeditions (1928–30 and 1933–35), Jack Dempsey's winning of the heavyweight title (1919–26), and Babe Ruth's home runs. The first network broadcast of a symphony orchestra in 1926 introduced the listening public to "culture" in the home. Meanwhile, however, women could listen to cooking expert Betty Crocker (Zella Layne) or learn the principles of good grooming from Hedda Hopper (1890–1966). At night, after supper, families listened to George Burns's closing quip, "Say Goodnight, Gracie."

For those addicted to news about Hollywood there was Louella Parsons interviewing movie stars over the radio. The movies gave an American family a world outside of its own particular home. They gave Americans a new way of looking at their own lives, with more tolerant, open minds. They broke down Victorian sexual hangups . . . somewhat. Home décor changed. Fashions changed. Attitudes toward life changed. As one British observer put it, the movies became "the national store window for fashions of all sorts." And young people became more assertive, more independent, more explorative.

Everyone loved Mary Pickford. Her curls, her girlish charm, her movie sorrows and joys, helped reassure conservative parents who had doubts about the advisability of motion-picture going. Lillian Gish, whom contemporary critics described as a "pure white flame," and as an "incomparable interpreter of the experience of sensitive women" brought great acting to the screen. Greta Garbo made worldly sophistication and detached remoteness a fascinating mystery. And as would happen

with the many movie stars who followed her, Clara Bow became the idol of young women across the country, who imitated her bob, her provocative pout, her short skirts, hoping to find in them her sex appeal. The cult that grew up around a leading lady of the screen—her ability to draw crowds at the box office and seemingly assure the success of a movie—was a phenomenon that gained strength through the decades. The fascination that Hollywood held for Americans, the success of its movies, its directors, and its big production companies, owes a great deal to the styles and talents of women in the movies.

World War I had prepared the American public to accept these burgeoning changes in fashion, and had speeded up the amazing proliferation of inventions and laborsaving devices. It had also brought working women into the public focus. Women were manning all kinds of jobs in all kinds of industries, among them high explosive, machine tool, copper smelting, iron refining, and the chemical industry. Temporarily working women's problems had been met by the World War I Women in Industry Service Committee, headed by Mary van Kleeck and her assistant Mary Anderson. On June 5, 1920, President Wilson signed into law a bill establishing a Women's Bureau in the Department of Labor, its purpose "to protect the welfare of working women."

Mary Anderson, the Women's Bureau's first director, who served from 1920 to 1944, set high standards for the bureau's activities. Its fact-finding investigations were so exhaustive and so thorough that Miss Anderson's reports were never challenged during these formative years. Its

Movie idol Clara Bow. Photoworld

standard-setting policies became a guide for a half-century of legislative action. Miss Anderson (1872–1964) knew working women's problems at first hand. She herself had worked for a time in a clothing factory as well as eighteen years in a shoe factory. She gave focus and leadership to the bureau's program. By World War II working women who manned industrial jobs worked under better conditions, for better wages, and better hours with premium pay for overtime because the Women's Bureau had focused public attention on the working women's problems.

Women were active in other areas of government as well. The first woman to be seated in the Senate was Rebecca L. Felton (1835–1930) of Georgia, though she occupied her senate seat for only one day. Mrs. Felton was appointed on October 3, 1922, to fill a vacancy to November 22, 1922, a term of twenty-five days. She was eighty-seven years old, an ardent suffragist, an experienced politician, and a tireless women's rights worker. Though she knew her successor had already been appointed, and that her own appointment was purely honorary, she insisted on taking her seat in the Senate. She traveled to Washington and was sworn in on November 21, 1922, the day before her term would expire, to the applause of suffragist women who packed the balconies.

Nine years later, Hattie W. Caraway of Arkansas (1878–1950) would become the first woman actually to serve in the Senate. Her term covered nearly 14 years (1931–45). Edith Nourse Rogers (1881–1960) of Massachusetts ran for the House of Representatives seat left vacant by her husband's death, and won it in 1925. She was elected to her Congressional seat for eighteen consecutive terms of office (covering 35 years) and was preparing to campaign for her nineteenth term, when she died two days before the 1960 primary election, at the age of 79.

Though New York's Governor Alfred E. Smith twice lost his bid for the presiden-

tial nomination, and in 1928 having won the bid, lost the presidential election, Belle Moskowitz (1877–1933) who worked as the governor's close counselor and political adviser never wavered in her efforts to win for him a presidential victory. She had "the greatest brain of anybody I ever knew," Smith once said of her. She had experience in labor relations, in politics, and in collaboration with her husband had entered the relatively new field of public relations (a field in which women would excel as the years passed). Although she had no real title during her long association with Governor Smith, she was sometimes called an "unofficial official," and managed to keep in the limelight those causes which she cared about—help for working women, free speech, housing aid for the poor.

By the year 1925 there were two women governors. Mrs. Nellie Taylor Ross was installed governor of Wyoming in 1925, just a few days before Mrs. Miriam Amanda Ferguson became governor of Texas. Mrs. Ross was later appointed the first woman director of the U.S. Mint, a position that she held for twenty years until resigning in 1953.

Women whose artistic contributions would assume major proportions for future generations were working in the 1920s (and the 1930s) with an energy that seemed to be unceasing. Some were well known; many were not, or had only small followings. Amy Lowell, Sara Teasdale, Edna St. Vincent Millay, and Marianne Moore were all writing poetry. Edna Ferber, Pearl Buck, and Dorothy Parker were writing novels and short stories. Willa Cather, whose 100th anniversary was cele-

Willa Cather, one of America's greatest novelists. Alfred A. Knopf, photograph by Steichen

brated in 1974, and whose "work stands as a monument more unshakable than she might have dreamed," a modern critic said, won the Pulitzer Prize in 1923 with *One of Ours.* Willa Cather's experience grew out of the western prairies, as did Georgia O'Keeffe's, a painter whose canvases of immense and boldly colored flowers and desert scenes reflected an observation of the natural world that was entirely new. When Alfred Stieglitz, the famous photographer, saw some of her drawings, he is said to have exclaimed, "Finally! A woman on paper!" In the field of dance, Doris Humphrey and Martha Graham who had trained with Ruth St. Denis, left her to work more deeply with their own movement instincts.

Martha Graham invented a totally new dance vocabulary for the body. Her use of the contraction and release of energy, her integration of the body's breath and weight and the earth's gravity to express what is deepest in human emotion became the basis of a technique that influenced every American modern dancer who came

Martha Graham in "Errand into the Maze."
Martha Graham Center of Contemporary Dance

Malvina Hoffman's work was commissioned all over the world. Here she works ninety feet above the street on the façade for Bush House, London. Malvina Hoffman Properties.

after her. Her instrument was herself, and "movement does not lie" was her first principle. Her total departure from ballet, symbolized perhaps, by the flexed rather than the pointed foot, shocked many. She said simply: "The flexing did something else for me that the pointed foot didn't have—a contact with the earth." Out of her company came many of the best-known and most innovative modern dancers of today.

Two women sculptors of the 1920s and '30s made important contributions to American art, though in somewhat different ways. Malvina Hoffman (1887–1966) studied in Paris with Rodin, study that was a prelude to receiving the largest sculptural commission ever given to a woman. She was chosen to execute 110 life-size bronze statues that now stand in the Chicago Field Museum's Hall of Man. She traveled all over the world to study and observe the countries and the people she would represent in her work—Sicilian fisherman, New Zealand Maoris, Mongolian dancers, among them. It was an assignment that required an anthropological as well as artistic sensitivity.

Both as a sculptor and as a patron of young American artists Gertrude Vanderbilt Whitney (1875–1942) made a notable contribution to emerging American art in the early 1900s. Her own studio in Greenwich Village was the meeting place for young artists trying to break away from traditions of the past. Miss Whitney was concerned that the work of American artists be shown to the public and her studio developed into the Whitney Studio Galleries, where painting and sculpture were not only exhibited but offered for sale. Later, in 1930, she founded the Whitney Museum of American Art in New York.

In New York another woman was giving commercial support and personal encouragement to the writers of her day. On January 2, 1920, Frances Steloff opened the Gotham Book and Art Shop in New York's theatre district, despite the fact that she had been told that actors don't read. Martha Graham was one of the bookshop's early patrons, and over the years it became a gathering place for creative men and women in all fields. Frances Steloff stocked the books of Gertrude Stein, T. S. Eliot, James Joyce, and Henry Miller (along with *The Little Review*) long before they were famous, often risking a run-in with the New York Vice Squad in order to do so. Miss Steloff did not believe in the censorship of serious creative writers, and Henry Miller once said of her: "In waging a lifelong battle against the forces of ignorance and intolerance Frances Steloff has rendered both the writer and the American public an inestimable service."

Frances Steloff in the bookstore she opened in the twenties that still flourishes today.
Frances Steloff, photograph by Victor Laredo

In Paris in 1919, Baltimore-born Sylvia Beach opened her bookstore, Shakespeare and Company, and almost simultaneously became involved in publishing for the first time James Joyce's *Ulysses*, a venture that would probably have shocked her long line of Presbyterian forebears. The publishing project took several years and almost ruined her financially, but by February 1922 she had brought out in print one of Joyce's greatest novels and she received a large measure of satisfaction from that.

Women writers were also concerned that the work of their contemporaries have an opportunity to be read and become known. Harriet Monroe (1861–1936), a poet herself, began publishing *Poetry: A Magazine of Verse* to give poets a chance to be heard. She had no money to invest in her project so she raised money from Chicago businessmen and made many personal sacrifices to give young poets a start. Marianne Moore, Edna St. Vincent Millay, Amy Lowell, Robert Frost, Ezra Pound, T. S. Eliot, James Joyce, were some of the young writers whose work appeared in *Poetry*. Miss Monroe not only published poems but paid for them, made annual awards for poetry, and saw to it that her magazine became a forum for literary discussion. Ezra Pound once said of her: "No one in our time or any time has ever served the cause of art with greater devotion, patience, and unflagging kindness."

The Little Review, published by Margaret Anderson (1891–1973) who also had no fortune and encountered frequent problems financing her magazine, rivaled *Poetry* for a while. "I wanted conversation with people who had ideas," she gave as her reason for founding *The Little Review*.

The work of Gertrude Stein, Marianne Moore, Wallace Stevens, and William Carlos Williams appeared in *The Little Review*, but its greatest coup was the United States publication of James Joyce's *Ulysses* (shipped over by Ezra Pound in installments). Miss Anderson and her assistant Jane Heap were hauled into court, tried on charges of obscenity, and fined one hundred dollars each. In 1929 both of them gave up *The Little Review* and moved to Paris, where there was already an ever-growing community of American expatriate artists.

Supporting and encouraging those who came to Paris, and night after night working on her own experiments with words, was Gertrude Stein (1874–1946). Though she wanted to be recognized as a writer first and foremost, she came to be known as a personality, through whose salon passed almost every great writer or artist of the twentieth century. She assembled, with some help from her brother Leo, a discriminating collection of modern art. Miss Stein seemed to know what was great before others did. Her walls were hung with paintings by Picasso, Matisse, Cézanne, Renoir, many of whom were her friends. Her early, serious writing, experiments with grammar and recurrence of expression, often left her readers bewildered or angry. *The Autobiography of Alice B. Toklas*, however, written in an easy and flowing style, established Miss Stein's fame as a writer, as did her *Four Saints in Three Acts*, which Virgil Thomson set to music and which opened in 1934. She was received warmly and avidly by students during a lecture tour to the United States in 1934.

Amelia Earhart waves to the crowd after her solo flight across the Atlantic. Photoworld

By 1922, Janet Flanner had also settled in Paris, to write and later to become the "Genêt" whose perceptive and discriminatingly written "Paris Letters" in *The New Yorker* magazine gave her an enthusiastic audience for fourteen years. In the 1930s she moved to London, and "London Letters" continued to inform Americans, as did her profiles on Hitler, Edith Wharton, Thomas Mann, and others.

American women were winning international distinction in the field of sports as well. On August 6, 1926, Gertrude Ederle, an eighteen-year-old New Yorker, became the first woman to swim the English Channel. She did it in 14 hours and 31 minutes, and her time broke the record of the fastest male swimmer by two hours. Helen Wills was amazing tennis audiences in America and England, where she won the Wimbledon singles eight times between 1927 and 1938. Mildred ("Babe") Didrikson Zaharias (1914–56) astounded sports fans with her excellence in almost every sport. She won the Associated Press Woman Athlete of the Year award eight times, and at the 1932 Olympic Games walked away with the gold medal for the 80-meter hurdle and the javelin throw. Ultimately she chose golf for her sports career and concentrated on the game until she was unequaled, winning 82 tournaments between 1935 and 1953. And Amelia Earhart (1898–1937), the first

Determined and agile, Helen Wills plays exciting tennis at Wimbledon. Photoworld

woman to fly a plane alone across the Atlantic (1932) and the first flyer to solo from Hawaii to the American mainland (1935), demonstrated the daring and courage of women in the field of aviation. During her brief flying career—it encompassed only nine years—Miss Earhart encouraged women to enter aviation. She was aviation editor of *Cosmopolitan*, wrote and spoke on aviation, and was a founding member of the Ninety-Nines, an international organization of licensed women pilots.

Another woman, not native-born but keenly respected by Americans who listened to her brilliant lectures, was traveling from Russia, to Sweden, to Germany, England and France during the 1920s. Emma Goldman, (1869–1940), "anarchist" and "radical," had immigrated to the United States from Russia. She traveled from coast to coast speaking on the anarchist movement, on the New Drama (Shaw, Ibsen, O'Neill, Strindberg), on Walt Whitman's poetry, advocating women's rights, supporting the growing birth control movement, free speech, and civil rights. When World War I broke out, she was sentenced to prison for her opposition to conscription. In prison she met Kate O'Hare, a Socialist whose programs for prison reform would be implemented in California thirty years later. Miss O'Hare was inspired by the care and support Emma gave other prisoners, and spoke of her as a "tender cosmic mother." In 1919 Miss Goldman was released from prison and deported to Russia. She spent the second part of her life wandering from country to country. Once, in 1934, she was allowed to enter the United States for ninety days. She left reluctantly. It was, she said, a country that had an "unbroken grip" on her "deepest feelings."

The United States to which Emma Goldman returned in 1934 was itself in the grip of a bitter depression. Ten years of peace, enjoyment of new inventions, and the thrill of emancipation had ended abruptly when the bottom fell out of the stock market on October 24, 1929, ushering in the Great Depression of the 1930s.

CHAPTER TWENTY-ONE

Depression and Another War

So first of all let me assert my firm belief that the only thing we have to fear is fear itself—nameless, unreasoning, unjustified terror which paralyzes needed efforts to convert retreat into advance.

With these words Franklin D. Roosevelt began his first Inaugural Address on March 4, 1933. From coast to coast the country lay shattered. The bank closings and a decline in the volume of business were among the successive depression catastrophes. There were breadlines and soup kitchens in large cities where thousands had lost their jobs and used up their resources. There were even homeless people who, unable to pay the rent, were living in tar-paper shacks on the fringes of cities. The Hoover government had hesitated uncertainly, hoping that "rugged individualism" would assert itself and right the economy. The Reconstruction Finance Corporation Bill, signed by President Hoover in January 1932, was designed to loan money to banks, railroads, industry, and so on, but had failed to restore the shattered economy.

The New Deal, under Franklin D. Roosevelt, brought new life, new impetus, and new hope to people and to the economy. In rapid succession agencies were created to meet people's most urgent problems and to establish public confidence—the Federal Emergency Relief Administration, the National Recovery Act, the Public Works Administration, the Tennessee Valley Authority, and many others. The therapy of action worked. People began to participate, to move forward together purposefully encouraged from time to time by President Roosevelt's morale-raising fireside radio talks.

But the momentum took time and Eu-

The woman in this picture told the photographer that she and her children had been living on frozen vegetables from the surrounding fields, and birds that the children killed. She had just sold the tires from her car to buy food. Library of Congress, photograph by Dorothea Lange

rope was in a state of disquiet. Over the world hung the threat of war as Hitler and Mussolini and Stalin began invading and annexing neighboring countries. Some women newspaper writers were perceptively viewing European heads of state and sending back dispatches to their newspapers. Anne O'Hare McCormick (1881–

1954) of *The New York Times* was cabling stories about Mussolini and the Soviet Union as early as the 1920s. She interviewed Hitler, Stalin, Churchill, and heads of state around the world. She became the first woman member of *The New York Times*'s Editorial Board, and was the first woman to win the Pulitzer Prize in journalism for excellence in European correspondence. Dorothy Thompson (1894–1961), whose syndicated *New York Herald Tribune* column reached 130 U.S. newspapers in 1936, vigorously attacked Hitler, Stalin, and Mussolini. Her public read her column diligently, and her radio broadcasts warning of the perils of Europe's dictators reached even the remotest American villages.

In Washington two women stood out during these years of lost prosperity at home and ominous turbulence abroad: Frances Perkins, for twelve years Secretary of Labor, the first woman ever to hold a cabinet post, and Eleanor Roosevelt, the First Lady. Indefatigable Eleanor Roosevelt (1884–1962) traveled the country and the world to bring goodwill and reassurance to people everywhere in those early depression years, listening, understanding, and caring about people's ideas and people's needs. She talked with disoriented young people, with despairing heads of families, with black people still alienated though emancipated, with bitter and cynical college students. Later she would visit soldiers in the far-flung Pacific bases of World War II. Her presence was a message of hope in the desolate years of the Great Depression.

Frances Perkins (1882–1965) was well prepared for her duties as Secretary of Labor when President Franklin D. Roosevelt appointed her to that position in 1933, setting precedent by appointing a woman to a Cabinet post. Miss Perkins already had had twenty years' experience in labor and industry and had served in top labor jobs under two New York State governors. Under Governor Roosevelt of New York she had served by appointment in 1929 as Industrial Commissioner, heading the State Department of Labor, administering the state's workmen's compensation law, its labor law, and issuing invaluable monthly employment statistics that were considered of national significance. As ex-officio member of the New York State Commission on Unemployment Problems (1930), she had been involved in industrial stabilization and social insurance programs. In Governor Smith's administration, Miss Perkins had been appointed to the State Industrial Commission in 1919, the first woman to hold a major political office in the state. Later Governor Smith appointed Miss Perkins a member (1924) of the State Industrial Board. She became its chairman in 1926.

Miss Perkins received her early baptism in the labor field in 1910 when, as executive secretary of the Consumers League, she investigated cellar bakeries and succeeded in abolishing them in New York. In 1911, following the tragic Triangle Shirtwaist Factory fire Miss Perkins, as executive secretary of the New York Committee on Safety (1911–17), secured legislation to prevent similar occurrences. She also worked successfully for the nine-hour working day for women, which passed the New York State Legislature in 1913, and for provisions for the safety of women in

Eleanor Roosevelt in the coal mines of Pennsylvania during the Depression years. Photoworld

industry. She was director of the New York State Factory Commission from 1912 to 1913.

Miss Perkins began her twelve-year term of service in Washington as Secretary of Labor with this impressive background in industry and labor, but there was criticism over her appointment. A man had always held the Labor Department post and both labor and industry grumbled about a woman holding what was considered a man's job. Miss Perkins proceeded unperturbed to expand the Bureau of Labor Statistics, to strengthen the Children's Bureau and the Woman's Bureau, and to call a conference of civic and labor leaders. At this conference a program was outlined, a large part of which found its way into the NRA's industry and trade codes. Recommendations were made concerning unemployment relief, public works, construction, shorter working hours, higher wages,

Secretary of Labor Frances Perkins at the Homestead Steel plant in Pittsburgh, Pennsylvania, 1933. Brown Brothers

abolition of child labor, revision of government purchasing standards, mediation boards. In a report on this conference Miss Perkins pointed out that these concepts were "economic factors for recovery and for the technique of industrial management in a mass production age." Unemployment insurance, low-cost housing, old-age pensions, the establishment of a division of labor standards and service, were also discussed and recommended at this conference. Miss Perkins's ability to formulate labor legislation acceptable to all concerned was one of the invaluable assets she brought to Washington. She was more interested in the achievement of goals than in taking personal credit for achievement. She worked quietly and un-

ostentatiously toward her objectives. By 1944, after serving eleven years as Secretary of Labor, Miss Perkins asked to be relieved of her duties, but President Roosevelt persuaded her to remain. After his death, in 1945, President Truman accepted her resignation but at his request she agreed to serve on the U.S. Civil Service Commission from 1946 to 1953.

President Roosevelt had promised the United States full employment in peacetime. The many projects of the Roosevelt administration did have an effect. Writing of the Tennessee Valley Authority region, Eleanor Roosevelt commented,

They were so poor; their houses were unpainted, their cars were dilapidated, and many grown-ups as well as children were without shoes or adequate garments. Scarcely eight years later, after the housing and educational and agricultural experiments had had time to take effect, I went through the same area, and a more prosperous area would have been hard to find.

Still, in 1938, there were ten million unemployed. Ultimately it was not any governmental administration that brought America out of its depression, but the country's entry into World War II. Pearl Harbor was attacked by the Japanese at 7:55 A.M. on December 7, 1941, and Americans mobilized to win the war.

For days and weeks after Pearl Harbor women by the thousands poured into mu-

nitions plants and war industry factories ready to do almost any kind of work offered them. As men were rapidly recruited for the armed services women were more and more enthusiastically welcomed by industry. They were hired by chemical, automobile, iron, steel, metal, electrical and machinery plants. They became welders in shipyards. They worked at plane dispatching, aerial photography, weather forecasting. By 1945, at the war's end, some four million women were employed at a wide variety of war-related jobs that women had never had access to before.

In addition, some 260,000 women enlisted in the Armed Forces. The WAC

During World War II maintenance crews composed entirely of women took over the job of cleaning locomotives and keeping them ready to roll. NYPL Picture Collection

(1942) (Women's Army Corps) enrolled and trained some 150,000 women. Mrs. Oveta Culp Hobby of Houston, Texas, became the corps' first director with the military rank of major, later of colonel. By 1943 the WAC had received full army status and served both in the United States and overseas. Miss Mildred McAfee, president of Wellesley College, became head of the WAVES, the navy unit. By 1945 some 86,000 women were serving in the WAVES, assigned to duty in such job fields as communications, logistics, administration, public relations, intelligence. Women Marines, totaling some 18,000, served in recruiting, photography, communications, motor transport, at stations in continental United States. The SPARS (Women's Reserve of the Coast Guard), headed by Captain Dorothy C. Stratton, took over many Coast Guard shore duties, releasing men for sea duty. About 11,000 women served in the SPARS, its name taken from *Semper Paratus* the Coast Guard motto meaning Always Ready.

Jacqueline Cochran, who had already attained fame as an aviator and who had set many records and won trophies for speed, distance, altitude flying, was appointed director of the Women's Airforce Service Pilots (WASP) in 1943. Some 1,000 women were graduated from the WASP's training program. They flew about 60 million miles for the Army Air Forces. Miss Cochran was commissioned lieutenant colonel in the Air Force Reserves in 1948.

The Women's Auxiliary Ferrying Squadron of the Air Transport Command, organized in 1942, was headed by Nancy Harkness Love and included fifty of the 250

women holding commercial licenses at that time. Some of these women aviators ferried trainers' and liaison planes from factories to airports. Some served as relief pilots on heavier aircraft. The Squadron conducted its own training school in Texas.

The WAC ground forces under the Air Service Command performed inestimable services in maintenance shops, sometimes manned by all-women service crews. One such crew of women mechanics completely rebuilt a crashed transport in 1943 at San Antonio, then offered to serve as ballast on the test flight. The test pilot accepted their offer. The transport passed the test. McClelland Field in Sacramento, California, had an all-woman crew of dispatchers in 1942. Women aircraft mechanics were sent to Africa before that campaign ended. The WAC trained thousands of women ground personnel for jobs as radio technicians, dispatchers, and mechanics during the war.

American women who remained at home during World War II participated in the Civil Defense program, training for emergency first aid, organizing community Civil Defense units, acting as medical aides, air-raid wardens, working in blood donation programs, in bond drives, and assisting the rationing administration. By 1942 some 12 million volunteers (men and women) were enrolled by the 12,000 Civil Defense councils operating throughout the country.

Some women continued their activities for peace. Emily Balch, who with Jane Addams, had taken a firm stand for peace during World War I, remained intransigent. She had worked closely with the

League of Nations, and in 1934–35 she worked as secretary for the Women's International League for Peace and Freedom without salary for eighteen months. In 1946 Miss Balch shared the Nobel Peace Prize with John R. Mott. In 1947, she was one of the signers of a letter to President Truman asking amnesty for conscientious objectors.

Some one million black men and women served in the armed forces during World War II, in the Army, the Navy, the Marine Corps, the Coast Guard, and approximately 600 black pilots had received their wings before the war's end. Four thonsand black women served in the WAC in World War II. Integration progressed slowly, however, though black Americans continually put pressure on the government to integrate the armed forces and to provide war jobs for black civilians. Some black and white platoons were integrated to fight on German soil in 1945, and the experiment proved successful, but on the whole integration did not make noticeable progress during World War II. "The Nation cannot expect colored people to feel that the United States is worth defending if the Negro continues to be treated as he is now," Mrs. Roosevelt had said, and her remark was to prove prophetic. As they welcomed their soldiers home, some with medals for bravery, and five wearing Distinguished Service Crosses, black Americans became more anxious than ever before to obtain civil rights.

CHAPTER TWENTY-TWO

The Black Revolution

BLACK WOMEN WALKED side by side with black men in the long march to freedom and integration in the 1960s. Black women took part in "sit-ins" at lunch counters. They refused to be seated in the back of buses, encouraged by Rosa Parks' determined stand in Montgomery, Alabama, in the 1950s. They joined the March on Washington for Jobs and Freedom in August 1963, when 200,000 black Americans crowded the plaza in front of the Lincoln Memorial. They marched from Salem to Montgomery, Alabama, in March 1965, listening to Nobel Peace Prize winner Ralph Bunche, speak out for freedom and Nobel Peace Prize winner Martin Luther King, Jr., say that "no tide of racism can stop us." And they wept at the funeral of the assassinated King, in April 1968, reaffirming his inspiring words, "We shall overcome." Black women, who had borne black men's babies and white men's babies for generations, who had worked side by side with fathers, brothers, husbands in cotton fields, who had kept their families together in shantytowns and urban slums, were on the march.

Black women had lived fearfully through Jim Crow years of the 1890s when rabble-rousers whipped up hate against Southern blacks. Fifty black women were among the 2,522 black lynchings that took place between 1889 and 1918. Whenever loved ones left their homes, fear and apprehension gripped the families. Black women had endured the separateness of those years when there were separate schools, separate public transportation, separate facilities, segregated housing.

The 1930s brought a faint ray of hope to black Americans. During the Roosevelt administration black Americans were given equal opportunity in New Deal job programs; the Agricultural Adjustment Act, the Tennessee Valley Authority, and the Works Progress Administration benefited both black and white Americans. Segregation in some federal offices in Washington was abolished. Defense industry jobs were opened up to black Americans by Roosevelt's Executive Order 8802, issued on June 25, 1941, prohibiting discrimination in employment in defense industries and government because of race, creed, color, or national origin. Some black Americans were appointed to high-ranking government jobs. Mrs. Mary McLeod Bethune was appointed director of the Division of Negro Affairs of the National Youth Administration. Mrs. Crystal Bird Fauset became racial relations adviser in the Office of Civilian Defense. From the late 1940s on, unions slowly increased their black membership. In Washington hotels began accepting black guests; motion picture houses and public restaurants were desegregated by the late 1950s. In 1955 the Interstate Commerce Commission decreed that all racial segregation must be stopped on interstate trains and buses by January 10, 1956.

All these developments were encouraging. But though the country appeared to be moving toward integration, the movement was painful and slow. There were still violent acts against blacks and brutality carried out by law enforcement officials. Though the Warren Supreme Court decision of May 17, 1954, outlawed segregated public schools, time passed before the decision was fully implemented.

Black Americans moved into the 1960s with an inspiring leader, the Reverend Martin Luther King, Jr., and with a new president, John F. Kennedy (1961–63). President Kennedy established the Committee on Equal Employment Opportunity with Vice President Lyndon B. Johnson as chairman. President Kennedy issued an order to prevent discrimination in new federally supported housing. He appointed several black Americans to important federal offices, among them Marjorie Lawson to the bench in the District of Columbia. When President Johnson came into office (1963–69) after the assassination of President Kennedy, he expressed deep concern for black Americans, stating that "until justice is blind to color, until education is unaware of race, until opportunity ceases to squint its eyes at human pigmentation, emancipation will be a proclamation, but it will not be a fact." By 1964 President Johnson had got through Congress the Civil Rights Act of 1964, outlawing discrimination in labor unions, in public facilities, in employment, and in the application of voting laws.

In 1967 Shirley Chisholm became the first black woman to be seated in Congress, Elizabeth Duncan Koontz was appointed director of the Women's Bureau of Labor Department, and President Johnson appointed the first black woman ambassador—Mrs. Patricia Roberts Harris became ambassador to Luxembourg.

Progress was being made. But still black Americans were not free. Desegregation was not a reality either in public schools or at lunch counters. Freedom marches continued, joined by an increasing number of concerned white Americans and by various national organizations. At the

Shirley Chisholm, the first black woman to be seated in Congress, was a nominee for president at the 1972 Democratic National Convention. Photograph by Diana Mara Henry

Lincoln Memorial demonstration in Washington on August 26, 1963, the Reverend Martin Luther King, Jr. brought tears to the eyes of many present with his moving words, "I have a dream."

His assassination on April 4, 1968, triggered riots in Washington, D.C., and the calling out of troops by President Johnson. There was racial violence in 29 states and 125 cities. Black Americans had lost the leader most capable of unifying the black population and of winning the respect of the country at large. There remained the National Association for the Advancement of Colored People, also the black power movement, that produced some controversial young leaders, among them Angela Davis, and other black freedom groups that organized across the country.

During the civil rights movement of the sixties—and before—black women were making names for themselves singing blues, gospel, jazz, and appearing on the stage, in motion pictures and on radio and TV. Bessie Smith (1896–1937) known as the Queen of the Blues, had a powerful contralto voice and "music in her soul." At the height of her career (1923–30) she made 160 recordings, many of them with Louis Armstrong. Ethel Waters was the first black American to star alone on the Broadway stage (*At Home with Ethel Waters*, 1954). She rose to fame in *Mamba's Daughters* (1938–39) and with her show-stopping singing in *Stormy Weather* and *Cabin in the Sky*, (1941), some of her several movies. Mahalia Jackson's "Singing to the Lord" established her as Queen of Gospel song. Miss Jackson (1911–72) gave recitals, had a weekly radio program in 1955, and appeared on TV. Blues singer Lena Horne was a featured motion picture actress, and in 1943 she was awarded the New York Newspaper Guild's Page One Medal as the "brightest singing star of the season." In opera and on the concert stage Marian Anderson, Dorothy Maynor, Leontyne Price, Grace Bumbry, Martina Arroyo, Shirley Verrett, Reri Grist all were winning large followings.

Actresses and TV personalities such as Pearl Bailey, Jane White, Barbara McNair, Mary Wilson, Dihann Carroll, Cicely Tyson, Leslie Uggams and Jackie "Moms" Mabley were becoming very well known.

Leontyne Price, opera singer. Metropolitan *Opera Association Press Department*

Gwendolyn Brooks, Pulitzer Prize winning poet. Harper & Row

In the dance there were dancers Carmen de Lavallade, Pearl Primus, Edna Guy, Mary Hinkson, Pearl Lang, and Judith Jamison.

The first black woman to win a Pulitzer Prize was Gwendolyn Brooks, whose volume of poetry entitled *Annie Allen* was a 1949 prizewinner. Maya Angelou's *I Know Why a Caged Bird Sings* and *Georgia, Georgia* and Nikki Giovanni's *My House* have brought their authors fame.

In the business world as early as the 1900s, C. J. Walker became one of the first black women millionaires, producing beauty products and establishing beauty schools all over the United States. In the 1970s many black women were carrying on successful and profitable enterprises— Mrs. Frances Murphy as the publisher of the Baltimore-based Afro-American newspapers, Mrs. Ida Lewis as the editor and publisher of the New York-based magazine *Encore*, Mrs. Ernesta Bowman Procope as owner of a large insurance company, and Mrs. Freddaye Henderson as executive vice-president of one of the nation's most successful travel agencies.

In the field of public affairs, Miss Marion Anderson, Mrs. Zelma Watson George, and Judge Edith Sampson served as alternate delegates to the United Nations during the Truman administration. Constance Baker Motley, the first black woman ever to serve in the New York State Senate, became borough president of Manhattan (1965) and judge in the U.S. District Court in New York City in 1966. Miss Barbara M. Watson became in 1966 the first black woman to attain a rank equivalent to Assistant Secretary of State, as administrator of the State Department Bureau of Security and Consular Affairs. Eleanor Holmes Norton became chairperson of the New York City Commission on Human Rights in 1970.

Four black Congresswomen served in the Ninety-third Congress—Shirley Chisholm from New York, Yvonne Brathwaite Burke, from California, Barbara Jordan from Texas, and Cardiss Collins from Illinois. Two women held important positions within the Democratic National Committee. Mrs. Patricia Roberts Harris, former dean of Howard University Law School, and former ambassador to Luxembourg, served as chairman of the Credentials Committee at the Democratic National Convention in 1972, and Mrs. Yvonne Brathwaite Burke served as co-chairman of the Democratic National Convention.

Many black women down through the centuries have stood out as pathbreakers, but one black woman has always been es-pecially revered. Mary McLeod Bethune, who on July 11, 1974, became the first black (or white) woman to have her statue placed in Lincoln Park in Washington, D.C., was born in 1875 in Mayesville, South Carolina, one of seventeen children. Education became her crusade.

Mary McLeod Bethune encouraged black women to assume leadership roles and implement social change. National Council of Negro Women

Through hard work and faith she founded the Bethune-Cookman Institute at Daytona Beach in 1904. She was adviser to four presidents on a wide range of issues. She was a member of the Planning Commission for a National Conference on the Education of Negroes in 1933, administrator of the Office of Minority Affairs of the National Youth Administration, special consultant at the United Nations Charter Convention in San Francisco, and founder of the National Council of Negro Women. In making the presentation of the Bethune Statue in 1974, Miss Dorothy Height, herself an outstanding black woman leader and President of the National Council of Negro Women, pointed out that Mrs. Bethune's statue was a recognition of both blacks and women. Mrs. Bethune's legacy engraved on the base of the statue reads:

I leave you love. I leave you hope. I leave you the challenge of developing confidence in one another. I leave you a thirst for education. I leave you respect for the use of power. I leave you faith. I leave you racial dignity.

CHAPTER TWENTY-THREE

Toward Full Liberation

WOMEN WHO ATTENDED the first meeting of the John F. Kennedy Commission on the Status of Women in 1961 must have left with somber thoughts about women's status during the forty-one years that had elapsed since the Woman Suffrage Amendment had been ratified in 1920. This, the first federal government commission in United State history to concern itself with women, was from one point of view a sobering event, from another point of view a hopeful event. The status of women certainly had not improved by leaps and bounds since 1920. But the Kennedy Commission provided women with an opportunity to make a fresh start with the blessings of the federal government. This was a challenge to women in the 1960s who sorely needed to take a new look at themselves. Way back in 1920, af-

ter the last difficult campaign was over and the Nineteenth Amendment signed by Secretary of State Bainbridge, Carrie Chapman Catt had looked ahead hopefully to women's future. In fact, suffragists all over the country—women who had worked long and devotedly for the vote—felt a sense of achievement and of elation that at last, at long, long, last, women had the vote. These veteran suffragists looked forward into the future, convinced that women would make memorable civic and political contributions to the nation. It did not happen quite that way. Women moved forward through the 1900s, but slowly. Though Alice Paul and members of the Woman's Party tried year after year, beginning in 1923, to get the Equal Rights Amendment through Congress, all efforts failed. The same dynamic, alert, concerned activists just didn't seem to be around to press on consistently and insistently for women's rights.

In the period between 1920 and the 1970s individual women did make names for themselves, achieve their goals, and forge ahead to the top of their professions. Dr. Maria Goeppert Mayer won the Nobel Prize for Physics in 1963, the second woman in the world to receive this honor, which she shared with two colleagues. Rachel Carson's concern for the environment alerted the country to its increasingly urgent environmental problems. Anthropologist Margaret Mead's enlightening books were a prelude to women's later liberation efforts. Muriel F. Siebert became the first woman member of the New York Stock Exchange in 1967, and headed a securities concern bearing her name. Katherine Graham was editor-publisher of the powerful *Washington Post* and Dorothy Schiff ran the *New York Post*. Mrs. Jean Westwood had held the responsible position of chairman of the Democratic National Committee and Anne Armstrong had been vice-chairman of the Republican party. Two women, Shirley Chisholm and Margaret Chase Smith, had announced their candidacy for the presidency, and Mrs. Chisholm had actually been among the nominees at the Democratic Convention in 1972. Women had continued to excel in the performing and creative arts, and in the field of sports. Pauline Frederick and Barbara Walters made names for themselves on television, and there were other successful women in a variety of fields. But there had been

few voices to prod women on to their complete fulfillment.

The first setback that women encountered after the passage of the woman suffrage amendment was the depression of the 1930s and that was hardly over when another catastrophe occurred—World War II. Women showed their stamina and turned out unhesitatingly to man war jobs. When the war was over, many women gave up their jobs and went home instead of staying on and working their way up through the ranks as engineers, or aviators, or radio technicians, or presidents of large companies, though this was not universally true. Some women did want to continue in their well-paid war jobs. But they were sometimes forced out, laid off, or lost their rightful seniority through technicalities, and had to accept low paying "woman" jobs to support themselves or their children. Women could have succeeded in reaching the top in many fields, but they believed, or they were told, that woman's place was in the home —as women had been told century after century. The joys of having a well-furnished house and many babies were alluringly dramatized in those postwar years by women's magazines along with the co-operation of delighted advertisers of "things." A wife's purchasing power made her a victim of appliances, detergents, swimming pools, two cars in the garage, cosmetics, and seasonally changing fashions, becoming or not. During the baby boom era, starting in the 1940s and continuing into the 1950s, the nation's birth rate rose from 2,559,000 in 1940 to

Well-known folk singer Joan Baez is one of many women in the performing arts who became involved in social and political issues of the 1960s and '70s. Vanguard Records

Betty Friedan gave voice to the feelings of many American women in her book The Feminine Mystique. *Photoworld*

3,632,000 in 1950. Even young girls in school got the message. One college junior interviewed by Betty Friedan explained that

> I don't want to be interested in a career I'll have to give up . . . I don't want to be interested in world affairs. I don't want to be interested in anything besides my home and being a wonderful wife and mother. Maybe education is a liability . . . Only sometimes I wonder how it would feel to be able to stretch and stretch, and learn all you want, and not have to hold yourself back. . . .

As time passed women in suburbia, living electrified lives in split-level ranch-type houses, chauffeuring husbands to the station and children to school day after day, began to feel the frustration of their lives. Betty Friedan wrote about their dilemma in her well-documented book, *The Feminine Mystique*, which appeared in 1963 and became a best seller.

Women began to recognize themselves as the "trapped American housewife," to feel the "hunger that food cannot fill," to be aware of the "problem that has no name," and to have the feeling that they "didn't exist" and that they were never being "truly themselves." The feminine mystique was described by Betty Friedan as a myth which makes "housewife-mothers" the model for all women and makes domestic aspects of feminine existence "into a religion, a pattern by which all women must now live or deny their femininity."

There had been a "woman problem" almost since the first woman set foot on American soil as a permanent settler, but it was never spelled out as Betty Friedan spelled it out. M. Carey Thomas, the young and dynamic president of Bryn Mawr, in 1908 described it as living in a "twilight life, a half life apart" and seeing "men as shadows walking" and knowing that you were living "in a man's world where the laws were men's laws, the government a man's government, the country a man's country." All this will change, Miss Thomas had hoped, and women would become "citizens of the state."

Making women feel themselves "citizens of the state," not just housewives, or nonpersons, was one of the many women issues that faced the Kennedy Commission on the Status of Women, headed by Eleanor Roosevelt (who brought the commission dignity and prestige), as they started their committee research in January 1961. There were fourteen women members, including Dr. Mary I. Bunting, president of Radcliffe College, who was later to serve on the Atomic Energy Commission, Marguerite Rawalt, attorney, and past president of the Federal Bar Association; Mary E. Callahan, member of the executive board, International Union of Electrical, Radio and Machine Workers; and there were twelve men.

While the Commission was preparing its reports, President Kennedy issued a few women-oriented directives on his own part. One reversed traditional interpretation of a federal law barring women from high-level civil service jobs. Congress, meanwhile, had passed the Equal Pay Act of 1963 requiring equal pay for men and women for equal work performed under equal conditions.

American Women, the Kennedy Commission's report on the status of American women which was issued on October 11,

1963, and listed 24 recommendations to combat sex discrimination, both triggered and fortified the women's liberation movement of the 1960s and the 1970s. Betty Friedan's *The Feminine Mystique* appeared at just about the same time.

President Kennedy acted promptly on two of the commission's recommendations. He established an Interdepartmental Committee on the Status of Women (its members government officials) and he established the Citizens' Advisory Council on the Status of Women, a continuing organization, its members private citizens.

Immediately things began happening.

The House of Representatives voted to add "sex" to race, color, religion, and national origin in the Civil Rights Bill in Title VII. By June 1964, twenty-four state commissions on the Status of Women had been formed, and had held a national conference. By July 1964 Congress enacted a Civil Rights Act including Title VII with a ban on sex discrimination. By July 1965 forty-four state commissions on the Status of Women had held a second convention.

By June 1966 the National Organization of Women (NOW) was formed and became a militant feminist organization, militant in the way that the Woman's Party was militant in the early 1900s. Other groups sprang up such as Bitch, Witch, Bread and Roses, Redstockings, Radical Mothers, some of them sponsoring rap groups and consciousness raising sessions. There were liberation groups in Chicago, San Francisco, Seattle and other cities.

On August 26, 1970, a day commemorating the 50th anniversary of women's right to vote, women of all ages, ten thousand of them, lawyers, housewives, secretaries, typists, marched arm in arm as sisters down New York's Fifth Avenue in a Woman's Strike for Equality demonstration, organized by Betty Friedan. All who watched from windows and sidewalks sensed their determination. "Give us the right to live, give us the right to compete, the right to a job regardless of sex," said Eleanor Homes Norton, chairperson of New York City's Commission on Human Rights. No one was there who remembered another march down Fifth Avenue in 1910, when suffragists timidly and daringly (so they thought) walked from 59th Street to Union Square carrying banners with slogans, one of which read: "New York State Denies the Vote to Idiots, Lunatics, Criminals, and Women." No one remembered except possibly one 79-year-old woman marcher who said, "I marched when I was 16. They used to call us suffrage-cats. It always does my heart good to see a few people thinking—thinking." And there was a 70-year-old grandmother who marched hand in hand with her daughter, 48, and her granddaughter, 23.

Women began their search for political power not only in their own behalf, but in behalf of brothers, sons, and relatives who had been away so long fighting an unwanted war in Vietnam. By the end of 1970, many women had worked long and hard to help bring the war in Vietnam to an end. Already, women had voting superiority (almost 4 million more women than men voted in the 1972 elections), but women needed to focus their voting strength. To help attain this end, the National Women's Political Caucus, its ob-

Bella Abzug, supported by NOW, campaigns for office. Photograph by Diana Mara Henry

jective to see more women gain political power, was organized in Washington, D.C., on July 10, 1971 by Representative Shirley Chisholm of New York, Representative Bella Abzug of New York, Betty Friedan, Gloria Steinem, and a group of 300 women representing 26 states, all major political parties, different ages, races, and economic backgrounds. Its objectives included among others such issues as free comprehensive child care programs, adequate shelter for all Americans, an end to discrimination against women in housing, strengthening enforcement clauses in existing antidiscrimination laws. As the words discrimination and libera-

tion began to spread throughout the country, thoughtful women experienced a period of self-examination, of anger, then of action, as they became aware of themselves as second-class citizens—discriminated against as American women had been discriminated against for almost four centuries.

Sex discrimination cases, based on two laws, the 1964 Civil Rights Act and the 1963 Equal Pay Act, began to come up in the federal courts by the early 1970s. Millions of dollars in back pay were awarded by the courts to women workers, proof that discrimination was a reality. The Equal Employment Opportunity Commission be-

Elizabeth Holtzman, congresswoman (left)*, and Billie Jean King* (right)*, at "An Evening of Tennis" sponsored by the National Women's Political Caucus.* *Photograph by Diana Mara Henry*

gan reexamining its guidelines. During the fiscal year 1973, 30,000 employees were found to have been underpaid by more than $18 million under the Equal Pay Act, nearly all of them women.

Gradually all segments of the nation's society began reexamining policies toward women—industry, universities, churches, banks, newspapers, magazines, advertisers. Union women began to assert their rights, and to run for union offices. Membership in labor unions increased by 333,000 between 1970 and 1972. A Coalition of Labor Union Women was formed in March 1974, with women from 58 labor unions joining together to make a stand against sex discrimination, and to work toward more women in policy-making positions in unions, toward legislation to provide child care facilities, and to encourage the organization into unions of the country's 34 million working women, something that six mill girls had tried to do (unsuccessfully) in Lowell, Massachusetts, in 1845. In universities, women's status slowly began to improve, with

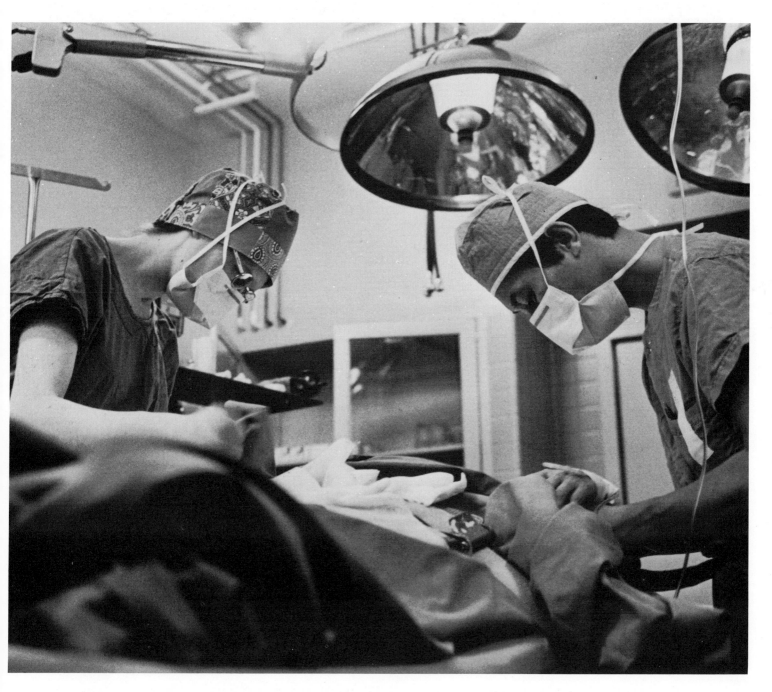

A woman surgeon operating. Downstate Medical Center, Brooklyn, N.Y., photograph by Bob West

women receiving more deserved rank and higher salaries. Sexism in textbooks and children's books came under fire. Girls were given more opportunities to compete in sports on an equal basis with boys.

The Citizen's Advisory Council on the Status of Women continued its search for ways of improving the status of women, issuing policy papers, legislative recommendations, its task force issuing reports on matters such as women's share in revenue sharing funds, the inclusion of household employees under the Fair Labor Standards Act, divorce practices, rape laws, and equality in the military services.

And finally came a major victory of the 1970s—the passage at long last of the Equal Rights Amendment by Congress on March 22, 1974, with Hawaii becoming the first state to ratify.

As Woman's International Year is celebrated in 1975 around the world, American women are doing more and more of the things they have not been able to do before. There are women coal miners, mining engineers, jockeys, firefighters,

More and more women are working alongside men in jobs from which they used to be excluded. Photograph by Bettye Lane

The demand for equal rights and
equal wages now has no age limit.
Photograph by Bettye Lane

women truck drivers, auctioneers, wine makers, subway motorwomen, telephone line crew women, horse trainers, carpenters, welders, disc jockeys, boxing judges, airplane pilots, women mayors, department store executives, ministers. Women's history is a field in its own right. American women, more than 92 million strong are on the march, asserting themselves as free and equal and first-class citizens of the United States of America.

Bibliography

Adams, Abigail. *Letters of Mrs. Adams, the Wife of John Adams.* Boston: C. C. Little and J. Brown, 1840.

Adams, Charles Francis. *Three Episodes of Massachusetts History: the Settlement of Boston Bay; the Antinomian Controversy; a Study of Church and Town Government.* Boston and New York: Houghton, Mifflin & Company, 1892.

Adams, Mildred. *The Right to Be People.* Philadelphia: J. B. Lippincott Company, 1967.

Addams, Jane. *Twenty Years at Hull House.* New York: The Macmillan Company, 1949.

Adamson, J. H., and Folland, H. E. F. *Sir Harry Vane: His Life and Times.* Boston: Gambit, 1973.

Aiken, Conrad, ed. *American Poetry 1671–1928.* New York: The Modern Library, 1929.

Allen, Frederick Lewis. *Only Yesterday (The 1920's).* New York and London: Harper and Brothers, 1931.

————. *Since Yesterday (1929–1939).* New York: Harper & Row, 1968.

American Heritage Editors. *The American Heritage Book of Indians.* New York: American Heritage Publishing Company, 1961.

Andrews, Charles M. *The Colonial Period of American History.* New Haven: Yale University Press, 1934.

Anthony, Katherine. *The First Lady of the Revolution.* New York: Doubleday and Company, 1958.

Beach, Cora M. *Women of Wyoming.* Casper, Wyoming: S. E. Boyer & Company, 1927.

Beard, Mary R. ed. *America Through Women's Eyes.* (reproduction of 1933 ed.) New York: Greenwood Press, 1968.

Beard, Charles. A., and Mary R. *The Rise of American Civilization.* Vol. 4. New York: The Macmillan Company, 1942.

Bird, Caroline. *Born Female.* New York: David McKay Company, 1968.

Blatch, Harriot Stanton, and Lutz, Alma. *Challenging Years.* New York: G. P. Putnam's Sons, 1940.

Blumenthal, Walter H. *Brides from Bridewell.* Rutland, Vt.: C. E. Tuttle Company, 1962.

Bowen, Catherine Drinker. *John Adams and the American Revolution.* New York: Grosset's Universal Library, 1950.

Bowers, Claude G. *The Tragic Era: The Revolution after Lincoln.* Cambridge, Mass.: The Riverside Press, 1929.

Bradstreet, Anne (Dudley). *Poems of Anne Bradstreet.* Introduction by Charles Eliot Norton. Boston: The Duodecimos, 1897.

Bridenbaugh, Carl. *Cities in the Wilderness.* New York: Ronald Press Co., 1938.

Brooks, Geraldine. *Dames and Daughters of*

Colonial Days. New York: Thomas Y. Crowell & Co., 1900.

Brown, Herbert Ross. *The Sentimental Novel in America, 1789–1860.* Durham, N.C.: Duke University Press, 1940.

Bryce, James B. *The American Commonwealth.* New York and London: Macmillan and Company, 1895.

Butts, R. Freeman. *A Cultural History of Western Education.* New York: McGraw-Hill Book Company, 1955.

Buxton, Frank, and Owen, Bill. *The Big Broadcast 1920–1950.* New York: The Viking Press, 1972.

Catt, Carrie Chapman, and Shuler, Nettie Rogers. *Woman Suffrage and Politics.* New York: Charles Scribner's Sons, 1923.

Chamberlin, Hope. *A Minority of Members: Women in the U.S. Congress.* New York, Washington, and London: Praeger, 1973.

Coigney, Virginia. *Margaret Sanger: Rebel with a Cause.* New York: Doubleday and Company, 1969.

Croly, J. C. *The History of the Woman's Club Movement in America.* New York: Henry G. Allen & Co., 1898.

Cromwell, Otelia. *Lucretia Mott.* Cambridge, Mass.: Harvard University Press, 1958.

Cubberley, Ellwood P. *Public Education in the U.S.* New York: Houghton Mifflin Company, 1947.

Dakin, Edwin Franden. *Mrs. Eddy.* New York: Charles Scribner's Sons, 1930.

Dannett, Sylvia G. L. *Music, Theatre and Fun in the American Revolution.* South Brunswick, N.J., and New York: A. S. Barnes and Company, 1973.

Dannett, Sylvia G. L. *Noble Women of the North.* New York and London: Thomas Yoseloff, 1959.

D'Arusmont, Frances Wright. *Views of Society and Manners in America 1818–1820.* London: Longman, Hurst, Rees, Orme and Brown, 1822.

De Beauvoir, Simone. *The Second Sex.* New York: Alfred A. Knopf, 1952.

Deen, Edith. *Great Women of the Christian Faith.* New York: Harper and Brothers, 1959.

Degen, Marie Louise. *The History of the Woman's Peace Party.* Baltimore: The Johns Hopkins Press, 1939.

De Tocqueville, Alexis. *Journey to America.* New York: Doubleday and Company, 1971.

Dexter, Elisabeth A. *Career Women of America 1776–1840.* Francestown, N.H.: Marshall Jones Company, 1950.

———. *Colonial Women of Affairs.* New York: Houghton Mifflin Company, 1924.

Dickinson, Anna. *A Ragged Register.* New York: Harper Brothers, 1879.

Dickinson, Emily. *The Poems of Emily Dickinson.* Boston: Little, Brown and Company, 1935.

Donovan, Frank. *The Benjamin Franklin Papers.* New York: Dodd, Mead & Company, 1962.

Douglas, Emily Taft. *Remember the Ladies.* New York: G. P. Putnam's Sons, 1966.

Drago, Harry Sinclair. *Notorious Ladies of the Frontier.* New York: Dodd, Mead and Company, 1969.

Drinnon, Richard. *Rebel in Paradise: A Biography of Emma Goldman.* Chicago: University of Chicago Press, 1961.

Duniway, Abigail Scott. *Path Breaking.* New York: Schocken Books, 1971.

Earhart, Mary. *Frances Willard.* Chicago: University of Chicago Press, 1944.

Earle, Alice Morse. *Colonial Dames and Goodwives.* New York: Houghton, Mifflin Company, 1896.

———. *Colonial Days in Old New York.* New York: Charles Scribner's Sons, 1896.

———. *Home Life in Colonial Days.* New York: Grosset and Dunlap, 1898.

———. *The Sabbath in Puritan New England.* New York: Charles Scribner's Sons, 1891.

———. *Two Centuries of Costume in*

America. London: The Macmillan Co., 1903.

Ellet, Elizabeth F. *Domestic History of the American Revolution*. New York: Charles Scribner's Sons, 1854.

————. *Queens of American Society*. Charles Scribner's Sons, 1868.

————. *Women of the American Revolution*. 2 vols. New York: Charles Scribner's Sons, 1854.

Ewen, David. *Popular American Composers*. New York: H. W. Wilson, 1966.

Federal Writers Project for the State of Massachusetts: *A Guide to Its Places and People*. Boston: Houghton Mifflin Company, 1937.

Federal Writers' Publications, Inc. *New York City Guide*. New York: Random House, 1939.

Fields, Annie. *Life and Letters of Harriet Beecher Stowe*. London: Sampson Low, Marston & Company, 1898.

Finley, Ruth E. *The Lady of Godey's: Sarah Josepha Hale*. Philadelphia and London: J. B. Lippincott Co., 1931.

Fleming, Alice. *Ida Tarbell: First of the Muckrakers*. New York: Thomas Y. Crowell Company, 1971.

Flexner, Eleanor. *Century of Struggle*. Cambridge, Mass.: Belknap Press of Harvard University Press, 1968.

Foner, Philip S. *Frederick Douglass*. New York: Citadel Press, 1969.

Franklin, John Hope. *From Slavery to Freedom: A History of Negro Americans*. New York: Alfred A. Knopf, 1967.

Friedan, Betty. *The Feminine Mystique*. New York: W. W. Norton & Company, 1963. Paperback. New York: Dell Publishing Company, 1964.

Gager, Nancy. *Women's Rights Almanac, 1974*. Bethesda: Elizabeth Cady Stanton Publishing Company, 1974.

Gallico, Paul. *The Golden People*. New York: Doubleday and Company, 1965.

Galt, Tom. *Peter Zenger*. New York: Thomas Y. Crowell Company, 1951.

Goldmark, Josephine. *Impatient Crusader: Florence Kelley's Life Story*. Urbana, Ill.: The University of Illinois Press, 1953.

Good, Harry G. *A History of American Education*. New York: The Macmillan Company, 1963.

Hays, Elinor Rice. *Lucy Stone*. Paperback. New York: Tower Publications, 1961.

Heffner, Richard D. *A Documentary History of the United States*. New York: New American Library, 1965.

Hewitt, Barnard. *Theatre, U.S.A. 1665–1957*. New York: McGraw-Hill Book Company, 1959.

Hildeburn, Charles R. *Sketches of Printers and Printing in Colonial New York*. New York: Dodd, Mead & Company, 1895.

Hole, Judith, and Levine, Ellen. *Rebirth of Feminism*. Chicago: Quadrangle Books, 1971.

Holliday, Carl. *Woman's Life in Colonial Days*. Williamstown, Mass.: Corner House Publishers, 1968.

Howe, Julia Ward. *Reminiscences: 1819–1899*. Boston: Houghton Mifflin Company, 1899.

Hughes, Langston. *Famous Negro Music Makers*. New York: Dodd, Mead & Company, 1955.

Hutchinson, Thomas. *The History of Massachusetts from the First Settlement Thereof in 1628 Until the Year 1750*. Salem, Mass.: Printed by Thomas C. Cushing for Thomas and Andrews, Boston, 1795–1828.

Irwin, Inez Haynes. *Angels and Amazons: A Hundred Years of American Women*. New York: Doubleday, Doran & Company, 1933.

James, Edward T., ed., James, Janet Wilson, assoc. ed., Boyer, Paul S., asst. ed. *Notable American Women 1607–1950: A Biographical Dictionary*. Cambridge, Mass.: The Belknap Press of Harvard University Press, 1971.

Johnston, Johanna. *Mrs. Satan: The Incredible Saga of Victoria C. Woodhull.* New York: G. P. Putnam's Sons, 1967.

Jones, Katherine M. *Heroines of Dixie: Confederate Women Tell Their Story of the War.* New York: Bobbs-Merrill Company, 1955.

Josephson, Hannah. *The Golden Threads. New England's Mills, Girls and Magnates.* New York: Russell and Russell, 1949. Reissued. New York: Atheneum House, 1967.

Kraditor, Aileen S., ed. *The Ideas of the Woman Suffrage Movement 1890–1929.* New York: Doubleday and Company, 1971.

———. *Up From the Pedestal.* Chicago: Quadrangle Books, 1970.

Larcom, Lucy. *A New England Girlhood, Outlined from Memory.* Boston and New York: Houghton Mifflin Company, 1889.

Lee, Richard Henry. *The Letters of Richard Henry Lee.* Edited by James C. Ballagh. New York: Da Capo Press, 1970.

Lerner, Gerda. *The Grimké Sisters from South Carolina.* Paperback. New York: Schocken Books, 1971.

Lewis, Captain Merriwether, and Clark, William. *Journals of Lewis and Clark.* Edited by Bernard DeVoto. New York: Houghton Mifflin Company, 1953.

Lloyd, Trevor. *Suffragettes International.* New York: American Heritage Press, 1971.

Lutz, Alma. *Emma Willard: Pioneer Educator of American Women.* Boston: Beacon Press, 1964.

———. *Susan B. Anthony.* Boston: Beacon Press, 1959.

Massey, Mary E. *Bonnet Brigades: American Women and the Civil War.* Alfred A. Knopf, 1966.

Merriam, Eve. *Growing Up Female in America: Ten Lives.* New York: Doubleday & Company, 1971.

Mill, John Stuart. *On the Subjection of Women.* Reprint. New York: Fawcett Publications, 1971.

Miller, John C. *The First Frontier: Life in Colonial America.* Paperback. New York: Dell Publishing Company, 1966.

Miller, Perry. *Errand into the Wilderness.* Cambridge, Mass.: The Belknap Press of Harvard University Press, 1956.

Morison, Samuel Eliot. *Admiral of the Ocean Sea: A Life of Christopher Columbus.* Boston: Little Brown and Company, 1942.

———. *The Oxford History of the American People.* New York: Oxford University Press, 1972.

Mott, Frank Luther. *Golden Multitudes: The Story of Best Sellers in the U.S.A.* New York: R. R. Bowker Co., 1947.

———. *A History of American Magazines.* Vol. I and II. New York: D. Appleton, 1930.

Nevins, Allan, and Commager, Henry Steele. *A Pocket History of the United States.* Reprint of 1945 original paperback by Pocket Books. New York: Washington Square Press, 1970.

Noble, Iris. *Nellie Bly: The First Woman Reporter.* New York: Julian Messner, 1956.

Nutting, Mary Adelaide, and Dock, Lavinia L. *A History of Nursing: The Evolution of Nursing Systems, etc.* New York and London: G. P. Putnam's Sons, 1907–12.

O'Neill, William L. *Everyone Was Brave.* Chicago: Quadrangle Books, 1969.

———. *The Woman Movement: Feminism in the United States.* Chicago: Quadrangle Paperbacks, 1971.

Ossoli, Margaret Fuller. *Memoirs.* Boston: Phillips, Sampson & Company, 1852.

———. *Woman in the Nineteenth Century.* New York: Greeley & McElrath, 1845.

Park, Maud Wood. Edna Lamprey Stantial, ed. *Front Door Lobby.* Boston: Beacon Press, 1960.

Parkman, Francis. *The Oregon Trail*. New York: The New American Library, 1950.

Perkins, Frances. *The Roosevelt I Knew*. New York: The Viking Press, 1946.

Piercy, Josephine K. *Anne Bradstreet*. New York: Twayne Publishers, 1965.

Porter, Sarah H. *The Life and Times of Anne Royall*. Cedar Rapids, Iowa: Torch Press Book Shop, c. 1909.

Randall, Mercedes M. *Improper Bostonian*. New York: Twayne Publishers, 1964.

Richards, Laura E., and Elliott, Maud H. *Julia Ward Howe, 1819–1910*. Vol. I. Boston: Houghton Mifflin Company, 1915.

Robbins, Russell Hope. *The Encyclopedia of Witchcraft and Demonology*. New York: Crown Publishers, 1970.

Rogers, Agnes. *Women Are Here to Stay*. New York: Harper & Brothers, 1949.

Rogers, W. G. *Ladies Bountiful*. New York: Harcourt Brace & World, 1968.

Roosevelt, Eleanor. *This I Remember*. New York: Harper & Brothers, 1949.

Ross, Ishbel. *Charmers and Cranks*. New York: Harper & Row, c. 1965.

———. *Ladies of the Press*. New York: Harper & Brothers, 1936.

———. *Sons of Adam, Daughters of Eve*. New York: Harper & Row, 1969.

Rossi, Alice S. *The Feminist Papers*. New York: Columbia University Press, 1973.

Rourke, Constance. *Troupers of the Gold Coast*. New York: Harcourt Brace & Company, 1928.

Rowlandson, Mary (White). *Narrative of the Captivity and Removes of Mrs. Mary Rowlandson, who was taken captive by the Indians at the Destruction of Lancaster (Mass.) in 1676, Written by herself*. 2nd edition at Lancaster, Mass.: Carter, Andrews & Co., 1828.

Rowse, Alfred L. *The Elizabethans and America*. New York: Harper & Brothers, 1959.

Royall, Anne Newport. *Letters from Alabama*. Washington, 1830.

Sablosky, Irving L. *American Music*. Chicago: The University of Chicago Press, 1971.

Shaw, Anna Howard, D.D. M.D. *The Story of a Pioneer*. New York and London: Harper & Brothers, 1915.

Sinclair, Andrew. *The Emancipation of the American Woman*. New York: Harper Colophon Books, Harper & Row, 1965.

Smith, Page. *Daughters of the Promised Land*. Boston, Toronto: Little, Brown and Company, 1970.

Smutz, Robert W. *Women and Work in America*. New York: Columbia University Press, 1971.

Sprague, William F. *Women and the West*. Reproduction of 1940 ed. New York: Arno Press, 1972.

Spruill, Julia Cherry. *Women's Life and Work in the Southern Colonies*. Paperback. New York: W. W. Norton & Company, 1972. 1938 University of North Carolina.

Stanton, Elizabeth Cady. *Eighty Years and More Reminiscences 1815–1897*. New York: Schocken Books, 1971.

———. (with Susan B. Anthony and Matilda Joslyn Gage for Vols. 1–3; Susan B. Anthony and Ida H. Harper Vol. 4; Ida H. Harper Vols. 5–6.) *The History of Woman Suffrage*. New York and Rochester, N.Y.: Fowler & Wells, 1881–1922.

Sterling, Dorothy. *Freedom Train*. New York: Doubleday & Company, 1954.

Stern, Madeleine B. *Queen of Publishers' Row: Mrs. Frank Leslie*. New York: Julian Messner, 1965.

———. *We, The Women*. Schulte Publishing Company, 1963.

Stevenson, Elizabeth. *The American 1920's*. New York: Crowell, Collier and Macmillan, 1970.

Stewart, Isabel M., and Austin, Anne L. *A History of Nursing*. New York: G. P. Putnam's Sons, 1962.

Still, Bayard. *The West: Contemporary Records of America's Expansion Across the Continent, 1607–1890*. New York: G. P. Putnam's Sons, 1961.

Stiller, Richard. *Queen of Populists (Mary Lease).* Crowell, 1970.

Sullivan, Mark. *Our Times: 1900–1925.* Reprint. New York: Charles Scribner's Sons, 1971.

Terry, Walter. *The Dance in America.* New York: Harper & Row, 1973.

Tharp, Louise Hall. *The Peabody Sisters of Salem.* Boston: Little, Brown and Company, 1950.

Trollope, Anthony. *North America.* London: Chapman & Hall, 1862. Paperback. Baltimore: Penguin English Library, 1968.

Trollope, Frances Milton. *Domestic Manners of the Americans.* Reprint. New York: Alfred A. Knopf, 1949.

United Nations, N.Y. *1967 Commission on the Status of Women. United Nations Assistance for the Advancement of Women, New York, 1967. Resources Available to Member States for the Advancement of Women, New York, 1966.*

Untermeyer, Louis. *Makers of the Modern World.* New York: Simon and Schuster, 1955.

Untermeyer, Sophie Guggenheimer, and Williamson, Alix. *Mother Is Minnie.* New York: Doubleday and Company, 1960.

U.S. Department of Labor Women's Bureau. *American Women at the Crossroads: Directions for the Future.* Fiftieth Anniversary Conference. The Women's Bureau, Washington, 1970.

Van Doren, Carl. *Benjamin Franklin.* New York: The Viking Press, 1938.

———. *Jane Mecom.* New York: The Viking Press, 1950.

———. *The Great Rehearsal.* New York: The Viking Press, 1948.

Wade, Mason. *Margaret Fuller: Whetstone of Genius.* New York: The Viking Press, 1940.

Wagenknecht, Edward. *The Movies in the Age of Innocence.* Norman, Okla.: University of Oklahoma Press, 1962.

Wald, Lillian D. *The House on Henry Street.* New York: Henry Holt and Company, 1915.

Werstein, Irving. *Labor's Defiant Lady: Mother Jones.* New York: Thomas Y. Crowell Company, 1969.

Wharton, Anne Hollingsworth. *Martha Washington.* Reprint. New York: Charles Scribner's Sons, 1967.

White, William Allen. *Autobiography.* New York: The Macmillan Company, 1946.

Whitney, Janet. *Abigail Adams.* Boston: Little, Brown and Company, 1947.

Willard, Frances E., and Livermore, Mary A. *A Woman of the Century: fourteen hundred-seventy biographical sketches accompanied by portraits of leading American women in all walks of life.* Buffalo, N.Y.: C. W. Moulton, 1893.

Willison, George F. *Saints and Strangers.* New York: Reynal & Hitchcock, 1945.

Winthrop, John (supposed author). *A Short Story of the Rise, Reign and Ruin of the Antinomians, Familists and Libertines that Infected the Churches of New England.* London: R. Smith, 1644.

———. James Kendall Hosmer, ed. *Winthrop's Journal. History of New England, 1630–1649.* New York: Charles Scribner's Sons, 1908.

Wissler, Clark. *Indians of the United States.* New York: Doubleday and Company, 1966.

Woody, Thomas. *History of Women's Education in the United States.* Lancaster, Pa.: The Science Press, 1929.

Wright, Louis B. *Life on the American Frontier.* New York: Capricorn Books, 1971.

Young, Agatha. *The Women and the Crisis: Women of the North in the Civil War.* New York: McDowell, Obolensky, 1959.

Index

Davis, Pauline Wright, 99
Day, Edith, 175
Debussy, Claude, 153
Declaration of Independence, 51, 52, 56, 58
Demorest, Ellen L. C., 124
Dempsey, Jack, 176–177
Depew, Chauncey M., 139
Depression, the Great, 187–192, 204
DeVries, Peter Rudolphus, 16
Dias, Bartholomeu, 1
Dickens, Charles, 92
Dickinson, Emily, 129–130
Dickson, John, 77
Didrickson, "Babe." *See* Zaharias
Dix, Dorothea, 105, 109
doctors, female, 126–128
Dodge, Grace, 143
Dodge, Mary Mapes, 128
Douglass, Frederick, 98, 131
Drake, Francis, 2, 3
Drew, Georgianna Emma (Mrs. Maurice Barrymore), 157
Drew, Louisa Lane, 157
Dudley, Mrs. Guilford, 172
Dudley, Thomas, 24
Duffy, Mary, 160
Duncan, Isadora, 154, *155*
Duniway, Abigail Scott, 121–122
Duston, Hannah, 23
Dyer, Mary, 26, 29–30, 31
Dyer, William, 29

E

Earhart, Amelia, *185*, 187
Eastman, Crystal, 162, 166
Eddy, Mary Baker, 130–131
Ederle, Gertrude, 185
Edmonds, Sarah Emma (Thompson, Franklin), 109–110
education, 69, 70–79, 128. *See also* colleges, women's; public schools
Edwards, Jonathan, 39

Edwards, Sarah Pierrepont, 39
Eliot, T. S., 183, 184
Elizabeth I, Queen, 1, 2, 3
Emancipation Proclamation, 90
Embury, Philip, 40
Emerson, Ralph Waldo, 90, 93, 116
Endecott, John, 31
Equal Employment Opportunity Commission, 210
Equal Pay Act, 207, 210
Equal Rights Amendment, 203, 213
Equal Rights Association, 116, 117
Equal Rights Convention, 90
Equality League of Self-Supporting Women, 160, 161
Estaugh, John, 36
Everett, Edward, 93

F

Family Limitation (Sanger), 151, 152
Farrar, Geraldine, 153
Fauset, Crystal Bird, 197
Felton, Rebecca L., 179
Female Labor Reform Association, 94
Ferber, Edna, 180
Ferdinand, King, 1, 2
Ferguson, Miriam Amanda, 179
Fiske, Minnie Maddern, 157
Fitzgerald, F. Scott, 175
Flanner, Janet (Genêt), 185
Fletcher, Alice Cunningham, 133
Foley, Margaret, 93
Forrest, Mistress, 7
Forty–Niners, 95
Foster, Abigail Kelley, 85, *101*, 102
Foster, Hannah Webster, 9
Foster, Stephen, 115
Fox, George, 29
Franklin, Anne S., 49–50

Franklin, Benjamin, 39, 47–49, *49*, 50, 51, 52, 54
Franklin, Deborah. *See* Read, Deborah
Franklin, Elizabeth, 49
Franklin, James, 49
Franklin, Jane. *See* Mecom, Jane Franklin
Franklin, Mary, 49
Franklin, Sally. *See* Bache, Sally Franklin
Frederick, Pauline, 204
Fremstad, Olive, *153*–154
Friedan, Betty, 204, *206*, 207, 208
Frost, Robert, 184
Fuller, Loie, 154
Fuller, Margaret, 74, 81–82

G

Garbo, Greta, 177
Garden, Mary, 153
Gardener, Helen, 165
Garrison, William Lloyd, 76–77, 85, 89, *101*, 115, 116
Gay, Mary Ann Harris, 112
George, Zelma Watson, 200
Gilbert, Sir Humphrey, 3
Gilson, Helen, 105
Giovanni, Nikki, 200
Gish, Lillian, 177
Goddard, Mary Katherine, 52
Goddard, Sarah, 52
Goddard, William, 52
Godey's Lady's Book, 124, *125*
gold, discovery of, 94–95
Goldman, Emma, 187
Gougar, Helen, 141
Gould, Jay, 143
Graham, Katherine, 204
Graham, Martha, *181*–182, 183
Gram, Betty, 173
Grant, President, 132
Great Religious Awakening, the, 38–43
Greeley, Horace, 82, 116

Lewis and Clark Expedition, 65, 67

Lewis and Clark Exposition, 67

Lincoln, Abraham, 103, 108, 110–111

Lindbergh, Charles A., 176

Little Review, The, 184

Lockwood, Belva, 131–*132*

Lockwood, Ezekiel, 132

Longfellow, Henry Wadsworth, 36, 104

Loos, Anita, 175

Lothrop, Harriett Mulford, 129

Love, Nancy Harkness, 194

Lowell, Amy, 180, 184

Lowell, Josephine Shaw, 143, 145

Lucas, Eliza, 45–47. *See also* Pinckney, Eliza Lucas

Lucas, Lieutenant Colonel, 45

Lucas, Polly, 47

Ludwig I, King, 96

Lyon, Mary, 72–73

M

McAfee, Mildred, 193

McClintock, Mary Ann, 97

McCormick, Anne O'Hare, 189

McDowell, Mary E., 149–150

McNair, Barbara, 199

Mabley, Jackie ("Moms"), 199–200

Madison, Dolley Payne Todd, 59, 63–65, *64*

Madison, James, 63, 64

magazines, women's, 124–125

Mann, Mary (Mrs. Horace), 73

Marco Polo, 1

Marlowe, Julia, 157

marriage contracts, 101–102

Martineau, Harriet, 92

Massasoit, 13

Mather, Increase, 34

Maulin, Anna Catherine. *See* Zenger, Catherine

Mayer, Maria Goeppert, 204

Mayflower, the, 11–13, 14

Maynor, Dorothy, 199

Mead, Lucy Ames, 166

Mead, Margaret, 204

Mecom, Jane Franklin, 47

medical books, 126

Metacom. *See* Philip, King

Metropolitan Opera House (N.Y.), 152, 153, 154

military service, women in, 193–195

Millay, Edna St. Vincent, 180, 184

Miller, Henry, 183

Mindell, Fania, 152

Minor, Virginia, 120

Mirror of Fashions, 125

Mitchell, Maria, 74–75

Monroe, Harriet, 184

Monroe, James, 71

Montez, Lola, 96

Montpelier, 64

Moody, Lady Deborah, 26, 31–32, 33

Moore, Marianne, 180, 184

Morris, Esther, 120–*121*

Moses, Emma Richardson, 113

Moskowitz, Belle, 179

motion pictures, 177

Motley, Constance Baker, 200

Mott, James, 90, 98

Mott, John R., 194

Mott, Lucretia, 85, 88, 89–90, 97, 98, 99, 117, 166

Mount Holyoke College, 73

Mount Vernon, 59–60, 63

Mullaney, Kate, 143

Murphy, Frances, 200

Murray, Judith Sargent, 69

N

National American Woman Suffrage Association, 117, 159, 160, 161, 162, 163, 169, 172, 174

National Association for the Advancement of Colored People, 199

National Council of Jewish Women, 136–137

National Council of Women, 137

National Equal Rights Party, 132

National League of Women Voters, 172

National Organization of Women (NOW), 208

National Woman Suffrage Association, 117, 131

National Women's Trade Union League, 146–148, 150

Neff, Mary, 23

Negroes, problems of, 196–199

New Northwest, The, 121, 122

New World, colonizing the, 2–9

Newsom, Ella King, 106

Nichols, Mary Grove, 81

Nightingale, Florence, 134

Nobel Prizes, 168, 204

Norton, Eleanor Holmes, 200, 208

novels, female-in-distress, 69–70

Nurse, Rebecca, 34

Nurses Settlement House (N.Y.), 148

nursing profession, 133–135

Nutting, Mary Adelaide, 133

O

O'Hare, Kate, 187

O'Keeffe, Georgia, 180–181

Opechancanough, 11

opera in America, 152–154, 199

Ossoli, Marchese d', 82

Overall Workers Union, 160

Owen, Robert Dale, 101, 126

P

pacifists, 166–167

painters, 152, 180. *See also* artists